Worker Self-Management
in Industry

edited by
G. David Garson

Worker Self-Management in Industry
The West European Experience

PRAEGER SPECIAL STUDIES IN INTERNATIONAL BUSINESS, FINANCE, AND TRADE

Praeger Publishers   New York   London

Library of Congress Cataloging in Publication Data

Main entry under title:

Worker self-management in industry.

    (Praeger special studies in international business,
finance, and trade)
    1. Employees' representation in management--Europe--
Case studies. I. Garson, G. David.
HD5660.E9W67   1977   658.31'52   77-2774
ISBN 0-03-022406-3

HD5660
E9
W67
1977

PRAEGER SPECIAL STUDIES
200 Park Avenue, New York, N.Y., 10017, U.S.A.

Published in the United States of America in 1977
by Praeger Publishers,
A Division of Holt, Rinehart and Winston, CBS, Inc.

789   038   987654321

To Richard, Paula, Tony, and Bobby

CONTENTS

MODELS OF WORKER SELF-MANAGEMENT: THE WEST EUROPEAN EXPERIENCE
G. David Garson

In a 1974 report, the director-general of the International Labor Organization (ILO) observed, "Labour relations in Europe are in a state of flux. . . . Participation is taking its place alongside collective bargaining as a framework for the conduct of these relations."[1] In fact, worker participation in management is the single most important labor relations issue in Europe today; previously an area of great stability, the organization of work has been undergoing rapid change. Such change is of the utmost interest not only to students of labor relations but to all those interested in social change in modern, industrialized societies.

I began an earlier study of developments in European workers' participation[2] with the remark by a prominent European unionist that 1968 would record the year industrial democracy advanced to the center of the industrial relations stage.[3] Since then, country after country in Western Europe has been marked by the passage of legislation, or by national collective agreements, placing worker representatives on company boards, increasing the powers of works councils, and establishing new forms of worker participation in the ownership of enterprises.

More significant, in countries oriented toward a traditional collective bargaining approach to labor issues, such as England and Scandinavia, the union movement has dramatically shifted from a purely voluntaristic approach to a position calling for legislation institutionalizing workers' participation. And in countries where Communist or radical influence has caused unions to reject board representation as a mere cooptive reform, workers' control has nonetheless become a significant slogan and social force, setting the scene for the de facto increase in participation changes even in these countries (for example, France, Italy, Belgium); indeed, except for Spain, Greece, and a few less developed European countries, the changes have been rapid. As David Peretz, head of Britain's Interbank Research Organization, has stated, "Everything is in the melting pot now."[4]

This volume seeks to present a detailed and current overview of this rapidly evolving situation. After the initial overview presented in this chapter, Alfred Diamant discusses the principal West European model of workers' participation: the West German system of codetermination, as revised by major legislative changes that came into effect in 1976. As Diamant demonstrates, codetermination is essentially a corporatist system, but its conservative implications are tempered by the advantages it provides the union movement and the frustration it poses to would-be technocratic elites.

The codetermination model represents an increasingly powerful political program that has injected itself into the affairs of a number of West European states. Even nations with strong traditions of voluntarism in labor relations, such as Sweden, are now moving toward a partial form of codetermination. Andrew Martin's chapter on the Swedish case shows how the political logic of the workers' participation issue has the capacity to draw the Social Democratic parties to the left. Rather similar forces are analyzed in Derek Jones's discussion of the British situation. Here, however, the voluntaristic tradition of collective bargaining has combined with a strong shop-steward's movement to develop workers' control demands in a different direction. While the British Trades Union Congress (TUC) has dramatically dropped its opposition to many aspects of codetermination, the model of workers' participation the TUC espouses envisions little emphasis on works councils or representation of labor on corporate boards. The chapter on France by Stephen Bornstein and Keitha S. Fine and the one on Italy by Martin Slater discuss situations where the issue of workers' control has been raised by labor movements in a more radical setting. Here the symbols of codetermination, particularly board representation of labor, are rejected in favor of a more confrontationist policy.

Consequently, the countries analyzed in this study do not represent discrete types of labor relations systems. Rather, there is a spectrum of systems ranging from enthusiastic espousal and expansion of the codetermination system (Germany), limited acceptance of codetermination (Sweden), and adherence to a liberal model of collective bargaining with concessions to codetermination (Britain), to rejection of the symbols of codetermination by labor (France, Italy). But in all states the tendency is clearly toward increased workers' participation in one form or another. And in no state can instruments of workers' participation (for example, works councils) be seen as possible vehicles for supplanting collective bargaining. This chapter will outline the alternative models of worker participation now "in the melting pot," and suggest the typically ideal form toward which West European nations are evolving, as well as the alternative concrete forms that illustrate present subregional diversity. Finally, the closing chapter will present some apparent paradoxes of workers' control as perceived from a U.S. vantage point, including why this issue has not caught on in the

United States in spite of numerous similarities in labor relations conditions.

Though participation has become a slogan in many West European countries, there is a profound underlying disagreement over the ends in view. Participation, yes. But instituted from above or from below? With powers of codetermination or of control? With worker rights in financial matters or just in social affairs? Reinforcing union power or competing with it? By indirect representation of workers or through direct participation? Consistent with existing shareholder's rights, or transferring the prerogatives of ownership to workers?

Dusted off and refurbished with contemporary language are the old debates over capitalism and socialism, even reform or revolution. Few think that the worker participation legislation of the 1970s is the ultimate end. This is a stepping stone to something else, but to what? Answers vary from the view that participation is the road to cooptation of the labor movement, to the view that socialist self-management will be the final result.

ALTERNATIVE MODELS OF ORGANIZATIONAL CONTROL

Before discussing trends in particular West European countries, it is helpful to outline briefly four of the major models of organizational democracy that form the basis for current proposals on workers' participation in management.

The Capitalist Model

The capitalist model of organizational control is not complex. As Figure 1 illustrates, in simple terms the individual controls organizations in two ways. As a consumer he/she participates in free market choices in which purchases of goods are a sort of vote that sustains the decisions of capitalist enterprises, which are thought to operate in cost-efficient and consumer-responsive manners. As a shareholder the individual also participates in the shareholders' meeting, electing the enterprise board of directors or supervisors.

Reforms aimed at sustaining this model of organizational democracy include both traditional antitrust legislation (aimed at restoring the lost meaningfulness of "free" market decisions) and the current efforts to allow workers more ownership of public shares. The latter is intended to democratize the base of stock ownership, as in the "people's capitalism" concept of Kelso Plan advocates in the United States, or in the more restrained ideology of Valery Giscard d'Estaing (to be discussed in Chapter 5).

In the capitalist model of organizational democracy, a central way to legitimize the economic system is by widening worker participation in shareholding. If markets are acknowledged to be monopolized and if shareholding is confined to the upper class, then the capitalist model lacks even the pretense of

FIGURE 1

A Simplified Capitalist Model

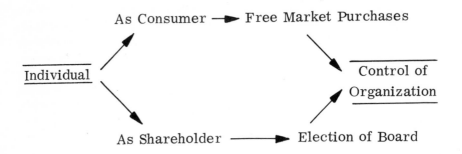

Source: Figures in this chapter have been compiled by the author.

democratic values. It is perhaps not surprising, then, that reforms to extend stock ownership to the working class are very much alive in West Europe.

In practice, however, actual West European reforms of this type diverge from democratic theory in two ways. First, in some countries such financial participation reforms have come to mean little more than that a system of forced internal savings accounts has been set up by companies for their employees without any significant progress toward actual stock ownership by individual workers. For example, the French ordinances of January 7, 1959 and of August 17, 1967, and the act of December 27, 1973 enabled enterprises to set up participation reserves, but only 3 percent of such funds have been used by workers for purchase of the firm's own shares. Even for that minority there is no effect on shareholders' meetings.[5] Similarly, in West Germany, acts of 1961, 1965, and 1970 resulted in savings systems that now cover some 60 percent of West German wage and salaried workers. But as in France, it is virtually impossible to discern any increase in organizational democracy as a result of financial participation in Germany.

A second and more radical variant of the shareholder-democracy idea has arisen in Sweden, Britain, and Denmark. In March 1973, the Swedish government allowed the National Complementary Retirement Fund to purchase shares in public companies. It further provided that the fund might be represented at shareholders' meetings by employees of the firms concerned. Since the fund is very large in relation to the value of Swedish corporate stock, this plan has the potential of substantially affecting corporate control. In 1976 the Swedish Confederation of Trade Unions adopted the so-called Meidner Plan, in principle, calling for legislation that would require a percentage of annual company profits (about 10 to 15 percent) be placed in a union fund devoted to the purchase of company shares. With the defeat of the Social Democrats in the September 1976 elections, however, progress in this direction has been postponed.

Somewhat similar proposals have arisen in other West European countries. In 1973 the British Labour party proposed a national workers' fund, to be created through a 1 percent tax on business equity. Though passage remains unlikely, this proposal would vest potential control over shareholders' meetings in the unions and the state. As another example, in Denmark the government has proposed a wage earners' fund, based primarily on an assessment against employers. Under this plan, over a 35-year span, workers could come to own half of all corporate stock. Though also bogged down in counterproposals and eclipsed by other issues, the Danish plan again illustrates how the "people's capitalist" solution to organizational democracy remains a viable program in West Europe.

The Statist Model

The statist model of organizational control is familiar to American readers. This is a mixed form, adding on to the capitalist model indicated in Figure 1; in addition to the consumer and shareholder roles (which are admitted to be limited in effect), the individual is said to control the organization in two other ways. As citizen, the individual elects a government that issues regulations controlling what the firm may or may not do. And as worker, the individual directly influences organizational behavior through union collective bargaining. Figure 2 illustrates this model in simplified form.

In West Europe as in North America, the declining meaningfulness of the free market has been associated with an increase in economic regulation.[6] Less publicized but probably of greater importance in the control of corporate organizations, however, has been the extension of union collective bargaining.

Many issues once associated with the jurisdiction of workers' councils proposed by radicals have now come within the domain of normal collective bargaining processes. These areas include negotiations over manpower policy, job security, corporate organizational control, changes in the working environment, disclosure of management information, and transfer of productive facilities.[7] Britain's TUC, for example, has called for negotiations over recruitment, training, transfers, speed of production, discipline, layoff policies, fringe benefit policies, dismissal policies, and the "opening of the books" on managerial information.

Similarly, in Italy collective bargaining has started to move into new arenas, such as the question of investment policies. The Montedison agreements of 1973 and 1974, for instance, committed that company to an extensive investment program to maintain employment levels. The Italian Metal Workers' Federation similarly forged an agreement with Fiat in late 1974, securing company

FIGURE 2

A Simplified Statist Model

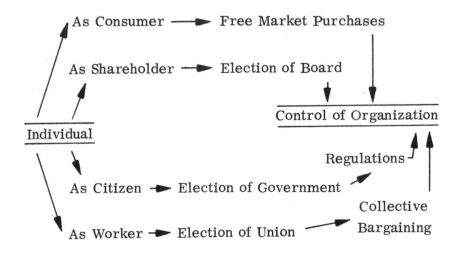

investment in the south of Italy.[8] Indeed, even workers' representation on company boards, works councils, and other participatory reforms have themselves become the subject of collective bargaining in a number of West European countries.[9] The expanding scope of collective bargaining has led even some Yugoslav advocates of socialist self-management to minimize the differences between the impact of collective bargaining compared to that of workers' councils.[10]

Workers' participation in management is not likely to proceed far in West Europe without strong union support, and unions are likely to press for the expansion of collective bargaining as the main vehicle for workers' power. In this context the statist model, which is a liberal one, remains prevalent not only in countries with social democratic union movements (Britain, Scandinavia) but also in those with strong Communist movements (Italy, France). This is illustrated in the chapter by Slater later in this volume.

The Worker Participation Model

The worker participation model is also a mixed one, adding on to the previous two as indicated in Figure 3. Though some view worker participation as a prelude to decentralized socialism, in the West European context this model accepts (but discounts the effectiveness of) capitalist and statist methods of organizational control such as collective bargaining, state regulation, and even

FIGURE 3

A Simplified Workers' Participation Model

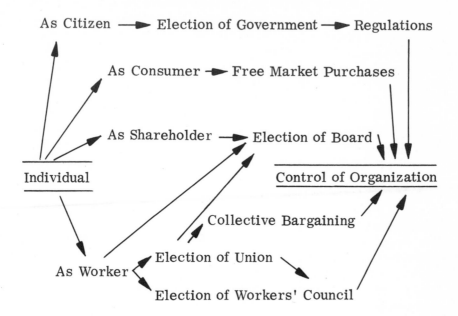

shareholders' meetings. Its innovation and emphasis, however, is control through direct organs of workers' participation.

The unique feature of the workers' participation model is usually the emphasis on worker representation at both the highest (board) and lowest (shop works council and work team) levels of the organization. Advocates of this model of organizational democracy seek majority or at least parity representation of labor with management at the board level, and 100 percent labor representation on participatory bodies at the shop-floor level. Numerous sympathizers advocate some variant of these proposals, often with reduced representation levels or reduced powers for the participatory organs in question. Indeed, many advocates of this model are advocates only in a reluctant sense, not in principle but only with the instrumental motivation of smoothing labor relations without disturbing capitalist power relationships.

The concept of worker or union representation on corporate boards has developed rapidly in Europe. Union or workers' representation on the boards of nationalized enterprises had been implemented for a number of years, but it is now becoming standard in the private sector as well.[11] West Germany, which established its system of one-third worker representation on supervisory boards in 1952, is no longer the sole example. And even in Germany the union movement has undertaken a major effort to upgrade this system to parity labor-management representation similar to that in the coal and steel industry. On July 1, 1976, legislation was passed providing 50-50 union-management board representation in some 800 of West Germany's largest firms, but under provisions giving a management-selected chairperson a tie-breaking vote.

Beginning in 1973, other West European countries began moving toward the West German example. France, which had had two advisory worker representatives on company boards since 1946, passed legislation in 1973 allowing a third representative. Sweden undertook a three-year test in 1973 providing for two union-appointed representatives. In the same year Norwegian legislation provided for an indirect system of elections enabling one-third worker representation on corporate boards. And the Netherlands gave its works councils the right to nominate board members; there the complex nomination-veto-appeal system allowed up to one-third labor representation, but representatives could not be enterprise employees.[12]

In 1974 further legislation was passed along codetermination lines. Austria enacted a bill providing one-third worker representation on enterprise boards. Luxembourg followed suit. Denmark passed legislation in 1974 providing for two worker representatives. And in countries such as Belgium and Italy, where unions opposed board representation as cooptive, action by the European Economic Community (EEC) raised the prospect of board representation anyway. This prospect emerged through the proposed EEC European Company Law, which would require companies incorporating under it to accept a system of one-third worker representation, one-third shareholder representation, with the remaining third to be coopted by both sides from among public individuals who are neither shareholders nor employees.[13]

While increased labor representation on company boards is now a major union goal in Britain, Scandinavia, Germany, the Netherlands, Austria, and Switzerland, there is general disenchantment among West European unionists with representation on works councils. A 1975 report of the International Confederation of Free Trade Unions (ICFTU) stated, for example, "All too often works councils tend to be mere talking shops and it is the management which decides how far the process of joint consultation is to be taken. They therefore lack real power [and may also] distract from the primary objective of building up an effective trade union structure."[14] The ILO similarly reported a general estrangement from the works council concept.[15] And a study by the Organization for Economic Cooperation and Development (OECD) concluded, "Summarizing all that has been said in the form of evaluation of the Works Council, we find the most striking feature is a general lack of enthusiasm."[16]

Nonetheless there is a positive side to the works councils, which explains their continued vitality as part of the workers' participation model of organizational control. The OECD study, for example, also noted that the councils have served to hold management more responsible to the work force and are "a practical example of genuine democratization."[17] Through the works councils, workers and unionists have been able to gain significantly greater access to corporate information compared to their U.S. counterparts, for instance.[18] Thus, in spite of widespread criticism, works council powers have been expanding.

In Belgium, as an example, a royal decree of November 1973 required companies to provide works councils with information on policies pertaining to recruitment, promotions, transfers, and the like. Belgian councils were also given powers to determine the general policy to be followed in the case of redundancy layoffs or reemployment.[19] Edward Wertheim has speculated that Belgian laws forcing information disclosure may lead eventually to workers gaining greater technical competence in management matters. Combined with the prospect of salaried employees and staff serving on works councils, Wertheim states that these organs may acquire significant decision-making powers in the future.[20] Pressures may also exist in Austria, France, the Netherlands, and West Germany to increase works councils' powers.[21]

In fact, a few councils already have co-decision-making powers in some fields; councils in West Germany, Belgium, and the Netherlands have formal co-decision-making powers on matters of training, pensions, hours, holidays, health and safety, company rules, and social affairs. In addition, German councils have powers in matters of layoffs and in payment/evaluation policies. French and Italian councils have the right to be consulted in these areas, while Belgian and Dutch councils have co-decision-making powers. In each country rights of information or consultation also exist in matters of productivity, expansion, relocation, and organizational structure.[22] In summary, the workers' participation model of organizational control, like the capitalist and statist models, is an important and still expanding concept of labor relations and political economy.

The Interest-Group Model

The interest-group model is even more eclectic, as indicated in Figure 4. As a system this approach preserves the fundamentally capitalist nature of management against the radical possibilities of the three previously discussed models (that is, against worker-owner capitalism, collective bargaining erosion of basic managerial prerogatives, or participatory control by workers). While acknowledging the partial validity of the previously-mentioned forms of organizational control, advocates of the interest-group model emphasize the need for balance among the various parties with an interest in the enterprise: shareholders, managers, workers, consumers, suppliers, the community, and the state. This balance is often proposed to take concrete form in tripartite or multiparty boards, composed not only of shareholder and worker representatives, but also representatives of other major interests.

The interest-group model is similar to that discussed by Eric Rhenman in

FIGURE 4

A Simplified Interest-Group Model

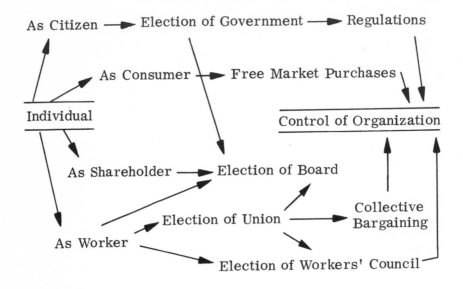

Industrial Democracy and Industrial Management (1968). Rhenman advocated a system under which each "stakeholder" in the firm—management, shareholders, workers, consumers, and so on—might be represented on corporate boards. This interest-group representation model has gained the attention of leading American pluralist scholars such as Robert Dahl,[23] and, indeed, it blends in with pluralist theory rather neatly. Ichak Adizes and Fred Weston have described its rationale: "The more interdependent the environment becomes, the greater will be the danger that decisions based on what is best from the standpoint of the individual or organization will not be best from the standpoint of society as a whole."[24] That is, all affected interests should be represented in the firm in order to obtain a higher level of social rationality in decision making. In this view boards should be composed of all interests, neither shareholder controlled nor worker controlled. As Diamant has noted in his analysis of the West German model of codetermination later in this volume, this philosophy is fundamentally corporatist and conservative. Though its form may provide greatly increased workers' participation in management, it is not ultimately compatible with workers' control.

Writing in the OECD study cited above, Michael Fogarty spelled out the interest-group model further. Fogarty argued that in practice modern company law does not support the shareholders' meeting playing a positive management role apart from its powers to veto certain managerial proposals, amend company statutes, and appoint and dismiss directors. Similarly, a condition of welcoming employee participation on corporate boards should be a clear understanding that positive functions of management—the decisions directors come to in the conduct of their business—are beyond the powers that the boards possess. In sum, worker representatives may influence management decisions through board participation, but they cannot acquire the right to actually make management decisions.[25] In this way, Fogarty explains, the West German codetermination system confers merely the right to be consulted and to hold up certain decisions, not the right to make the decision. Even the TUC, which has come to advocate board representation, has not done so with a view toward taking over management decision making directly. The right to decision is to rest with management, regardless of what interests may come to gain influence on corporate boards.

The Common Market's proposed European Company Law follows the general interest-group model. Since it represents the product of a very comprehensive process of compromise among thousands of West German businessmen, government officials, and unionists, its provisions may be indicative for the future; as mentioned previously, this statute provides for one-third worker, one-third shareholder, and one-third other-interest representation on boards, with the latter to be derived from the state, the business community, and consumers.

Two political observations on the interest-group model deserve emphasis. First, significant pressures exist in West Europe in this direction. The 1975 Green Paper on European company structure and workers' participation makes clear that the Common Market wishes to discourage "too diverse developments" in workers' participation "as this would impede investment flow between the countries."[26] Second, the tripartite plan of the interest-group model clearly institutionalizes a subordinate position for labor. In 1975 Edmund Fawcett predicted the West German government would, in the interest of encouraging foreign investment, back away from majority or parity labor representation on boards. Instead, some sort of tripartite system was anticipated.[27] While the 1976 legislation in West Germany did not in fact fall back on interest-group tripartism (unlike the recommendation of the Sudreau Commission in France, discussed by Bornstein and Fine in Chapter 5), it did fall short of parity. Few expect this will be the end of the matter, however, and the West Germans may yet be forced to choose between extending the workers' participation model toward its logical conclusion (parity or majority workers' control) or toward the interest-group model, which seems to be the form of organizational control most generally accepted by West European Business, labor, and government leaders.

SUBREGIONAL DIVERSITY

West European labor relations are too diverse to be subsumed under any one model of organizational control. In a few more conservative and stable countries, authorities have felt little need to adjust traditional labor practices. Elsewhere labor movement may be so militant or so Communist influenced that the West German type of workers' participation model may seem too cooptive or conservative. In such countries labor representation on corporate boards may be perceived as serving only to legitimize the capitalist order. In spite of much social ferment, consequently, little progress may be made toward institutionalizing the workers' participation model. And in yet other nations, the workers' participation model or the interest-group model is expanding in an orderly manner. In the remainder of this chapter these varying subregional trends will be surveyed.

The Worker Participation Model in West Germany

In West Germany the codetermination system of workers' participation in management is steadily evolving. As previously discussed, near-parity labor representation was created in the coal and steel industry at the board level in 1951. This was followed by a system of one-third labor representation in other industries starting in 1952. At the same time works councils were established with significant veto powers in regard to hours, shifts, rest periods, leave plans, pensions, regulation of piece work, discipline; and with co-decision-making powers changes having a substantial effect on employees, such as shutdowns, relocations, mergers, and fundamental technology or production changes. The 1972 Works Constitution Act increased worker council responsibilities further. Powers were conferred to police union contracts and to handle immediate employee grievances regarding hiring, firing, transfer, and promotions.

These reforms increased the factory-constitutional rights of individual employees and helped assure due process in the workplace. After 1972 councils were given the right to codetermine preparation of company personnel questionnaires, wage scales and special remuneration plans, training programs, and related matters. In addition three weeks paid leave was provided for training of worker councillors each term of office. These reforms also established representation of youth in works councils an an institutionalized special interest.[28]

At the level of board representation, workers' participation has expanded as well. In December 1975, industrial codetermination just short of parity won the endorsement of all major West German parties. Passed in July 1976, new legislation upgraded board representation outside coal and steel from one-third to one-half labor representation. This fell just short of true parity, however, since management was given the right to appoint the board chairperson, who holds the tie-breaking vote.[29] These reforms are discussed in the Diamant chapter later in this volume.

The Interest-Group Model in the Netherlands

The West German model of workers' participation confers on labor more power than is contemplated in the interest-group model, with regard to proposed EEC Company Law. While it is certain that German unions would strongly resist "stepping down" to the proposed European Company Law patter, for other countries such a change would be an advance for workers' participation.[30]

In the Netherlands the increase in workers' participation in management has proceeded under a philosophy more consistent with the interest-group model than with the codetermination model of workers' participation. In the Netherlands the union movement generally favors the tripartite system symbolized by the proposed EEC Company Law. Holland was the first nation in West Europe to follow the West German practice of labor representation on company boards. But the 1971 law (which came into force in 1973) establishing representation provided for indirect participation, quite unlike the West German system.

Under the 1971 law, works councils may nominate corporate board members, but actual selection remains a process of cooptation by the board itself. More significant, coopted members may not represent workers or the union directly. Instead, coopted members must be other public individuals—reflecting a belief in the desirability of representation of general interests. On the other hand, the works councils have a right of veto over the board's choice of coopted members, but even this veto is appealable to the national Social Economic Council.

In the Netherlands the works councils themselves included a management representative as president until reforms in 1976, again reflecting a past orientation biased against having only workers' representation at any organizational level. These reforms also gave the councils advisory powers on investments, mergers, expansions, cutbacks, and appointment of senior managers; the 1971 reforms had given the councils veto rights over work schedule changes, holidays, health and safety matters, plus an increase in information rights. All three national union federations support further extension of works council powers. Thus it is by no means clear whether the Netherlands will eventually establish workers' direct participation as one element within an overall interest-group model, or if the union movements in Holland will press toward greater representation under some model of workers' participation closer to the West German type.

Partial Workers' Participation Models in Luxembourg, Austria, and Scandinavia

In several other West European nations direct labor participation in management is at the level of works councils, with expanding powers, plus board representation not greater than one-third labor seats. In such environments the possibility exists to move toward either a workers' participation or an interest-group model.

In April 1973, the government of Luxembourg introduced a proposal (which became law in 1974) establishing one-third worker representation on boards of companies with over 1,000 employees and of companies with state financing. Though less than the union goal of parity, this reform represented a major step toward the codetermination model of labor relations. The same law also established mixed employer-employee committees (50:50 ratio) with powers of decision over health and safety, hiring, firing, transfer, promotion, and methods of employee surveillance. In addition the committees were given consultation rights on matters of manpower, training, production changes, and access to management information.[31]

Austria has similarly moved toward the workers' participation model, though it too has not yet reached the level of parity representation of labor and management. Legislation in 1973 increased the number of worker representatives on corporate boards from two to one-third, elected by the works councils. This fell short of the parity goal sought by the Austrian Federation of Trade Unions. In addition, 1971 legislation strengthened the works councils by conferring co-decision-making powers on incentive payments and bonuses, and by increasing information rights regarding investments, reorganizations, and other matters.

In Scandinavia, partial workers' participation is also the emerging norm. Norwegian legislation of 1973 established, for example, a new company organ, the "company assembly," with one-third worker representation. This assembly was given final jurisdiction over major investments, reorganizations, and other major decisions. The assembly also nominates the company board, doing so by proportional representation in nominations requested by one-third of assembly representatives; this enables one-third board representation by labor, with a legal minimum of two worker representatives. This system has been or is being extended outside the manufacturing sector (for example, to construction, publishing, and transportation).[32] Norwegian works councils, established in 1945, have been relatively neglected by the union movement and by the Social Democratic government. The government has been strongly attracted to the interest-group model, however, and has established a commission to investigate the possibility of one-third of board representatives being appointed by municipal authorities. It is likely that at least one such representative will be mandated in the near future.

In Denmark greater emphasis has been placed on expanding workers' control through the works councils than through board representation, though 1973 legislation gives labor at least two seats on boards of firms with over 50 employees. Earlier, 1971 legislation renamed the joint consultation committees (Danish works councils, created in 1947) as "collaboration committees." These bodies were then given the right to participate in personnel policy decisions, and in decisions on working conditions. The 1973 national basic labor agreement further required employers to cooperate with the councils on questions of change in work distribution. In addition, the Social Democrats have been interested in democratizing the capitalist model of organizational control. In this regard they have put forward a proposal for a Wage Earners Investment and Profit Fund. Overall, however, Denmark illustrates a national setting relatively less advanced toward any one of the models discussed earlier, and with varied flirtations with each.

The Statist Model in Sweden, Britain, Italy, France, and Belgium

Sweden, in spite of the much-publicized image[33] of involvement with direct worker participation, represents a Scandinavian country in which the central line of expansion of workers' control is through enhancement of the collective bargaining process. Works committees, created in 1966, have increased little in powers in spite of a 1971 labor federation resolution favoring such increase. Board representation was increased in 1972, but this legislation provided for only two labor seats.[34] Somewhat more significant was the establishment in 1975 of joint economic committees (three management and three worker representatives) at the plant level. These committees gave Swedish workers the right to examine management financial matters for the first time.

These minor developments are overshadowed by the expansion of collective bargaining in Sweden,[35] culminating in the Democracy at Work Act of 1976 (which took effect on January 1, 1977).[36] This act authorizes unions to bargain collectively about all issues hitherto considered "management prerogatives." In effect, employers may not take action on significant matters until after consultation and bargaining. Moreover, if bargaining does not lead to agreement, the employer is liable to strike action. Refusal to negotiate makes the employer liable to assessment for substantial damages. In the words of the minister of labor, "The principle is that it must never be economically worthwhile for an employer to sacrifice the rights of his employees for the sake of other interests."[37] Civil servants are to be covered by similar legislation now in preparation. The Democracy at Work Act has the potential to extend workers' influence greatly through the liberal or statist model of organizational democracy, with only limited involvement with organs of direct workers' participation. The substance of powers achieved may well not be very different, however.

Britain, like Sweden, is a country with a strong background of voluntaristic collective bargaining. But lately, labor movements in both nations have reassessed voluntarism, dramatically endorsing various measures to legislate workers' powers. In Britain, however, the labor movement has been less successful.

The major shift came in 1973, when the TUC dropped its longstanding opposition to works councils and board representation. Prompted by the need to develop policy demands vis-a-vis the proposed EEC Company Law, the TUC called for parity labor representation at the board level. It also demanded the board be given veto powers over management and over the shareholders' meeting, quite in contrast to the interest-group model. The British employers' federation has opposed these demands. Caught amid controversy, the Labor government issued an election manifesto in 1974 vaguely favoring a "radical extension of industrial democracy," and established a Commission on Industrial Democracy to develop concrete proposals for legislation.[38] The very composition of the commission, however, promised much watering-down of the TUC position. This topic is further discussed by Jones in Chapter 4.

What advances in workers' power in management have come about in Britain are primarily attributable to the vitality of the shop-steward movement. The shop stewards are the basis for the movement for workers' control, though a few top TUC officials (for example, Jack Jones, general secretary of the Transport Workers) have been outspoken as well. The stewards have played an increasingly important role in plant-level bargaining; there has abeena a corresponding decline in the meaningfulness of the works councils.

Although Prime Minister Wilson called for establishment of works councils in all enterprises of over 100 employees in 1973, the Labour party has since evinced little interest in pressing this sort of reform. On the contrary, TUC opinion has increasingly favored "a single channel of representation" (the unions). The TUC favors participative bodies only as an integrated part of union structure, subordinated to the strategy of collective bargaining.

Ireland presents a similar situation. In spite of a deep commitment to voluntaristic collective bargaining, a 1973 subcommittee of the national Employer-Labor Conference called for establishment of works councils in enterprises of over 25 employees. The following year the minister of labor announced plans for encouraging works councils in state enterprises and possibly board representation as well. The Irish Congress of Trade Unions supported both councils and board representation, though insisting on control of the employee representation process. These developments, however, are exceptions to the general emphasis on an increasingly centralized collective bargaining process.[39]

On the continent a number of countries remain firmly committed to the emphasis of the statist model on increasing workers' control through collective bargaining. In Switzerland, for example, the Swiss Labor Federation in conjunction with two Christian labor groups has developed a united stand in favor of a constitutional amendment permitting workers' participation at the shop, plant, and board levels. Both this and a more limited government proposal, however, were rejected by a substantial margin in initiative elections on March 21, 1976. This reflected the success of a major employers' propaganda drive raising the specter of the "syndicalization" of the economy.[40] As a result Swiss unions have

been forced to pursue collective bargaining approaches to expanding labor influence, though the direct worker participation model will undoubtedly be pressed
again.

In Italy, France, and Belgium, the statist model's emphasis on collective
bargaining occurs in a more radical setting. In these countries labor is committed
to workers' "control" only as contrasted with workers' "participation" of the
works council and board representation sort. In Italy, for example, the works
councils (known as internal committees) have been eclipsed by much more militant, union-controlled factory delegate councils. These developed after the social
crisis of 1968-69 and brought Italy an analogy to the shop-stewards movement;
this was a form of decentralization quite in contrast to the highly hierarchical
form of Italian collective bargaining prior to 1969. The councils formed the
practical basis for various workers' "control" demands.

The 1970 Law on Workers' Rights legalized and encouraged such shop-
floor union activity. Most of the factory delegate councils formed after 1969
have become accepted into the union structure. The Trade Union Agreement,
forming a single federation among the three major labor groups, states that the
councils are "the basic units of the trade unions," functioning to negotiate
industrial agreements.[41]

Through this new system employers have been forced to accept councils
composed in many cases of activists (sometimes including radical factions such
as Lotta Continua) as well as union and party officials. Though not mandated by
legislation, as in Sweden, in practice virtually all management issues have become
negotiable through collective bargining since 1969. Old concepts of reserved
managerial prerogatives have been shattered. The 1974 contract at Fiat, for
example, asserted unprecedented control affecting not only working terms and
conditions but also location of investments and the basic plan of production.[42]
It is hardly surprising that successful factory delegate councils at such plants see
codetermination as a conservative alternative.[43] In general, the factory delegate
system has brought about decentralized, detailed negotiations for collective
agreements of unprecedented scope.

The French case is similar and only somewhat less intense in terms of labor
relations. Though characterized by a greater degree of direct workers' participation in management, here, too, collective bargaining remains the central avenue
for expansion of workers' "control." Though "*la participation*" has become a
popular general slogan in France, employed by the Gaullists as well as radicals,
for the Communists who head the *Confederation Générale du Travail* (the dominant labor federation), the same sharp distinction between "control" and "participation" is drawn as in Italy.

In spite of communist resistance, France has slowly expanded its system of
direct participation. Following the social crisis of May 1968, unionists came to
control over half of the seats on the works councils, which had been set up in
1945.[44] In this context a 1969 national collective agreement required employers

to consult with the councils in advance of proposed layoffs. 1971 legislation gave the councils consultation rights on worker training, and 1973 legislation expanded rights to consider working conditions. At the level of board
participation, an act in 1972 expanded the number of nonvoting labor representatives from two (the level established in 1945) to four (but one was to be a
representative of managerial employees and engineers). In 1975 a commission
headed by industrialist Pierre Sudreau recommended one-third representation, in
accord with the proposed EEC model and similar to the tripartite system already
in effect in nationalized French industry.[45] Legislation emerging from the
Sudreau Commission is still under debate (see Chapter 5).

In spite of these reforms, participative organs hold little power in France.
In a 1976 closing of the Rhone-Poulenc plant, for instance, the works council
was not even informed; major strife followed.[46] Since the 1973 LIP watch
factory strike brought worldwide attention to rank-and-file workers' control
demands, numerous other factory occupations have occurred: over 200 between
July 1974 and July 1975. In over a dozen such instances workers continued to
run the enterprise, sell products, and pay themselves.[47]

While such militant activities have not crystallized in any equivalent to the
Italian factory delegate council system, they do reinforce intense interest in ongoing discussions of workers' democracy by the unions and government.[48] The
two major union federations are skeptical about the Sudreau Commission plan,
feeling meaningful industrial democracy can only come under a government of
the left. Nonetheless, François Lagrange, an author of the proposed participative
reforms, remains optimistic: "I do not guarantee we will get it all through in two
years. It will go in steps, probably piecemeal. But I guarantee that ten years from
now this pattern of labor participation will be established. That is the way
society is going."[49]

Finally, the Belgian General Federation of Labor (FGTB) has also combined skepticism toward direct participative bodies with an ideology of workers'
control. Although Belgian management experts may accept the EEC model of
participation, the FGTB opposes it as cooptive. The unions look with greater
favor on increasing the powers of the works councils, however. A national collective agreement in 1970 gave the councils rights of information, along with
partial control over labor regulations, over criteria for hiring and firing hourly
workers, over vacation and job rotation schedules, and over administration of
employee facilities. Management retains the right of veto. And in 1971 a royal
decree granted shop-floor union delegations the right to be informed of and
respond to proposed wages and hours changes.[50] In sum, the councils are still
chaired by the managing director, board participation is absent, and the unions
are not strongly in favor of workers' participation reforms. Instead Belgium
adheres to its system of national collective bargaining involving equal numbers of
representatives of unions and employers, chaired by an independent figure. As in
Britain, Italy, and France, in spite of pressure to move toward an EEC model,

collective bargaining within a statist model remains the clear ideological preference of the union movements of these countries, at least in the short run.

CONCLUSION

No single or simple model of organizational democracy at the workplace
emerges from the experience of West European countries. It is tempting to
correlate successful movements for workers' power with intensity of militant
unionism. One could cite, for example, the case of Italy, where the factory delegate councils that emerged from the social ferment of the 1960s have been the
basis for extending collective bargaining into wholly new and basic areas of
decision making. On the other hand, the maturing powers of the German system
of direct workers' participation in management cannot be belittled. These are
popular with workers and unionists because they have placed the labor movement in a relatively powerful position. France, though having a more militant
union movement, is more likely to drift into the relatively conservative tripartite
interest-group model than is West Germany, for instance.

Whether labor relations proceed under collective bargaining or under
organs of workers' participation is a matter of emphasis. The underlying
substance may not be much different. In either case, rank-and-file pressure and
strong unionism are essential to the vitality of the system from the point of
view of protecting workers' interests. Unionism benefits from formal systems of
participation in the form of control over policing of contracts, greater access to
information, use of the councils as footholds in unorganized enterprises, and not
insubstantial actual control over many enterprise conditions important to the
worker—social conditions, personnel policies, and work assignments, for
example. There is, in general, an interdependent relationship between unionism
and participative organs wherever both have coexisted. Workers' participation is
most successful when it is part of an overall strategy involving efforts to increase
workers' influence at all organizational levels and through all channels simultaneously.[51]

The problems that emerge from partial work democratization strategies—
involving only one level of the organization—is illustrated in the Swedish "job
humanization" experiments. These were widely heralded in the United States as
desirable efforts to break up the assembly line, form autonomous work groups,
enlarge and rotate jobs, and so on. And it is true, as a 1974 ILO study concluded, that such experiments generally lead to increased productivity and job
satisfaction.[52] Similar conclusions have also been reached in a survey for the
OECD by Lars Ødegaard.[53]

The problem of such participative experiments is not intrinsic to their
operation but rather derives from the failure of these examples to spread outside
a small experimental sector. Ødegaard found in fact that such experiments

become encapsulated and stagnate. "This seems to take place," he wrote, "in the phase of development when it becomes ncessary to consider fundamental conditions or features of the superimposed organizational authority structure in order to establish necessary conditions for continued growth and development on the factory floor level of the organization."[54] That is, stagnation is associated with managerial unwillingness to subject higher levels of the power structure to democratization.

Such one-level experimental approaches embody untenable assumptions. As Edward Greenberg has noted, the group dynamics philosophy behind such reforms envisions an intense and gratifying (and productivity-enhancing) worker experience on the one hand, wedded to a very narrow scope of decision making on the other.[55] The attempt to democratize organizations without altering the control structure is ultimately absurd. Giscard d'Estaing's call for "participation without risk," discussed by Bornstein and Fine in Chapter 5, is such an absurdist philosophy.

Each of the models of organizational control discussed earlier—the capitalist, the statist, the workers' participation, and the interest-group models—can be defended as part of a coherent social philosophy. What is untenable is the raising of the symbols of one model (for example, the workers' participation model) while proceeding in the direction of another (for example, the statist model). In particular, one cannot pretend that participatory reforms as part of a strategy based on an EEC-type interest-group model are a meaningful step toward socialist self-management.

In the West European setting it is still possible to obscure this issue. This is because, as the ICFTU has reported, many of the short-run aims of self-management (a workers' participation model with majority or 100 percent labor representation on decision-making organs) are compatible with other models. For example, reforms for information disclosure, or for establishment of autonomous work groups, can play a role in extending collective bargaining along statist model lines, as well as being reinforcing parts of a system of workers' control of a direct type. Advocates of self-management may even support limited participatory reforms on the principle that such participation whets the appetite for power among workers and unionists. In the long run, however, the EEC's interest-group model is incompatible with democratic socialist aspirations of self-management. And even within the workers' participation model, there is a tremendous difference between the nominal-parity labor representation of the West German codetermination system and genuine majority labor control sought by radicals.[56]

Though Communist or radical control of a West European government is more than a mere fantasy, the majority workers' control version of the workers' participation model of organizational democracy is not on the European agenda. And even if it were, it is not clear that the 1970s is an advantageous time for its introduction. Alan Whitehorn and David Walden have written persuasively on this point. "Premature attempts to introduce a fully workers' self-managing system," they write, "generates participation, but participation based on uncertainty and anxiety due to dramatic role changes. Such premature attempts at full participation are considerably negative and likely to lead to despair and cynicism. . . . What is required, therefore, is a transitional stage or system in which learning experiences and expectations can grow cumulatively."[57]

The central question in West European labor relations, examined in this book, is whether European labor is now forging such a transitional stage—or whether what passes for reform forestalls more radical democratization. The eventual outcome depends critically on whether one believes that the participative experience is essentially coopting or whether its net effect is to encourage greater demands for ever more extensive powers until a conscious and overt confrontation with capitalist authority is brought about.

The crucial transitional goal of advocates of majority workers' control must be the forming of a supporting, democratic, participative culture at local and national levels. In a limited way, this is coming to be recognized among West European unionists. International labor conferences, for example, have issued frequent calls for more education of worker representatives, union control over worker training, and integration of training with the schools of education for purposes of participation at the workplace. A number of reforms have been achieved already: paid leave for training, works council control over training, and access to independent, expert advocates who can aid worker representatives in responding to technical management proposals.[58]

Radicals advocate wedding such limited reforms to the slogan, "knowledge equals power." Such is the perspective in the program on workers' control of the Belgian federation of trade unions, for example.[59] This program calls for workers' control over both training and learning a trade, and for a radical expansion of workers' influence in the area of press information, radio, and television.[60] Such radicalization of the socialization process is a critical element in the transition to socialist self-management. "The drive for an egalitarian and liberating educational system," a major 1976 study concluded, "must be an essential element of a socialist movement; . . . socialist educational reform must consciously move toward equating liberated education with economic democracy."[61] The seemingly rapid changes in European labor relations in the 1960s and 1970s are part of a long-term struggle over the texture of labor-management relations and, more broadly, over participation as a social value and its integration into national culture. The interest-group model of organizational control may be the immediate beneficiary of these changes, or the workers' participation model may be halted at a nominal parity level, but the eventual outcome may be significantly more far-reaching.[62]

NOTES

1. International Labor Organization, "Human Values in Social Policy: An ILO Agenda for Europe," Report of the Director-General of the ILO to the Second European Regional Conference, Geneva, January 1974, pp. 79–80.

2. G. David Garson, "Recent Developments in Workers' Participation in Europe," in *Self-Management: Liberation of Man*, ed. Jaroslav Vanek (Baltimore: Penguin, 1975), pp. 161–86.

3. Charles Levinson, "Collective Bargaining in Perspective," Report 1B of the Trade Union Seminar on New Perspectives in Collective Bargaining, Social Affairs Division, Organization for Economic Co-operation and Development, Paris, 1969, p. 6.

4. "Why Nothing Works in Britain," *Business Week*, February 10, 1975, p. 60.

5. G. Chavanes, "Financial Participation," in OECD, "Workers' Participation: Documents Prepared for an International Management Seminar Convened by the OECD," Versailles, March 5–8, 1975 (Paris: OECD, 1975), p. 80 (hereafter cited as "Workers' Participation").

6. See Gregory Grossman, *Economic Systems* (Englewood Cliffs, N.J.: Prentice-Hall, 1967): chap. 5, for a basic review. On balance, however, European economic planning seems to have enhanced rather than diminished the flow of power toward the executive. See Andrew Shonfield, *Modern Capitalism: The Changing Balance of Public and Private Power* (New York: Oxford University Press, 1965), p. 236.

7. International Confederation of Free Trade Unions, "Industrial Democracy," Agenda Item 10, 11th World Congress of the ICFTU, Mexico City, October 17–25, 1975, pp. 3–6.

8. Commission of the European Communities, "Employee Participation and Company Structure in the European Community," Document COM(75)570, Luxembourg, November 12, 1975, p. 26 (hereafter cited as "Employee Participation").

9. Cf. Gerry Dempsey, "Collective Bargaining," pp. 53–61 in "Workers' Participation," p. 59.

10. See Josip Zupanov, "Two Patterns of Conflict Management in Industry," *Industrial Relations* 12, no. 2 (Mary 1973): 213–33. See also J. Schregle, "Symposium on Worker Participation in Decisions Within Undertakings: Summary of Discussions," Oslo, August 20–30, 1974, Document 82 (Geneva: ILO, 1974), p. 8. Schregle takes the view that "collective bargaining and joint consultation are one and the same process," and urges works councils be integrated into union structure, citing Germany, France and Austria as countries where unionists already dominate.

11. See Schregle, op. cit., p. 10. Worker representation in the public sector exists in Austria, Belgium, France, Ireland, Italy, Norway, Switzerland, and the United Kingdom.

12. See Rolf Thüsing, "Participation at the Board Level," in "Workers' Participation," p. 33.

13. Commission of the European Communities, "Green Paper on Employee Participation and Company Structure in the European Communities," Document P-70 (Brussels: CED, November 1975), p. 4 (hereafter cited as "Green Paper").

14. ICFTU, op. cit., p. 7.

15. Schregle, op. cit., p. 8.

16. J. A. P. van Hoof, "The Works Council," in "Workers' Participation," p. 50.

17. Ibid., p. 51.

18. Roger Blanpain, "Provision of Information," in "Workers' Participation," p. 94.

19. International Labor Organization, "Symposium on Workers' Participation in Decisions Within Undertakings. Background Paper," Document D-1 of a conference at Oslo,

August 20–30, 1974 (Geneva: ILO, 1974), p. 8. Reprinted as *Labor-Management Relations Series*, no. 48, ILO, 1976).

20. Edward G. Wertheim, "The Impact of European Worker Participation on Managerial Decision-Making" (paper presented at the Northeast Aids Meeting, Amherst, Mass., April 1975), p. 6

21. For a review, see G. David Garson, *On Democratic Administration and Socialist Self-Management: A Comparative Survey*, Sage Professional Papers, Administrative and Policy Studies Series, vol. 2, no. 03-015 (Beverly Hills, Calif.: Sage Publications, 1974), pp. 26–31.

22. Van Hoof, op. cit., p. 70.

23. Robert Dahl, *After the Revolution?* (New Haven: Yale University Press, 1970), pp. 115–39. Surprisingly, Dahl rejects the interest-group model in favor of a self-management model, feeling the former to be an inadequate motivational system.

24. Ichak Adizes and J. Fred Weston, "Comparative Models of Social Responsibility," *Academy of Management Journal* 16, no. 1 (March 1973): 121.

25. Michael Fogarty, "Relevance of the Nature and Structure of the Enterprise," in "Workers' Participation," pp. 7–10.

26. "Green Paper," p. 2.

27. Edmund Fawcett, "European Companies," *European Communities*, no. 188 (July-August 1975): 3.

28. See German Information Center, *Codetermination: How Labor Shares in German Industry* (New York: GIC, n.d.). See also "Employee Participation," pp. 95–107.

29. German Information Center, *Economic Reports* 2, no. 31 (December 18, 1975).

30. See Herman J. Teigelkamp, "Gewerkschaften und Mitbestimmung am Arbeitsplatz," *Soziale Welt* 24, no. 2-3 (1973): 271–95.

31. "Employee Participation," pp. 146–51; Raymond Weydert, *Recueil de Législation Sur les Comités Mixtes d'Entreprise et les Délégations du Personnel* (Luxembourg: Ministère d'Etat, Service Central de Législation, 1974); Fédération des Industriels Luxembourgeois, *Les Comités Mixtes d'Entreprise* (Luxembourg: FIL, 1975).

32. ILO, Document D-1, op. cit., p. 6.

33. See G. David Garson, "Workers Participation in Europe in the 1970s" (Paper presented at the Conference on Workers' Participation and Control, Maxwell Graduate School of Citizenship and Public Affairs, February 21, 1975, Syracuse, N.Y.), pp. 11–16.

34. Sweden, Ministry of Labor, *Issues of the Working Environment: Current Features of Swedish Policy* (Stockholm: Ministry of Labor, September 1975), p. 11.

35. See review by Lars Erik Karlsson, "Experiences in Employee Participation in Sweden, 1969–1974," *Economic Analysis and Workers' Management* 9, no. 3-4 (1975): 296–327.

36. Sweden, Ministry of Labor, "Draft Legislation Concerning Democracy at Work," Press Release, January 19, 1976, Stockholm.

37. Ibid., p. 4.

38. *Workers' Control Bulletin* (Nottingham), no. 31 (February-March 1976): 1.

39. "Employee Participation," pp. 126–31.

40. "La Participation: Le programme de l'Union syndicale suisse," *Revue Syndicale Suisse* 63, no. 10 (October 1971): 269–79; M. Andréas Thommen, *La 'Participation' en Suisse* (Zurich: Schweizerischer Arbeitgeber-organisation Zentrolverband, 1972); Union Syndicale Suisse-Schweizerischer Gewerkschaft Bund (USS-SGB), "Participation: Conception des syndicats," mimeographed (Bern: USS-SGB, Sept. 1973); USS-SGB, "De la démocratie politique a la démocratie économique" mimeographed (Bern: USS-SGB, Dec. 1975); Charles Lattman, *Die Humanisierung Der Arbeit und Die Demokratisierung Der Unternehmung* (Bern: Haupt, 1975); Werner Stauffacher, *Gefahrdet Mitbestimmung Dem Arbeitsfrieden?* (Zurich: Schulthess Polygraphischer Verlag, 1975).

41. "Employee Participation," p. 138.

42. See Garson, "Worker Participation in Europe in the 1970s," op. cit., pp. 4-8.

43. Enrico Finzi, "La Cogestione delle Fabbriche: E invece in Italia il sindicato dice: grazie, no!", news article reprinted by the Italian Embassy, Washington, D.C., 1975.

44. "Employee Participation," p. 114.

45. Flora Lewis, "Labor Relations in Europe," New York *Times*, March 25, 1975, p. 1. Note 1975 legislation also provided that enterprise committees be consulted on layoff matters.

46. Clyde Farnsworth, "Plant Closing Plan Brings Strife in France," New York *Times*, April 8, 1976, p. 55.

47. Steve Bodington, "Offspring of LIP," *Workers' Control Bulletin* (Nottingham), no. 29 (November 1975): 9-12.

48. The Confédération francaise democratique du travail (DFDT) has long demanded worker participation at all levels of the enterprise. In contrast the CGT has only reluctantly come to advocate workers' control, and then only in contrast to worker participation. See Fred L. Williams, "Union Democracy in France; The French Democratic Confederation of Labor" (Ph.D. diss., University of Illinois, 1974).

49. Lewis, op. cit., p. 1.

50. "Royal Decree on the Disclosures to the Works Council," *Commerce in Belgium* (January 1974): 13-19. A decree of November 1973, gave the councils rights of information over personnel recruitment, promotion and transfer, and determination of general layoff policies in cases of economic downturn or technological changes. A further increase in powers and provision for young workers' delegates was provided in 1975.

51. Schregle, op. cit., p. 13.

52. ILO, Document D-1, pp. 24-25. The ILO emphasizes the necessity of strong union support for wider democratization experiments.

53. Lars Ødegaard, "Direct Forms of Participation," in "Workers' Participation," pp. 62-75.

54. Ibid., p. 66. For similar conclusions regarding an Italian setting, see Federico Butera, "Partecipazione Poeraia dell' Organizzazione del Lavoro e Gruppi Autonomi di Lavora," *La Critica Sociologica* 30 (Summer 1974): 23-48.

55. Edward Greenberg, "The Consequences of Worker Participation: A Clarification of the Theoretical Literature," *Social Science Quarterly* 56, no. 2 (September 1975): 191-209.

56. ICFTU, op. cit., p. 2.

57. Alan Whitehorn and David Walden, "Some Considerations in the Development of a Pluralist Model of Self-Managing Socialism" (paper presented at the Caucus for a New Political Science, American Political Science Association, annual meeting, San Francisco, September 1975), pp. 2-3.

58. Flemming Agersnap, "Preparation of Management Staff, Workers, and Their Representatives for Participation," in "Workers' Participation," p. 105. See also Schregle, op. cit., pp. 13-14. See also Center for Economic Studies, "18th Month Report: Educational Requirements for Industrial Democracy," (Palo Alto, Calif.: CES, 1975).

59. Wertheim, op. cit., pp. 11-12.

60. Ken Coates, ed., *FGTB, A Trade Union Strategy in the Common Market* (Nottingham: Spokesman Books, 1971), pp. 117-18.

61. Samuel Bowles and Herbert Gintis, *Schooling in Capitalist America* (New York: Basic Books, 1976), p. 287.

62. Lewis, op. cit., p. 1.

2

DEMOCRATIZING THE WORKPLACE: THE MYTH AND REALITY OF *MITBESTIMMUNG* IN THE FEDERAL REPUBLIC OF GERMANY

Alfred Diamant

Worker participation in industrial decision making has been a goal of the German labor movement and of its political ally, the Social Democratic party (SPD), almost since their inception. The struggle to assure worker representatives places on the boards of industrial and other enterprises reached a milestone on July 1, 1976, when legislation extending the coverage of worker *Mitbestimmung* (codetermination) went into effect. However, the event did not give rise to wild celebrations by the German Trade Union Federation (DGB) or by the SPD, for the 1976 *Mitbestimmung* law did not provide for full-parity representation for labor with managers and shareholders as demanded by both DGB and SPD. Instead the law arranged matters in such a way that on issues on which labor and capital representatives disagreed, the latter would be able to prevail. This deficiency of the 1976 law, from the workers' perspective, can be traced chiefly to the fact that the coalition of the SPD and the Free Democratic party (FDP), which has governed the Federal Republic of Germany (FRG) since 1969, had not been able to agree on the terms of *Mitbestimmung* legislation. The FDP, representing chiefly business and professional people, had resisted full-parity codetermination to the end and had forced a compromise formula on its coalition partner. That the political climate on such matters had probably been assessed correctly by the FDP was confirmed by the results of the national elections held on October 3, 1976, in which the so-called social-liberal coalition of SPD and FDP barely retained power. The opposition Christian Democratic Union/Christian Social Union (CDU/CSU) captured 48.6 percent of the popular

Work on the Federal Republic of Germany was made possible by the John Simon Guggenheim Foundation, the Fulbright-Hays Program, and a sabbatic-leave grant from Indiana University.

vote and reduced the SPD-FDP majority in the federal parliament from 46 to 10 seats.

Neither the passage of the 1976 law nor the results of the October election, however, has stilled the demand of the unions for full-parity codetermination. The conviction that only by gaining a fully equal voice with managers and owners could social democracy be achieved is deeply anchored in the German labor movement. But a full understanding of this phenomenon cannot be attained by restricting this discussion to the German scene; we must begin by examining the nature of large-scale organizations and the problems people confront who must function in such organizations.

Concern for the life of people in large-scale organizations has taken forms as varied as the chronicle of the life of K. in Franz Kafka's work, the mathematical models of organizational behavior found in the *Administrative Science Quarterly*, or the computer-based management decision games of the Harvard Business School. One theme—or concern—that is common to much of this output is the ability or inability of people in such organizations to have a say in the decisions that are made about the organizations, the manner in which these decisions are carried out, and—most importantly—the manner in which they impinge on their lives. Given this concern, the next step would clearly be a demand to have a decisive say in the decisions being made in the organizations, and especially those decisions that affect people most directly.

At the same time, there has come a recognition that having control over one's immediate environment is not enough, for decisions made in distant places can be as far-reaching and decisive as those made in one's immediate organizational environment. The disillusionment with life in large-scale organizations has given rise to the sentiment that "small is beautiful" or, at least, "small is better than large." But the preoccupation with one's immediate circle can be a cruel hoax if it leads to a romanticizing of the small and a neglect of the forces that can then, without disturbance, control the wider environment, whose significance has been overlooked in the search for meaningfulness in mom-and-pop stores, neighborhoods, and newly discovered ethnic togetherness. This paradox of longing for face-to-face contact while watching helplessly the creation of ever larger units is not irrelevant to this examination of worker participation in industrial decision making in the FRG today. For if the German workers through their organizational instrumentalities would concentrate only on gaining a voice at the plant level, they would be falling into the trap suggested above. However, there has been considerable awareness in the German labor movement that a multiple strategy is needed, that is to say, that *Mitbestimmung* at the plant or even enterprise level is insufficient to protect the interests of workers in a highly interdependent national economy, which is tied not only into a European economic community but into a world economy, part capitalist, part socialist.

Moreover, the issue of participation is an issue of the distribution of power—political power—in organizations: Any move to secure participation rights that go beyond advice to a share in making binding decisions will require that those who heretofore have been solely responsible for these decisions must yield at least some share of that power. Thus, the shareholders, or more realistically the corporate managers, who have had an exclusive say about how work should be organized, what compensation workers should receive, and so on, might now have to face an equal number of workers' representatives on the supervisory board of the firm or enterprise; and if decisions require a majority vote, then they must have deemed to have yielded decision-making power if a majority vote requires the votes of workers. One might add that the receptivity of existing organizations and organization managers to such claims for participation varies considerably, depending on the structure and purposes of the organization; it might well be that the workers' demands for *Mitbestimmung* once seemed as outrageous to capitalist owners and managers as to today's medical managers, who hear the proposition that patients ought to have a voice in how hospitals are run and what treatment they ought to receive.

The purpose of this chapter is not to make judgments about the claims of either workers or capitalists/managers, but to examine the nature of certain participation claims, the manner in which these claims have been handled by a particular society over a span of time, and the outcome of the developments.

Seen from this perspective, the discourse about participation tends to involve three groups: those who view participation as a means of radically transforming existing organizations;[1] those who expect that participation will have positive consequences for those making the demand, but do not want or expect more than incremental changes in the existing organizational order;[2] and those who see it only as an end in itself, a sort of therapeutic perspective which, with all its humanistic concerns, tend to leave the people in organizations pretty much where they were before, except that they now feel better adjusted to life in their particular factory.[3] One notes that a discourse between the first two of these groups is not always a model of intelligence and usefulness. Too often, it simply degenerates into name calling—idealistic dreamer cum subversive revolutionary versus lackeys of the establishment, cooptation, sellout, and so on. It is, of course, the claim of any investigator that he can rise above the din of such battles. But if he is to do so successfully, he has to indicate what he proposes to examine and what benefits, if any, he expects will flow from his analysis.

An examination of the German labor movement's drive for industrial democracy—that is to say, assuring the workers a binding voice in industrial decisions, from the shop floor and plant level up—might yield several results, depending on the scope and detail of the examination. One might learn something useful to industrial organization and functioning in the United States. This is clearly the aim of the World of Work organization established in 1975 with support from major foundations.[4] Going beyond dissemination activities like those of the World of Work projects, one might argue that the German experience might throw some light on how to modify, more or less radically, the U.S.

capitalist order using a German prescription. One might, on the other hand, be tempted to look at the German pattern simply with the hope of discovering what it is that makes and keeps workers in the FRG as happy, disciplined, and productive as they seem to be. But the prospects for such discovery are dimmed as soon as we realize that we face a double difficulty: the data might not be in a form that permits cross-national comparison, and an appropriate methodology for such cross-national comparisons might not exist; and the past record and future prospects of efforts at institutional transfer of such complex social practices as industrial codetermination are highly discouraging. Perhaps the most modest set of benefits are those that would enable us to gain a better insight, as social scientists, into the functioning of a highly industrialized society, one of a group of societies have have constituted a major segment of the industrialized economy. This leaves the present study open to the charge that it is only a case study. Without trying to make a virtue out of necessity, it is hoped that the following analysis will demonstrate the richness and complexity of the fabric of German industrial organization and will thereby support the exercise of strong caution about facile cross-national generalizations or about cross-national institutional transfers. It might well be that the German trade unions' persistent demand for worker representation on industry boards is a fairly direct consequence of the German variant of the Roman law tradition, as has been argued.[5] But such an explanation surely constitutes an illegitimate abstracting of one explanatory factor from a multitude of historical, social, economic, and other factors that must be taken into account.

Over the past century, the German labor movement has sought for the workers not only political recognition through political parties and industrial recognition through trade unions, but places on the governing committees of industrial enterprises, generally under the slogan of *Mitbestimmung*. To what extent the persistence of these demands can be understood best in terms of a neocorporativist explanation of German social organization will be explored more fully later; there have been many observers of modern Germany who have focused their attention on the nearly unbroken strand in both social thought and social organization that reaches not only from Jean Baptiste Colbert (the French mercantilist) to Hjalmar Horace Greeley Schacht (the German finance minister), but beyond Schacht to the *Konzertierte Aktion*. The fact is that since the 1920s, the German labor movement has succeeded in firmly anchoring a trade union structure and works councils in industrial organization, and since World War II has been able to place worker representatives on the governing councils of industrial enterprises, in varying numbers and with greater or lesser success in having these representatives effectively voice and enforce worker demands.

Given this history, the questions this chapter will try to answer are these: What has been the record of the German labor movement in achieving various forms of *Mitbestimmung*? Why have the demands for participation taken the particular forms associated with the German labor movement? What difference, if any, has *Mitbestimmung* made in the functioning of the German economy?

HISTORICAL CONTEXT OF THE 1976 *MITBESTIMMUNG* LEGISLATION

Though the year 1945 seemed for Germany at that time to be year zero, we know today that the reconstruction of Germany was just that: not a new beginning in all aspects of polity and society, but a reemergence of some very important and persistent elements of past German life. Perhaps the most important of these were the twin institutional forces of the labor movement: its political party, the SPD, and its industrial organization, the unified trade union movement. To be sure, the present DGB differs somewhat from its pre-1933 prececessors, but the major orientation of the trade unions did not change appreciably. What is most significant in that pre-1933 structure, using that term loosely, that has survived and that merits our attention in understanding the developments of the postwar period?

The German labor movement was the principal locus of the major issues confronting socialism before 1914: revolutionary versus evolutionary socialism, expressed in the contrasting views of Karl Kautsky and Eduard Bernstein. It is not much of an exaggeration to say that in the case of both the German and the Austrian labor movements, the voice was often that of Kautsky, but the hand was that of Bernstein; that is to say, the program and the rhetoric (using the term in a nonpejorative manner) were those of Kautsky, but the movement in action was an evolutionary one, eventually abandoning the last remnants of the Marxist tradition in the Godesberg Program in 1959. But up to 1918 and even to 1933, the voice of the SPD was that of class struggle and conflict, and as long as it retained that voice, the SPD sought in vain to gain status as a majority party.

A second important characteristic of the German labor movement was its rapid bureaucratization. The labor movement, which originated in a spirit of revolution against the existing state and bureaucracy, seemed to adopt quickly the central features of the system that the movement was dedicated to opposing. How quickly this bureaucratization of party and trade union took shape can be judged by the fact that Roberto Michels's classic statement of the iron law of oligarchy bears the date 1915, and the subject of his inquiry was the German labor movement. This bureaucratic heritage continues to leave its mark on the contemporary labor movement as well. The tightness of the organization, the union discipline that reaches up in the level of obedience to national leadership (with some notable exceptions) constitute one of the strengths of the contemporary organizations. Party and trade union do not always speak or move in unison, but when they do the constitute a major force in the polity.

A third major historical element that will aid in understanding the contemporary labor movement is its commitment to economic democracy.[6] The most dramatic and significant form of this commitment was in the *Rätebewegung* (Works Council Movement), through which the workers were to take into their own hands the direction not only of industry, but of the state as well. Again, we encounter a paradox between theory/ideology and the actual practice of the movement. The Works Council Movement in Germany was clearly part of a wider social phenomenon: a rejection of parliamentary government and the territorial state, which found expression in Russian soviets and, though in a very different form, in fascist corporatism.[7] Yet when the Hohenzollern Monarchy collapsed, the leaders of the SPD took over the state machinery, found themselves comfortable in their new bureaucratic roles, and in short order were at odds with the Works Council Movement, which seemed to threaten the power base the SPD had just acquired. The SPD was not prepared to overturn completely the government and administrative machinery that seemed to be bulwarks against chaos, and in the end the works councils were restricted to an intraenterprise scope of action. However, within that context, the works councils became an established element in German social organization, though clearly stripped of their functionalist character. In this they probably fared no worse than the Russian soviets and much better than the Italian corporations. But it is this functionalist parentage that has given the works councils their staying power and that accounts for the manner in which they seem to fit easily into the FRG's social corporatism; more on this last point later.

One of the more dramatic elements of German reconstruction after 1945 was the reemergence of the SPD and the trade union organization. Though treated with more or less favor, depending on the policies of the occupying power, party and unions provided a framework for the reemergence of organized political and economic action. Because these institutions continue to function in the FRG, we more nearly appreciate fully their role in reconstruction. What is almost forgotten today is that the social climate in the western occupation zones of Germany was decidedly anticapitalist and strongly reformist. Clauses authorizing the socialization of the means of production were written into some of the early *Land* (state) constitutions (Hessen, Nordrhein-Westfalen), and the so-called *Ahlener Programm* of the present-day CDU advocated far-reaching restraints on the functioning of the capitalist system. Partly this reflected the social concerns of the Roman Catholic church expressed in the papal encyclicals of Leo XIII and Pius XI, but the manner in which German business and industry had coexisted comfortably with the Nazi regime also played a role in producing a liberal, reformist climate of opinion, not duplicated in the FRG since those reconstruction years.

The reform impetus reached its apogee in 1951 with the passage of legislation setting up worker participation in the governing councils of the coal and steel industry, *Montanmitbestimmung*. After that, only minor adjustments were made in provisions for worker participation in industrial decision making, and even the 1976 law stops considerably short of parity codetermination, the goal of the labor movement. Under the impact of the so-called economic miracle and the long reign of Konrad Adenauer and the CDU, the FRG's social climate became increasingly conservative, with 25 years elapsing between the coal and steel bill and the present extension of worker participation. Thus, the SPD and the unions became integrated into FRG polity and society.

The features of the FRG that help define the significance of industrial democracy are the following. Persistent assertions of the CDU governing elite and of its U.S. supporters notwithstanding, what we can observe in the FRG is not a market economy, or even a social market economy, but the emergence of democraticic corporatism—perhaps pluralistic corporatism would be more accurate. What has actually developed in the FRG is a pluralistic political system in which the major parties are based in good part, though not entirely, on class voting. In the 1972 national election the SPD had been able to attract white-collar, middle-class voters. But in *Land* elections held between 1972 and 1976, and in the 1976 national election, many of these swing voters seemed to have returned to their natural conservative home in the CDU/CSU. Thus, while the FRG meets many of the normative standards of a democratic political system, its socioeconomic patterns are essentially corporatist; that is to say, social and economic action take place in a framework of legally defined and publicly sanctioned functional organizations. In this respect the FRG must be distinguished from the group politics system of the United States. To be sure, the appearances are similar; in both, there are labor organizations, business organizations, churches, and so on, attempting to influence public policy. In the United States some of the rules of that game are defined by law, and organized groups have legally defined rights of input, social life, and economic decision making, which are to a considerable extent independent of legally defined organizations. In the FRG, by contrast, functional organizations in society and economy have structures, procedures, and so on, defined by law, and their interactions take place in the context of governmental procedures. Furthermore, these functional organizations are entitled to be consulted and have a significant say in shaping public policy regarding their particular economic or social sectors. Seen from either a left-libertarian or right-libertarian perspective, worker participation in industrial decision making might be no more than a clever device to tame and coopt the working class; but seen from the strong tradition of socio-economic corporatism, demands to have worker representatives on enterprise boards is a legitimate way of making demands and assuring their satisfaction in a corporatist system. Much of the debate and the action involving *Mitbestimmung* becomes unintelligible when seen from the perspective of industrial relations in Great Britain or the United States. It requires the historical context of the German labor movement and contemporary German neocorporatism to gain an accurate perspective on these developments.

One final element of the post-1949 historical context must be specified: the dynamics of coalition politics, already briefly noted, which has shaped the thrust of national policy since 1966. Beginning with the Great Coalition of 1966–69, the SPD, participating in the government for the first time since the Second World War, has attempted to reshape the FRG along lines congenial to its own basic ideology and policy preferences. With regard to worker participation, this led to the appointment of a commission to study the issue and make recommendations.[8] Headed by a man who has since become secretary general of the CDU, Kurt Biedenkopf, the commission's report fell considerably short of what the SPD, and especially the trade unions had set as their goal. It is worth noting here that the 1976 legislation in the form in which it was finally passed more nearly resembles the Biedenkopf report than often-voiced trade union demands. One can give no more effective evidence about the limits imposed on the labor movement as a result of the relatively stable distribution of party strength in the FRG.

The Great Coalition was succeeded in 1969 by the present governing constellation in which the SPD became the senior partner, but remained dependent on the FDP for a majority in the federal legislature.* After having successfully tackled *Ostpolitik* in the first three years of its life, the social-liberal coalition then attempted to enact major domestic policy reforms, but with little success. For the bipartisan agreement on *Ostpolitik* was replaced by persistent and often major disagreement on social policy. As a result, the SPD was unable to redeem more than a fraction of the far-reaching social programs on which it had contested the 1972 election: *Mitbestimmung*, profit sharing, and urban land use regulation. The present coalition has definitely abandoned any hope for the last two, in good part because of the energy crisis and the subsequent economic decline; to what extent it was able to pass worker participation legislation that approached the full-parity goal of the trade unions will be examined below. It is in this historic context that we must approach an analysis and understanding of *Mitbestimmung* legislation in the FRG.

---

*The narrow margin by which the social-liberal coalition remains in power at the national level is further complicated by the manner in which the federal system divides power without necessarily dividing responsibility in the same measure. In a number of major policy areas the coalition can get its way in the *Bundestag* but is blocked by the *Bundesrat* because the CDU opposition controls a sufficient number of *Land* governments to be able to block or force the modification of social-liberal legislation in such bitterly contested policy areas as abortion, education, legal and penal reforms, and so on. In the present study it will generally not be necessary to take into account this federal component in policy making.

THE 1976 LAW

Rather than provide a historically structured accounting of the various forms *Mitbestimmung* legislation has taken since the founding of the FRG, it seems preferable to begin by examining the latest step in this historical sequence and then show how the 1976 legislation reflects earlier enactments, which remain in force side-by-side with the newly enacted provisions. We will then have a full picture of the variety of *Mitbestimmung* formulas that are governing FRG industrial relations.

A first step in the analysis of the 1976 law will have to be basic terminology. Under FRG company law, the types of enterprises covered by this legislation have, in effect, two governing boards: the supervisory board, which is a policy-making organ, and the managing board, which is responsible for day-to-day operations. Worker representation has never been claimed for the managing board, though ever since the legislation providing for coal and steel *Mitbestimmung*, a so-called labor director has been appointed by the chief operating officer upon trade union nomination; this labor director has been concerned with personnel affairs. The 1976 legislation retained the labor director but eliminated the requirement for trade union nomination and also said nothing about his policy assignments.[9] Thus all discussion about worker representation is centered on the supervisory board.

A second terminological problem is the distinction, still made in the 1976 legislation, between *Arbeiter* (workers—usually blue-collar) and *Angestellte* (white-collar). Historically, these categories represented profound distinctions in social status, compensation, security of tenure, and so on. Though most of these distinctions have become blurred, functional labor force organizations still reflect this worker distinction—there being separate trade union organizations based on it—and the 1976 law has retained it. To complicate still further efforts to make sense of the composition of the worker side of the supervisory board, a category of *leitende Angestellte* (loosely translated as executive staff personnel) has been established.[10] Here the terms worker and employee will be used interchangeably in the Anglo-American sense, with the German words *Arbeiter* and *Angestellte* designating the peculiar German categories of members of the work force.

The 1976 legislation affects enterprises of a corporation type that employ more than 2,000 workers; branch enterprises with less than 2,000 workers are also covered if the entire corporate undertaking exceeds 2,000. The act does not cover political, religious, and charitable organizations and also excludes news and opinion media; various proposals for extending codetermination to the mass media are being actively discussed.

In all such enterprises the representatives of the stockholders and the representatives of labor will have the same number of seats, the total varying from 12 to 20, depending on the size of the work force. On the typical 20-member board, the ten labor representatives are divided up as follows: seven members must come from within the enterprise and three can be nominated by the trade unions and be from the outside. This latter point was bitterly contested by the employer side, who bridled at the thought of outside directors on the labor side of the table. It seemed that outside directors were acceptable if they represented banks, but not if they represented trade unions.

One of the more complex and obscure sets of provisions of the 1976 act is that specifying the modes of election for worker board members. In smaller enterprises (up to a labor force of 8,000) the labor representatives can be elected directly; in all others they must be chosen through the intermediary of an electoral college (smaller enterprises can also opt for the electoral college method). Assuming the use of the electoral college method, the four types of worker representatives are nominated as follows (two candidates being offered for each position): trade unions represented in the enterprise nominate the three trade union representatives; *Arbeiter* vote for their electoral college members; *Angestellte* vote for their electors as well as those of the *leitende Angestellte*, though the latter nominate their own candidates for the *Angestellte* ballot. The seven labor force members of the board are apportioned among the three categories according to their number in the enterprise, with each group being entitled to at least one member. Thus, in fact, the *leitende Angestellte* are always assured of one seat; the salaried, white-collar group will probably have two or three, with the remainder going to the *Arbeiter*, though the exact ratio between *Arbeiter* and *Angestellte* will vary considerably with the nature of the enterprise.

At this point, at least a few observations are in order about this most complex electoral machinery. The FDP was the principal proponent of a separate seat on the worker side for the executive staff. The trade unions considered this to be simply a method for assuring an employer-point-of-view majority on the board, and it would take a considerable dose of antiunion partisanship to see this feature of the law as anything else. There is strong evidence that the survival of the coalition seemed to hang on this issue, for the FDP believed that its continued existence as a party hinged on its championing the cause of the executive staff seat. The SPD on the other hand seemed to have been in favor of indirect elections because it believed that the trade unions would be able to control the process for nominating electors. The employer side generally favored direct election, as it favored any sort of move that would reduce the influence of the unions over the worker representatives. There is also little doubt, as one reflects on this electoral monster, that the splintering of the workers' bench could only weaken the influence that the worker members of an enterprise might have over policy decisions. The perpetuation of the *Arbeiter-Angestellte* distinction alone is very likely to do just that.

Though it might be argued that the electoral provisions of the 1976 act do not necessarily derogate from the parity principle, the sections dealing with the chairmanship of the board and with the method for breaking tie votes constitute such clear derogations. The chairman and the vice chairman of the board must be elected by a two-thirds majority; assuming that in most cases a corporate manager is to be chairman, he must be able to carry with him at least some worker votes; the same would hold true for the vice chairman, who might well be a worker representative. However, if a two-thirds majority cannot be obtained, the stockholder representatives elect the chairman and the worker representatives the vice chairman. Such arrangement still might leave the board facing tie votes. In such cases a second vote must be taken and if the result is again a tie, the chairman has the tie-breaking vote. Here, then, is the heart of the case against any notion that the 1976 legislation constitutes parity codetermination. The full scope of the argument that parity codetermination would alter the system of property rights in the FRG, that it would be in violation of a number of provisions in the basic law, will be examined later. At this point it might be useful to observe that the coal and steel codetermination law provides for parity, though it also adds a neutral member who could break ties. However, in the over 25 years of operation of this act, there has been no formal tie-breaking action by the neutral members. Radical critics might argue that no clearer proof is needed of the coopting of trade unions in the FRG; but the evidence also permits the observation that frequent recourse to the neutral tie breaker would quickly lead to very difficult industrial relations problems for which mechanical tie-breaking devices will be of little aid.

The management board, which will also include a labor director, is elected by a two-thirds vote of the supervisory board, with the 1976 act providing elaborate machinery for overcoming the failure to obtain such a majority. Here, as well, the decisive vote rests with the stockholder-elected chairman in cases of conflict and disagreement between the two benches.

The act went into force on July 1, 1976, but there will be a two-year transition period during which supervisory boards of enterprises subject to the law must be reorganized. Thus, at present, we have only a set of legal provisions that are the terminal point of a debate, often emotional and bitter, which has extended over decades. A judgment about its possible impact will be presented at the end of this chapter.

A fuller understanding of the 1976 legislation can be obtained by viewing it as simply another step in the fight over industrial democracy. The parentage of the 1976 act is clearly shown by the *Montanmitbestimmung* Act of 1951 and the Works Constitution Act of 1952. Both acts have been amended several times, as recently as 1974, and both continue in force for the types of enterprises covered by them.

In the *Montan* model there is apparent parity on the supervisory board, but the addition of a neutral member provides a tie-breaking mechanism; however, that could redound to the advantage of labor as well as management. One should note that the selection of the board has to go through the annual stock-holders' meeting, with the works councils and the unions making their recommendations to this stockholder instrument. The principle of outside directors nominated by the trade unions was established here and was incorporated into the 1976 law, but only after a bitter struggle. From the *Montan* model has also come the institution of the labor director of the management board, who is nominated by the trade unions and has personnel policy responsibility. The 1976 law divorced the labor director from union nomination and personnel policy responsibilities, though SPD and CDU are embroiled in a controversy over the intent of the legislation in this respect.

As shown previously, the passage of the coal and steel codetermination bill marked the high-water mark of the push toward the parity formula. The Works Constitution act of 1952 (as amended) provided considerably less than its predecessor. Worker representatives were limited to one-third of the supervisory board membership and all the labor members had to come from within the enterprise; nobody on the management board represented labor directly in the day-to-day operation of the enterprise. One would be hard pressed to categorize the 1952 legislation as anything but a small bone thrown to the labor dog, and there is little evidence that this *Drittel-Parität* (one-third representation) either satisfied the trade unions or that it had a significant impact on industrial relations. After 1966, and especially after 1969, the social-liberal coalition tried to strengthen the position and powers of the *Betriebsräte* (works councils) while also pushing for full-parity codetermination. They succeeded in the former effort—there being intracoalition agreement in that respect—but clearly failed in the latter.

As a result, the machinery for industrial relations in the FRG is varied. The modalities represented reach all the way from no codetermination in small enterprises employing less than five persons, to the 1976 *Mitbestimmung* law, which, it is estimated, will apply to about 625 enterprises, employing about four million workers. Of the six models, three provide for worker representation on supervisory boards, though taken together they employ only a minority of the work force. The other three models provide for worker representation through the, by now, traditional form of the works council, whose significance in industrial relations and enterprise decision making should not be minimized. The public service sector utilizes a comparable device, the *Personalrat*, which covers much the same ground as the works council in the private and semipublic sector. But with all the publicity about codetermination—the benefits claimed for it by its proponents and the dire consequences predicted for political freedom and the survival of the capitalist order by its opponents—well over half (or two-thirds if the public service sector is included) of the work force do not enjoy the benefits of this form of industrial democracy. They must be content with representation through the *Betriebsrat* (or *Personalrat*) or are deprived of any formal input whatsoever.

Though one might gain some benefit from a more detailed examination of how the existing forms of codetermination have fared, all of that would still be a fairly sterile exercise, for whatever exists now or is planned for the future functions, or will function, in the structural context of the FGR polity, society, and economy. Thus before a full critical evaluation of *Mitbestimmung* is possible, it will be necessary to examine that structural context.

INSTITUTIONAL AND POLICY CONTEXT

The elements of the structural context that bear most directly on the nature of industrial relations in the FRG are discussed below in a descending measure of centrality with regard to *Mitbestimmung*. These are clearly not logically distinct variables, but it is hoped that in their totality they will provide a reasonably complete or at least adequate understanding of the place of industrial democracy in the present context of the FRG.

Trade Unions and Collective Bargaining

Though trade unions are no longer elements of a social movement that provides workers with a total socialist environment from which much of the bourgeois world and culture are excluded, they are still the central institution of working-class loyalty and identity. Their relationship to the SPD, especially when the party is in power, is not always an easy one, but the discipline on behalf of the trade unions in Bonn remains strong—in no small measure because trade unions claim their share (and some say more than their share) of seats in the federal parliament and cabinet. It is this strength and discipline that are the foundation of the effectiveness of collective bargaining as the principal instrument for making and enforcing worker demands. Given the corporatist quality of social organization in the FRG, there is general acceptance of collective bargaining as a formal and legitimate decision-making process in FRG corporatism. Thus whatever is done through works councils or through worker representation on supervisory boards is always done within the context of collective bargaining between labor and capital, a process in which government often intervenes indirectly, with the nature of the intervention depending quite naturally on who controls the federal political machinery. But such intervention is generally considered illegitimate. The legitimacy of collective bargaining, strikes, and all the elements of employer-employee conflict, are fully accepted not only in the private but the public sector as well.

Though collective bargaining has been concerned with the, by now, traditional elements of industrial relations, some of the progressive unions, the metal workers among them (a union which includes all automobile workers in the

FRG), have moved on to issues of the quality of the workplace; there have been some notable successes on this front.[11]

Evidence of the strength of trade union discipline and effectiveness, as well as for trade union responsibility (seen by more radical critics as bona fide proof of union sellout) can be seen in the manner in which the FRG leads industrialized countries in low incidence of strikes, moderation in wage increases, high worker productivity, and so on. But the unions are intent on extending the scope of their intervention into economic decision making by pressing for formal trade union participation in the institutionalization of industrial democracy. It is this push that has generated a heated and often vicious debate over the threatening *Gewerkschaftstaat* (trade union state) that classical liberals and conservatives see just over the horizon.[12] Given the strong evidence that FRG workers in crisis conditions turn to conservative, if not right-radical, parties, left-radical trade union bureaucrats might soon find themselves as so many generals without the necessary footfolk to do battle.[13] It would be unprofitable to take this trade-union-state debate seriously, but it ought to be mentioned, at least, for it testifies to the significance of trade unions, their collective bargaining, general social policy concerns, and the manner in which the issue of codetermination fits into the general framework of the trade unions as one of the major corporative pillars of the FRG regime. There is one other aspect of trade union involvement in industrial democracy that deserves some consideration. Given trade union power in the general area of industrial relations, their influence over the existing works council machinery, the possibility of future profit-sharing schemes in which trade unions would administer workers' shares, and central government investment control (*Investitionslenkung*) by a government in which trade unions play a major role, conservative critics would seem to be justified in raising the issue of *Überparität* (dominant representation). If, under such conditions, workers (for which conservatives always say "trade unions") have numerical parity on supervisory boards, the total impact of this trade union power would overbear the voice and influence of the shareholders/managers. Still, a good part of this is only a future possibility whose realization might be cut short easily by a CDU success in a forthcoming election—not at all an unlikely possibility, in 1980, given the very narrow margin of the SPD-FDP victory in 1976.

FRG and Democratic/Pluralist Corporatism

It is hoped that some evidence, at least, has been presented to sustain the original conception of the FRG as a pluralist corporatist system. The question that remains is whether the movement toward codetermination adds to the corporative quality of FRG social structure. To the extent that the 1976 law does not really provide for full-parity codetermination, capitalist company law has not really been superseded. But the notion that in moving toward parity one moves toward some new synthesis would tend to support the present analysis of trends in the FRG.

Legally anchored and government-sponsored labor-management relations take other forms, as well. One, developed in the days of the Great Coalition and under the impact of an economic crisis, is the *Konzertierte Aktion*, which is tripartite machinery for labor, management, and government to discuss economic trends and to shape short- and intermediate-run wage and price policies. Labor has complained that the *Aktion* always produces much talk about how wages must be kept in check but often says little and does less about prices. Yet, government does not simply impose itself on the two partners in industrial relations, and the machinery of the *Konzertierte Aktion* contributes some measure to the persistence of corporative perspectives in the FRG. It is not really possible to make an incontrovertible case for FRG corporatism, for there is evidence from the economic sphere that very traditional capitalist state controls through the central banking structure cannot possibly be subsumed under a corporative framework. The same can be said for the undeniable clout of big business and industry in the economic realm and the continued conservative qualities of FRG social patterns. Furthermore, proposals for investment control by the central state authority would certainly undercut the political pluralism and the social corporatism of the FRG; proponents of such state control and direction of investment generally stand on the radical-to-moderate left, either inside the SPD or outside it.[14] However, to the extent that corporative features can be identified in the FRG, they would tend to be strengthened by codetermination.

FRG as a Welfare State

Along with collective bargaining, welfare state legislation contributes to insuring the material welfare of members of the labor force. Though provisions that protect the worker from the consequences of ill health, old age, and unemployment are major elements of the FRG welfare state, they are not necessarily substititutes for giving the worker a voice in industrial decision making that might affect his employment, his health, the quality of his workplace. For example, adequate provisions for periods of unemployment are considered to be among minimal provisions of social security—using the term in its broad sense. But workers and unions have realized that a share in investment, production, marketing, and other entrepreneurial decisions might secure steady employment—a condition clearly preferable to unemployment, no matter how generous unemployment protection services might otherwise be. To be sure, if working yields less than collecting unemployment compensation, there will be little incentive to work. But contrary to much conservative propaganda, such cases are marginal in modern industrial societies and thus the welfare state might well supplement codetermination, but it is not a substitute for it.

The Structure of FRG Politics

Looking at the FRG from a political perspective, yet one which is broader than that of partisan politics in the usual sense, most observers agree that the nearly 15-year rule of Adenauer and his immediate successors has made the FRG into what many observers have termed a "CDU state," that is to say, a conservative state, socially, politically, and economically. To be sure, there is as much evidence about generational cleavages in the FRG as in other European societies, but the pervasive conservatism of the FRG is really not much in dispute between those who take pride in it and those who condemn it. In this CDU state the SPD has never been able to gain a clear majority of votes and govern the country unimpeded by coalition ties. Radical critics will probably suggest that even as the sole majority party the SPD would not have governed much differently from the record it has made since 1966; no reliable response to such a proposition is possible. But there is no doubt that the slow and cautious advance toward parity codetermination must be traced in part to the pervasive conservatism of FRG society and to the continuing need for coalition politics; the often bitter conflict between the coalition partners as the result of the FCP's holding of a white-collar/executive staff brief is evidence of the tensions within the coalition.[15] The problems of the SPD in developing a consistent policy line in the socioeconomic field can also be traced to intraparty tensions between the party's mainstream people in city halls, state and federal parliaments, and the cabinet on one hand, and its youth and constituency organizations on the other. Over time the SPD had to disown three youth organizations that had moved too far to the left to be acceptable to the mainstream leadership and the rank and file. Some of the earlier youth rebels have, of course, found their way into the mainstream— Helmut Schmidt being perhaps the most prominent example—but successive generations of young radicals have not been so easily contained. Fortunately for the leadership, the young radicals are themselves divided into warring ideological factions, but their wild schemes for nationalizing major economic sectors, imposing controls on press lords like Axel Springer, and investment controls to be assumed by the state even over those economic sectors remaining in private hands, have tended to scare SPD coalition partners, the opposition, and the public at large to such an estent that even the more modest social reforms of the mainstream SPD have had tough sledding.[16]

Given this degree of intractability of the political situation, it is not surprising that the SPD was unable, as has been pointed out above, to make good on most of its major reform promises of the 1972 election. It failed completely on profit-sharing and land use legislation, and the need to compromise on parity codetermination was so far-reaching that SPD trade unionists were taunted by the left wing of the CDU, the so-called social committees, for succumbing to trade union and party discipline and voting for a *Mitbestimmung* act that was unacceptable even to the small CDU trade union wing.

Mitbestimmung and the Constitutional Framework of the FRG

A comment about the chances for codetermination in British enterprises noted that if the FRG trade unions, after a 25-year struggle, had been unable to achieve it, how much less the chances would be in Britain.[17] Such a comment is misleading not only because it fails to take into account the complex political situation faced by the SPD, the FRG counterpart of the British Labour party, but because it also fails to take into account the profound differences in the constitutional framework of these two political systems. While in Britain, parliamentary supremacy and the unwritten constitution would permit Parliament to enact whatever sort of codetermination legislation would be politically feasible, that is, by a clear Labour party majority and Labour-Trades Union Congress (TUC) agreement on the nature of such legislation, comparable legislation would, and indeed does, face a number of serious constitutional obstacles in the FRG.

These constitutional obstacles are of two sorts: procedural and substantive. The existence of a Federal Constitutional Court and the availability of judicial review make it possible for opponents and critics of certain forms of *Mitbestimmung* to raise constitutional issues in the appropriate federal tribunal; one might add that *Land* governments controlled by anti-codetermination forces could also raise constitutional issues arising from the federal distribution of powers in the FRG. The possibility of questioning the constitutionality of full-parity *Mitbestimmung* was raised repeatedly during the debate over the then-proposed 1976 law, and at one stage the U.S. Chamber of Commerce office in the FRG hinted at the possibility of claiming in the Constitutional Court that the proposed codetermination legislation contravened an existing treaty of friendship and commerce between the United States and the FRG.

The thrust of the substantive constitutional issues against full-parity codetermination was raised along two lines: that full-parity *Mitbestimmung* would interfere with the protection of private property, contained in paragraph 14 of the basic law; and that the presence of an equal number of worker and stockholder representatives on the board would not only alter the nature of collective bargaining between capital and labor as equal partners (*Tarifautonomie*), but it would also interfere with labor's rights of free association (*Koalitionsfreiheit*), contained in paragraph 9, section 3, of the basic law. Because the 1976 legislation is so greatly compromised, chiefly in the direction of weakening the parity formula, none of these constitutional challenges will now occur, simply because the legislation clearly does not represent a threat to private property in the form of stock ownership and its fruits. Considering the fact that the freedom-of-association provision in German constitutions was meant to protect bona fide trade unions against company unions, it seems more than a little strange that present-day opponents of codetermination now express such tender concern for the independence of trade unions, which might be threatened if their members sat on company boards.[18]

This discussion of issues of constitutionality involving *Mitbestimmung* was not meant to provide a definitive juridical answer to these problems. What it meant to do was to highlight still another structural element of the FRG context that has or might have an impact on the nature of *Mitbestimmung*.

Mitbestimmung in the European Community

For the present time and even for the near short term, installing systems of codetermination will be determined chiefly by domestic factors. Thus at the present time there exist profound variations in the approach to industrial democracy in the European context.[19] But one ought to keep in mind that developments are under way on the supranational level that will eventually create constraints on national decision making in that arena. Though a common European company law is still far from being realized, once such harmonization has been achieved, the manner in which workers will be able to participate in company decision making will then have to be fitted into such a supranational instrument. It might also be that demands for codetermination that cannot be obtained in a purely national arena could be secured under the pressure of a common front of transnational trade unions and a common European company law.[20]

Mitbestimmung as a Symbol

The mainstream trade union view of codetermination in the FRG has always been one of a means to an end; generally speaking, trade unions have taken an instrumental, a utilitarian view of such measures. This mainstream view has also eschewed a view of *Mitbestimmung* as an instrument for transforming the existing economic order.[21] Rather, it was to lead to a full equality of labor and capital and not to the elimination of the capitalist order as such. This has been the line taken by the DGB and it is difficult to read into such pronouncements any sort of revolutionary intentions. Thus, taking into account the generally moderate ideology of most of the DGB constituent unions and of the mainstream SPD, and considering also the development of the FRG economy as one of the healthiest of capitalist economies, albeit functioning in a modified corporative framework, one is tempted to ask what the *Mitbestimmung* shouting has been all about. Has *Mitbestimmung* become a historic demand of the labor movement that no one has the courage to remove from its pedestal? Has modified codetermination, either in its coal and steel, its *Drittel-Parität*, or its works council model really improved the lot of the worker? Has it really served to constrain the capitalist managers from their preferred alternatives in industrial relations and economic policy? In short, has the voice of the working man and of his representatives received a genuine hearing, and have worker members of supervisory boards and the elaborate machinery of works councils altered eco-

economic policy and industrial relations in the post-1945 FRG? Unless unambig-uous answers can be given to these questions—a doubtful possibility—the record of the struggle over *Mitbestimmung*, at least in the years since 1969, has many of the earmarks of an exercise in symbolic representation. To say so is not to denigrate the importance of symbols in the political process. At the same time, if *Mitbestimmung* has become only a symbol, might not the trade unions and the SPD have channeled their energies into another direction, if they wanted to have a greater say in FRG social policy and economic decision making?

CONCLUSIONS

In this chapter answers to three questions were sought: What has been the FRG record in achieving codetermination in industrial decision making? Why have particular models of codetermination been adopted in the FRG? And finally, what difference has it all made in the structure and functioning of the FRG economy and in the nature of industrial relations in particular? Answers to the first two of these queries have taken up the bulk of this chapter; some con-sideration of the third question will follow. But before turning to this task, let us summarize briefly what has been said with regard to the first two.

The various models of *Mitbestimmung* presently in force in the FRG range from no codetermination in very small establishments to the 1976 model of balanced, but not parity, codetermination in large corporate enterprises employ-ing more than 2,000 workers. There are three types of codetermination in which worker representatives sit on the supervisory boards, in equal numbers in the newly adopted one and in the *Montan* model of 1951, and in less-than-equal numbers in the *Drittel-Parität* model of 1952. Thus worker representatives are either clearly outnumbered, or where they are equal in number of shareholders' representatives, the latter effectively can override the voice of the workers. In the public service and in the works council model of 1952 workers are limited to representation in the *Personalrat* and *Betriebsrat*, respectively, though one must not minimize the significance of this representative device for inserting the workers' (and their unions') voice into industrial decision making, covering working conditions and the nature of work and of the workplace in the widest sense. There is also a strong record of worker consultation by management on a wide range of issues, as well as a strong sense of worker solidarity behind the works councils.

The reasons why a complex social relations pattern like codetermination takes a particular form in a given national society are always multifarious and most difficult to disentangle. An effort has been made to specify two sets of contextual conditions. Thus, historical forces reaching back a century and con-temporary structural elements have combined to give FRG codetermination its particular quality.

The specific form of codetermination, which has focused on having worker representatives sit on company boards, has been shaped by the German labor movement's historic preference for evolutionary over revolutionary methods of social change and by strong bureaucratic tendencies that have reinforced its evolutionary preferences. At the same time, the strength of the Works Council Movement in post-1918 Germany made this form of worker representation an important weapon in the arsenal of the German labor movement. Yet even here the evolutionary and bureaucratizing tendencies of the movement quickly stripped the Works Council Movement of its broader political aims and of its radical political ambitions.

The manner in which codetermination evolved after 1949 has been strongly influenced by the sort of structural variables analyzed above. The first four of these—collective bargaining, pluralistic corporatism, the welfare state, and the political dynamics of the FRG—clearly have had a decisive influence on the manner in which codetermination has developed and functioned in the FRG. The acceptance of collective bargaining as a legitimate form of industrial relations strongly supplements the representation of the workers on the boards and in the works councils, thus adding to the FRG's socioeconomic corporatism. The ability of the labor movement to create and expand the welfare state in the FRG has demonstrated its political strength, though one must note that the FRG welfare state in its current shape rests on a wide national consensus that cuts across all major political formations and had its origin in the well-known antisocialist strategy of Bismarck a century ago. In the context of the first three of the four structural elements, codetermination should be seen as one of several weapons at the disposal of the labor movement to make and enforce demands on behalf of its members. To do so is not to denigrate representative machinery; however, it does suggest that one see codetermination in a more realistic and complete perspective.

The fourth factor, FRG political dynamics, serves more to indicate the limits—or weaknesses—of the FRG labor movement than its strengths. The inability of the SPD and the unions to muster a majority for its programs is clearly a limiting factor, especially as long as these twin organization giants remain committed to democratic politics and to the ballot box. By contrast, the hurdles represented by the FRG basic law would become insignificant in the face of a determined majoritarian thrust. But here, too, SPD and the unions might be confronted with internal conflict, should they try to use their majoritarian strength to override in an undemocratic manner minority views voiced on the national level or those opposition views that draw their strength from the operation of the federal system. How much direct impact the developments on the supranational level—in the European Community and beyond—have on the shape of codetermination in the FRG is relatively easy to assess: very little, at least for the short run. But even in the long run the problems of putting the DGB under the same roof with France's *Confédération Général du Travail* (CGT) and Italy's

Confederazione Generale Italiana del Lavoro (CGIL) rather boggle the imagination.

Can we say, then, with any degree of confidence that *Mitbestimmung* has been a significant instrument in the hands of the FRG labor movement in its effort to transform the country's economy and economic relations in conformity with its goals? Obviously, we will never be able to say how different industrial relations, defined broadly, would have been if the labor movement had concentrated solely on collective bargaining in the economic realm and welfare legislation in the political arena. What is being suggested here is this: the German (or since 1949 the FRG) version of industrial democracy clearly bears the stamp of the peculiar national experience of that particular labor movement. But the achievements on the road to industrial democracy so far are more nearly system maintaining than system transforming in character. This has been so not only, or perhaps not even chiefly, because of the political and economic constraints imposed on the labor movement, but because the movement—at least since 1949—has moved almost entirely within a moderate, evolutionary ambience. What has been achieved, though it is quite far removed from full-parity codetermination, does not do as much violence to the labor movement's realistic goals as the spokesmen for that movement would declare. At the same time—and without meaning to contradict what has just been said—even if full-parity codetermination had been achieved, it would not have been the occasion for a radical transformation of the FRG society and economy, even though the DGB is clearly on record with its determination to continue its push for full parity.

Thomas Mann constructed a conversation between Consul Buddenbrook and his employees during the revolutionary days of the 1848 republic. Sensing the political dissatisfaction of his workers he asks them: "What do you want? Tell me." To which one of them replies: "Well, Consul Buddenbrook, all I can say is that we want a republic." "But we already have a republic, you stupid man," Buddenbrook replies with some exasperation. "Well, Consul Buddenbrook," the worker's response comes, "in that case we want another one."[22] A sizable segment of party and trade unions must surely feel that very same way about the 1976 codetermination law: if that is *Mitbestimmung* then we simply have to have another one. But given the German society's record with republics in 1848 and later, one would no more be justified in expecting radical results in the realm of economic democracy than in that of political democracy. Most observers agree today that, with the adoption and the coming into force of the 1976 *Mitbestimmung* law, the issue of industrial democracy has been, for all practical purposes, removed from a top position on the FRG's political agenda. But this says less about the intrinsic significance of the FRG's methods for insuring industrial democracy than about the conservative cast of the FRG.

Thus it would seem that the prospects for full-parity *Mitbestimmung* in the FRG are not very bright. Any further efforts to limit the power of the managers/shareholders will surely be resisted strongly. Yet the German labor movement has achieved a considerable degree of influence over economic decision making through collective bargaining and works councils, as well as through the working of the corporatist machinery. Is this experience relevant to other industrial societies? Three very tentative suggestions might be advanced. First, formulas for industrial democracy, like those for political democracy, are just that: instrumentalities that must be made to work in a complex environment and whose success depends chiefly on the manner in which these instrumentalities fit into the larger social context. Second, socioeconomic corporatism on the FRG model is likely to be a conservative influence; that is to say, it will serve to maintain the social and political status quo, even though it might permit a large measure of technological innovation. Such systems will look very modern in the technological sense but will tend to maintain a very traditional sociopolitical set of institutional arrangements. Third, in such a corporatist system the technocrats will more likely remain confined to their realm of expertise and will not reach out for power in other realms, as might be the case in non-corporatist systems. Such a hypothesis runs contrary to much of what is being said about the growing power of technocrats—military or civilian—in various parts of the world. It would seem that in socioeconomic corporatism wedded to a pluralist political arrangement, as is the case of the FRG, the technocrats will more nearly confine themselves to their realm of expertise, for the corporative structure vests them with considerable influence in such a role.

Because the FRG might be such a strongly deviant case, it might be difficult to construct a sound framework for comparative analysis with other industrial or industrializing nations. However, there is little that deserves more attention than gaining an understanding of the interaction between demands for industrial democracy and the increasing tendencies toward socioeconomic corporatism in such nations. It is this concern that has justified the present analysis and that ought to encourage further exploration elsewhere, both in the form of case studies and of comparative analyses.

NOTES

1. See, for example, Chapter 5 of this book and the literature cited there.

2. A good example of this is Detlef Hensche, "Zur aktuellen Mitbestimmungs-Diskussion," in *Vom Sozialistentesetz zur Mitbestimmung*, ed. Heinz Oskar Vetter (Cologne: Bund-Verlag, 1975), pp. 465–87 (hereafter cited as Vetter, *Sozialistengesetz*).

3. It would be no more than a debater's trick to dispose of this body of thought and practice with some cheap shots at the Hawthorne experiments; it is also the case that much organization theoretic work has the same sort of manipulative qualities; see my "The Temporal Dimension in Models of Administration and Organization," in *Temporal Dimensions of Development Administration*, ed. Dwight Waldo (Durham, N.C.: Duke University Press, 1970), pp. 90–132. Nevertheless, humanistic sociologists and psychologists do express some genuine concerns here that transcend any sort of manipulative dimension.

4. *The World of Work Report* is published by the Work in America Institute, whose work is being supported by the German Marshall Fund in the United States and the Ford Foundation. The former has been underwriting a program of research under the general world-of-work scheme and has also subsidized two installments of Bill Moyers's TV program devoted to that theme. Much of the reporting on European conditions for the institute is being done by David Jenkins, the author of *Job Power: Blue and White Collar Democracy* (Baltimore: Penguin, 1974).

5. Carl J. Friedrich, "Participation without Responsibility: Co-determination in Industry and University," in *Participation in Politics*, ed. J. Roland Pennock and John W. Chapman (New York: American Society for Political and Legal Philosophy, 1975), pp. 195-212. The tendentiousness of Friedrich's study is revealed by its title. Friedrich's conjecture about the influence of Roman law is an intriguing one, but his partisanship mars most of his contribution in other respects.

6. Rudolf Kuda, "Das Konzept der Wirtschaftsdemocratie," in Vetter, *Sozialisten-gesetz*, pp. 253-74. There is a voluminous literature on the Works Council Movement, some of which is cited by Kuda and in a general bibliography in the Vetter volume, pp. 513-32.

7. I am much indebted here to Henry Jacoby, *The Bureaucratization of the World* (Berkeley: University of California Press, 1973), pp. 181-90. This is a synthetic work in the best sense of the term and raises some important questions about the place and role of complex organizations.

8. The report is contained in Drucksache VI/334. *Deutscher Bundestag* 6 (1970). A condensed and translated version of the Biedenkopf Report is now available from the Anglo-German Foundation for the Study of Industrial Society, London.

9. For statements by leading CDU and SPD spokesmen, see *Die Zeit*, July 9 and 16, 1976.

10. For a sample of the preoccupation with the problem of the leitende Angestellte, see *Süddeutsche Zeitung*, April 19, 1974 and *Frankfurter Allgemeine Zeitung*, April 22, 1974. The problem was also explored at length during extended hearings on the codetermination bill; see *Deutscher Bundestag* 7, Drucksache 6/21/72, Stenographic transcript of hearings conducted by the Committee for Labor and Social Affairs, October 16, November 4 and 7, and December 19, 1974; the portion of the hearings relevant here can be found in the transcript for November 7, pp. 1-31 (the whole set is hereafter cited as *Hearings*).

11. See "Germany's 'Work Humanization' Program Aims at Major Advances in Work Reform," *World of Work Report* 1, no. 3 (May 1976): 3-5. For a report on a work humanization conference sponsored by IG Metall, the metal workers' union, see *Vorwärts*, January 31, 1974.

12. The polemics about the threat of a trade union state ebbed and flowed in the FRG all throughout the early 1970s. Typical of studies viewing this topic with alarm is one in *Frankfurter Allgemeine Zeitung*, March 8 and 27, 1974. *Die Zeit* devoted several pages in two successive issues to the topic, importing Ralf Darendorf and Lord Kaldor from England for a symposium with a number of trade union leaders, under the headline "Marsch in den Gewerkschaftsstaat?" (December 6 and 13, 1974). *Die Zeit*, at least, had the grace to put a question mark after its title; other media showed much less of an open mind on that issue.

13. A glimpse of the possible ideological distance between some of the trade union bureaucrats and their rank and file is reported in "Der radikale Doktor," *Die Zeit*, May 14, 1976.

14. Proposals to establish state control over the investment plans of the private sector came to be major items in the left-right debate in the FRG; see *Die Zeit*, October 18, 1974, and October 10 and 17, 1975.

15. For a major statement by an FDP cabinet member see *Frankfurter Allgemeine Zeitung*, March 13, 1974.

16. The rhetoric and the activities of the Young Socialists (*Jusos*) became a preoccupation of the centrist and right-wing press; see for example *Frankfurter Allgemeine Zeitung*, June 10, 1974; *Die Zeit*, April 19, 1974. It seemed to matter little that within the SPD the Jusos have lost ground steadily, and even *Die Zeit*, November 21, 1975, was moved to observe: "Those among the socialists who continue to hold fast to radical socialist goals as well as to radical socialist means, still determine opinion *about* the SPD, but not opinion *within* the SPD." (My emphases.)

17. *World of Work Report* 1, no. 3 (May 1976): 5.

18. See Hensche, op. cit., pp. 478–80.

19. Gerhard Leminsky, "Entwicklung und Formen der Mitbestimmung in einigen europäischen Ländern," in Vetter, *Sozialistengesetz*, pp. 427–63. See also Chapter 1 of this book.

20. The relation of the 1976 law to developments in the European Communities is explored in *Hearings*, November 4, 1974, pp. 62–68. See also *Die Zeit*, December 12, 1975.

21. See Hensche, op. cit., pp. 466–74.

22. I am indebted for this to Dieter Piel, "Ein ungeliebter Wechselbalg," *Die Zeit*, December 12, 1976.

3

SWEDEN: INDUSTRIAL
DEMOCRACY AND SOCIAL
DEMOCRATIC STRATEGY

Andrew Martin

INTRODUCTION

The structure of authority within Swedish enterprise has been substantially altered by a series of laws enacted since 1971. The essence of the legislation is that it sharply curtails long-established managerial prerogatives. It does so mainly by bringing the whole range of managerial decisions within the scope of collective bargaining, from which much of it had previously been excluded, or directly within the legally prescribed authority of unions or government agencies. These changes have been heralded by the Social Democratic government that had initiated them as opening the way for a thoroughgoing democratization of work life. According to Olof Palme, who was then the prime minister, they amount to the "greatest diffusion of power and influence that has taken place in our land since the introduction of universal suffrage."[1] While such claims may be a bit extravagant, the legislation undoubtedly lays the basis for a significant

---

This study is part of a larger project on the politics of economic policy in Sweden. An earlier version was presented at the American Political Science Association meeting in September 1976, and at the Seminar on the State and Capitalism, Harvard University. A travel grant from the Political Economy of Labor project at Harvard made possible research for the study in Sweden during the summer of 1975. As on previous visits, a large number of persons in government, unions, and business organizations gave generously of their time and help in securing materials. Since many of them wish to remain anonymous, however, none of them will be referred to by name. I can record my deep appreciation for the kindness and hospitality of my friends, Gösta and Ingeborg Edberg and their family.

redistribution of workplace power. The extent to which it actually occurs, the ways in which if affects workers' ability to influence decisions shaping their work experience, and its significance in the light of alternative conceptions of industrial democracy remain to be seen. What we will do here is try to explain how the issue of industrial democracy emerged in Sweden and why the response to it took the particular form it did in the new legislation. We will suggest that the explanation lies in an effort by the Social Democrats and unions associated with them to cope with basic problems of economic and political strategy that became increasingly pressing in the 1960s. But first a description of the legislation must be provided.

THE LEGISLATIVE ATTACK
ON MANAGERIAL PREROGATIVES

The first in the series of laws enacted since 1971 that introduced major innovations was a 1973 revision of the 1949 Work Safety Law (the 1971 and 1972 legislation will just be noted in connection with subsequent legislation that went further in the same directions). The 1973 revision expands the scope of health and safety regulations, extends their application to virtually all employment, and substantially strengthens the position of union safety stewards. Among other things, it gives the safety steward the right to halt any process he regards as imminently and seriously dangerous, pending a judgment from a state safety inspector. It also guarantees the safety steward's job security and right to do what he regards as necessary to perform his duties, as well as training and time to perform them without loss of pay. A safety steward who disputes any change in his job status, including reassignment or dismissal, is entitled to retain his job, pay, and working conditions unless and until the employer can get a judgment to the contrary from the Labor Court—an institution previously in existence. Thus, the law introduces the principle that the union's view of a disputed matter should prevail while it is being adjudicated, transferring what is referred to as the "interpretation prerogative" from the employer to the union. In doing so, it shifts the burden of initiating a legal challenge and of proof from the union, on which it had lain in the past, to the employer. The safety steward's right to stop imminently hazardous processes rather than having to first summon a safety inspector, leaving workers subjected to the hazard in the meantime, can be seen as a special instance of the principle, which was given progressively wider application in subsequent legislation.

Another innovation made in the work safety law revision that has more long-term implications for participation in decisions is that the authority of safety stewards and unions members of the obligatory safety committees is extended beyond existing conditions to the planning of changes. Employers must provide them with information about anticipated changes in plant layout, equipment, new construction, and so on, in advance of the changes, which can be held up by the union representatives on grounds of health and safety. Moreover, the concept of health and safety is widened to embrace the work environment in broad terms, including its impact on workers' psychological as well as physical well-being. All these provisions are expected to be strengthened in a new comprehensive law on the work environment now being drafted.[2]

Several of the laws in the series impose restrictions on management's authority to hire and fire, with particular emphasis on protecting those vulnerable to job insecurity because of age or union activity. Two laws in 1971 made modest beginnings in this direction, followed by three in 1974 that went much further. One was the Security of Employment Act. It requires employers to give notice of termination ranging from one to six months in advance, depending on length of service and age. It makes all unreasonable dismissals illegal, the conception of unreasonable being framed in such a way as to especially protect older workers and union officials. In cases where a union disputes the reasonableness of a decision to terminate someone's employment, the interpretation prerogative is assigned to the union as in the work safety law, so the affected person is entitled to retain his or her job at full pay pending adjudication of the employer's claim—if he chooses to press it—by the Labor Court.

Another in this series was the Law on Employment Promoting Measures designed primarily to increase employment opportunities for older and otherwise disadvantaged workers. Employers must notify both the local union and local employment office (provincial labor board) of impending layoffs up to six months in advance, depending on the number of workers involved. Tripartite committees—including employer, union, and employment office representatives—are thereupon supposed to be set up to seek ways to assure continued employment, such as postponing layoffs, temporary subsidization, or intrafirm transfers. In addition, tripartite "adjustment groups" are supposed to be set up to modify personnel policy and redesign jobs so as to adapt local demand for labor to the locally available labor supply. Local employment offices are not only authorized to require employers to supply information on these matters but also to change their practices and even hire only persons referred to them by the offices.

The third law in this group, the Law on Union Officials' Status at the Workplace, essentially extends to all union officials the protection provided to safety stewards in the work safety law. It lays down various rights of officials, including rights to information, and time and training for union work at the employer's expense, as well as further guarantees against discrimination in earnings and job assignments. Again, in any disputes over these rights, the union's view of the matter prevails unless and until the Labor Court upholds the employer's contrary view.[3]

Another group of laws in the series provides for employee representation on boards of directors. The first is a 1972 law giving unions the right to select two representatives to serve as regular members of the boards of most private industrial corporations and cooperatives with 100 employees or more. This was put into effect for an experimental period of three years. In 1976, it was replaced by a permanent statute, extending employee board representation to all industrial firms with 25 employees or more and strengthening employee representatives' rights in some respects. Simultaneously with the enactment of these temporary and permanent laws, legislation was enacted establishing the same employee membership on bank and insurance company boards. Also, a modified form of employee representation on the decision-making bodies of central and local government agencies has been provided for. What must be stressed in this connection is that the small size of employee board representation—not even approaching parity, much less control—is not conceived as a first, timid step toward West German-style *Mitbestimmung*. On the contrary, it reflects the Swedish unions' basic decision against following the West German unions' route to participation in decision making through board membership. Instead, board representation is looked upon mainly as a way of increasing the unions' access to information needed to put them in a better position to influence decision making at all levels, from the enterprise as a whole down to the shop floor, through the alternative route of collective bargaining.[4]

The main effort down this route so far is embodied in the Law on Codetermination in Work, enacted in June 1976. It replaces the three laws that established the basic legal framework of industrial relations in the 1920s and 1930s, retaining most of the essential features of that framework but strengthening the union's position within the enterprise in crucial respects. Most importantly, it specifies that unions can negotiate agreements providing for codetermination rights in all matters concerning hiring and firing, work organization, and management of the enterprise generally. The Swedish Employers Confederation (*Svenska Arbetsgivare föreningen* [SAF]) has long insisted that this whole range of matters are managerial prerogatives, lying outside the scope of collective bargaining. This principle of managerial prerogatives is explicitly asserted in paragraph 32 of SAF's rules; to emphasize its nullification, the declaration that collective bargaining applies to all these matters is made in paragraph 32 of the new law. The 1976 law also gives so-called "residual right to strike" if settlements on codetermination are not reached, even though there may be an agreement in force on other issues and strikes over such issues remain illegal during the life of the agreement.

Whatever additional rights might be won in codetermination agreements, certain minimum standards are set by the law. One is that management is required to initiate negotiations in advance of important changes in operations, such as expansion, contraction, and reorganization, as well as in an individual's tasks and working conditions. With respect to all other changes, management is obliged to negotiate if called upon to do so by the union. In the latter case as well, management has to postpone implementation of any decision until negotiations are completed, except under exceptional circumstances like emergencies. Management is also obliged to supply information from company accounts and other data concerning company operations and plans to unions, and to conduct whatever studies may be needed to supply any additional information that unions request.

The presumption in favor of the union's view of a disputed question introduced in the earlier safety and job security legislation is extended by the 1976 law to all disputes involving codetermination agreements as well as work assignments and discipline. In disputes over wage issues, the employer retains the interpretation prerogative subject to a time limit within which he is obliged to enter negotiations over the issue and, if not settled, submit it to the Labor Court. Otherwise, the union's view is to prevail. Unions are also given a veto right over work given to outside contractors if they regard this as circumventing collective agreements or the law.[5]

Like the general legal framework of industrial relations, the principle of codetermination through collective bargaining is applies to the public as well as private sector. However, while public sector employees have collective bargaining rights, spelled out in laws enacted in 1965, that legislation contained a counterpart to SAF's paragraph 32 that limited the scope of collective bargaining even further. This limitation is excluded in a new Law on Public Employment, replacing the 1965 legislation, enacted along with the general Codetermination in Work law. On the other hand, a partial equivalent remains in the form of some provisions concerning hiring and firing, statements accompanying submission of the bill to parliament, and a draft agreement between various public sector negotiating bodies and the affected unions. That agreement acknowledges that collective bargaining cannot "infringe on political democracy." Thus, the "purposes, character, extent, and quality" of public administration that are decided by elected bodies are placed beyond the scope of collective bargaining. Where the line is to be drawn is to be determined on a case-to-case basis by a committee on which the unions have minority representation.[6]

In calling for the legislation just summarized, the federation of blue-collar unions—*Landsorganisationen i sverige* (LO)—claimed that it was necessary because employers' insistence on their managerial prerogatives made it impossible to achieve the changes embodied in the legislation through collective bargaining. While this may well be true, the alternative of achieving those changes through legislation was available for a long time before it was pursued. Since its founding at the end of the nineteenth century, LO has been closely linked to the Social Democratic party, providing the latter with its main financial, organizational, and electoral resources. The party, in turn, controlled the government almost continuously since 1932. Thus, if the social democratic labor movement, consisting of LO and the party, had wanted to overcome employer resistance to the expansion of union power at the workplace through legislation, that option would seem to have been open to it for decades. Yet it was only taken up in the 1970s—why not long before then?

The answer to be suggested here is that the legislative onslaught on managerial prerogatives reflects a significant shift in strategy by the social democratic labor movement in response to basic strategic problems that became increasingly serious in the late 1960s. These problems took essentially two forms: one concerned the movement's relationship to Swedish capitalism; the other concerned its relationship to the federation of white-collar unions—*Tjänstemannens Centralorganisation* (TCO)—which is formally outside the social democratic labor movement. The nature of these problems, the reasons why they became intensified in the 1960s, and how a legislative attack on managerial prerogatives offered a way of coping with these problems can perhaps be best understood in the light of how the social democratic labor movement's previous positions concerning managerial prerogatives were shaped under changing political and economic conditions.

THE INDUSTRIAL RELATIONS SYSTEM BEFORE THE ERA OF SOCIAL DEMOCRATIC RULE

The basic terms of the relationship between unions and management that prevailed in Sweden until the 1970s were essentially defined in the first decade of this century. It was a decade of intense conflict over these terms, and the status of managerial prerogatives was the central issue in that conflict. The outcome of the conflict was shaped by a complex interaction of organizational developments in both the labor market and political arena, and by the contrasting effects of economic conditions and political issues on the ability of employer associations and unions to achieve their respective aims.

The employer associations, of course, came into being in response to the emergence of unions. When the traditional mercantilist-corporate economic order was replaced by a liberal economic order in Sweden during the middle of the nineteenth century, employers were freed of virtually all restrictions on their rights to run their operations as they saw fit. But the Swedish version of a liberal economic order also did not replace guild regulations with new barriers to union organization like the Le Chapelier law and the common-law conspiracy doctrine with which the French and British versions, respectively, inhibited worker organization at comparable stages of industrialization. Nonetheless, employers did see the growth of unions as a threat to their rights—especially since most of the unions were closely tied to the Social Democratic party, whose declared aim was to replace the liberal economic order with a socialist one.

Founded in 1889, the Social Democratic party stimulated and largely dominated the initial spurt of union growth. The earliest Swedish unions, started in the 1860s and 1870s, were liberal in their political orientation insofar as they had any. But the union movement was still tiny when the first socialist clubs came on the scene in 1881. Union growth accelerated largely because of the socialists' organizing efforts, consciously competing with the liberals to create a socialist labor movement. For a while, the party even performed the functions of a central union federation. Partly to facilitate the unionization of nonsocialist or antisocialist workers, however, the political and labor market functions of the labor movement were organizationally separated by the establishment of the LO in 1898. Nevertheless, the party and LO remained organizationally linked at local levels, and the idea of a single labor movement, whose political and labor market struggles were completely interdependent, remained deeply imbedded in the ideologies of both party and LO unions at all levels.

The broad character of the movement's challenge to the status quo was especially dramatized in 1902 by a three-day general strike in protest against suffrage and eligibility restrictions that made the Swedish parliament "one of the most reactionary" in Europe, "surpassed only by the Prussian Landtag."[7] The strike was part of a campaign to democratize Swedish political institutions that drew mass support far beyond the labor movement. This support was largely mobilized by liberal political formations that together sustained the largest party in the Second Chamber during the century's first decade. However, by joining with the liberals in the drive for universal suffrage and parliamentary supremacy, the social democratic labor movement added important and increasing strength to that drive. Their alliance in the suffrage drive also proved to be a decisive factor in shaping the role of the state during the crucial decade of conflict over the terms of union-management relationships.

The 1902 general strike jolted employers into mobilization in both the political arena and the labor market. Along with other conservatives, particularly large landholders and state bureaucrats, employers built up a national party organization, formally launched in 1904 with a program including limited suffrage reform and legislation to secure the sanctity of labor contracts and the "right to work," in the sense of the Taft-Hartley Act's section 14-B.[8] SAF was formed in 1902, along with two other employer associations, while the already established Metal Trades Employers Association—*Verkstadsföreningen* (VF)— was reorganized in preparation for an offensive against the unions. There were widely divergent views within these organizations about how the challenge of the social democratic labor movement should be met—just as there were within the latter wide differences about how to press the challenge. However, the employers found common ground in the conception of managerial prerogatives that SAF formally incorporated in its constitution in 1905 as paragraph 23, which later became paragraph 32 and which the 1976 Law on Codetermination was particularly aimed at nullifying.

Specifically, paragraph 32 required the association's member organizations and firms to include in any collective agreements they might make with unions a clause "stipulating the right of the employer to engage and dismiss workers at his own discretion; to direct and allot work; and to avail himself of workers belonging to any organization whatsoever, or to none."[9] While reflecting the importance employers attached to defending their exclusive rights to make the enumerated decisions, this language also implied acceptance of collective bargaining over other matters, principally wages. It thereby suggested a less hostile attitude to unions than that of employers who rejected them outright and sought to destroy them. Nonetheless, it sharply limited the scope of collective bargaining by placing hiring, firing, and work organization beyond its reach.

Not surprisingly, the unions resisted this effort to restrict the scope of collective bargaining, many of them refusing to sign agreements containing the prescribed clause. Their main concern was not with the employers' right to organize work, which they largely conceded, but to hire and fire, which they saw as a weapon that could be—and was—used against their organizing efforts. Disputes over this issue led to the first national negotiations between LO and SAF, culminating in the so-called December Compromise of 1906. In it, LO conceded the employer's right to manage, as formulated in SAF's paragraph 32, in exchange for SAF's acceptance of the unions' right to organize. That the respective rights could come into conflict was recognized in a clause entitling workers to "call through their organization for an investigation with a view to seeking restitution" in case of a dismissal, "which might be interpreted as an infringement of the worker's free right of association." But the circumstances under which a dismissal could be interpreted as victimization for union activity and what could be done about it were left unclear.[10]

As it turned out, the broad terms on which union-management relations developed in Sweden until now were essentially those laid down in the December Compromise, but they were by no means regarded as settled at the time. Many on each side were not reconciled to either collective bargaining or managerial prerogatives, and among those who were, there remained substantial differences over what the agreement really meant. In particular, disputes broke out over how the "right of association" applied to strikebreakers, with the unions insisting that refusal to work with strikebreakers was not a violation of the agreement, while the more intransigent SAF faction called for a general lockout to force all unions to acknowledge the employer's right to hire and fire whomever he pleases, including those who exercised their "right to work" while a strike was going on. In 1907 and 1908, the employers were dissuaded from resorting to this tactic lest it alienate the support of liberal farmers needed in parliament for passage of the conservative government's limited suffrage reform, designed to head off more radical change. In 1909, however, after the constitutional change had gone through its final stage, and after the international recession that had begun in 1907 had seriously weakened the unions' position, the employers proceeded to force a showdown by again threatening a lockout against all LO unions unless LO negotiated a national settlement ending all outstanding disputes. Under tremendous pressure to fight back, LO countered with a general strike. The unions' capacity for resistance was exhausted after five weeks and the strike ended with a major defeat for the LO unions, which lost half of their membership.

SAF then tried to consolidate its victory, first by codifying its interpretation of managerial prerogatives in a new national agreement with LO. Although the strike left the unions too weak to contest the employers' view in practice, however, LO could not be compelled to enter into a formal agreement committing itself to SAF's interpretation. Having failed to translate its labor market victory into the set of rules for the private government of industrial relations that it wanted, SAF then tried to get some broadly equivalent rules incorporated into public law. However, legislation to that effect introduced by the conservative government was defeated as a result of liberal opposition. The liberals had opposed the general strike while it was going on, severely straining their alliance with the Social Democrats in the struggle for political democratization. But once the strike was over, the primacy of the still uncompleted business of establishing universal, equal suffrage and parliamentary supremacy was reasserted and the liberal-Social Democratic alliance was revived.[11] Thus, the structure of issues and balance of forces in the political arena precluded the use of public authority to reinforce the outcome of the test of strength in the labor market. The result was to leave the private government of industrial relations essentially as it had been laid down in the December Compromise, vague and ambiguous though it was in crucial respects.

It was not until nearly two decades later that SAF was able to achieve a measure of success in its quest for legal reinforcement of the industrial relations system shaped by the course of conflict in the labor market. In 1928, a pair of laws, on Collective Agreements and on the Labor Court, was enacted in the face of intense labor movement opposition. The first made collective agreements legally binding and ruled out strikes and lockouts in disputes over the interpretation of such agreements. Disputes of that kind were instead to be brought to the new Labor Court set up by the second law. The legislation said nothing about managerial prerogatives or anything else concerning the substance of collective agreements. However, the court's subsequent decisions had the effect of giving legal sanction to paragraph 32. In the absence of anything to the contrary in collective agreements, which paragraph 32 was intended to rule out anyway, the employers' view of managerial prerogatives was regarded by the court as an implied part of the agreements. In this way, strikes over workplace issues were made illegal during the life of the agreements, although there can be strikes over any kinds of issues when there is no longer an agreement in force.[12]

What made passage of the 1928 laws possible was liberal support; liberal opposition had prevented enactment of legislation reflecting the employers' point of view in 1910. In the interim, a basic realignment had taken place in

Swedish politics. The cleavage over political democratization, in which the liberals were allied with the Social Democrats, was replaced by a "bourgeois-socialist" cleavage over economic issues, in which the liberals were allied with the conservatives and a new agrarian party. As long as this bourgeois coalition held, it effectively offset the power of the social democratic labor movement, despite its growth in both the political arena and the labor market.

The strength of the Social Democratic party had increased rapidly during the campaign for democratization. By 1915, it replaced the liberals as the largest party in the Second Chamber, although it was still a minority. Social Democrats occupied cabinet positions for the first time in 1917 in a coalition government formed with the liberals. In the protorevolutionary atmosphere accompanying the end of the First World War and the Russian and German revolutions, that government was able to bring the struggle for universal, equal suffrage and parliamentary supremacy to a successful conclusion—helped by leading industrialists who weakened conservative opposition in order to head off what they feared might be more radical change.[13] However, this brought to an end the alliance between the liberals and the Social Democrats, as the latter followed the logic of their ideology and called for the use of political democracy to bring about economic democracy—althrough they had as yet little idea of how this was to be done. It also brought a pause in the Social Democrats' growth, disappointing their expectation that political democracy would enable them to win the power to proceed toward economic democracy. Instead, a period of shifting parliamentary coalitions set in, during which the bourgeois parties repeatedly joined forces to carry out measures aimed at curbing union power.

In the years after the 1909 strike, union membership recovered—by 1915—and resumed its rapid growth—quadrupling its 1915 level by 1928. But during the 1920s, union power was subjected to new tests as employers tried to reduce wages in response to recessionary tendencies, and as public authority was used to weaken the unions' capacity for resistance in such ways as manipulating unemployment assistance. Efforts to prevent this by altering unemployment assistance regulations were what precipitated the downfall of two Social Democratic minority governments in the 1920s. In addition, SAF renewed its call for labor legislation, citing strike activity as proof of the need for it to perserve "industrial peace" and protect the rights of neutral third parties. This time, the Liberals, having formed a minority government, went along and introduced legislation along the lines advocated by SAF, which the three bourgeois parties together had sufficient strength to pass. Accordingly, while mass demonstrations were jointly mounted by LO and the Social Democratic party all over the country, there was little they could do about the legislation within the framework of the parliamentary system to which they had long since been thoroughly commited and which, after all, left open the possibility of winning the power to change this legislation as well as other things.[14]

As it turned out, it was not long before that possibility was realized, though with important limits. In 1932, in the depths of the Great Depression, the Social Democrats came into office, where they stayed continuously for 44 years, except for a brief period in 1936. Paradoxically, however, they did not proceed to repeal the legislation they had denounced only six years earlier, nor did they do anything to alter it until the 1970s. In retrospect, the failure to repeal the 1928 law is now seen by many as a big mistake. But at the time, it was not evident that the social democratic labor movement had the political power to do so, nor was it any longer certain that the movement wanted to.

MANAGERIAL PREROGATIVES IN THE SOCIAL DEMOCRATIC ERA

Still a minority in parliament when they came into office in 1932, the Social Democrats needed some additional support to enact the antiunemployment program on which they campaigned in the election. The program involved what was then a major innovation in economic policy, breaking with balanced-budget orthodoxy by deficit-financed expansion along Keynesian lines. Coupling it with support for agriculture, the party managed to break up the bourgeois coalition, winning enough votes from the agrarian party to get its program through. Any effort to repeal the 1928 labor laws at that point might have cost the votes needed to pass the program and brought down the government, just as the two preceding minority Social Democratic governments had been brought down over industrial relations issues. That risk was all the greater since a major construction strike in 1933-34 intensified pressures for new legislation to assure industrial peace. Even after the apparent effectivness of the Social Democrats' economic program—it was actually too little and too late to contribute much to the recovery that occurred—led to further gains in the 1936 election, giving them more seats than the three bourgeois parties together, though just short of a majority, a repeal effort still seemed risky.[15]

At the same time, the pressures for repeal within the unions and especially at the national LO level receded. For one thing, while the legislation could impair unions' ability to make the most of their opportunities during the boom period in which it was enacted, it turned out to provide protection against victimization for members of unions most weakened by massive unemployment. For another, while there was still some risk that any changes in the rules of industrial relations brought about by legislation would not turn out to be what the unions wanted, there was much less risk than ever before that any changes brought about through negotiations with employers would be unfavorable. The overwhelming majority of industrial workers had been brought into the LO unions, putting them in a stronger position than they had ever been in.

As for SAF, the political context had changed sufficiently to increase the risk that further labor legislation would not turn out to its satisfaction. The Social Democratic government then in office was clearly stronger than its predecessors and was even more so when it returned to office with more seats following the 1936 election. That legislation had indeed become riskier for SAF was confirmed by the one new labor law that was passed during the 1930s: the Law on Rights of Association and Negotiation, guaranteeing workers' rights to belong to unions and requiring employers to negotiate with those unions.[16] Enacted in 1936, it had been opposed by SAF, which, in contrast with its position in the 1920s, expressed "general distrust of labor legislation." The LO on the other hand supported it, not to assist its organization of blue-collar workers that had already been largely accomplished but to overcome employer resistance to white-collar unionization, which LO concluded would have to be carried out by unions outside LO. The law had precisely this effect, opening the way for the rapid growth of the unions affiliated with the TCO, especially after the Second World War. While SAF could not hope to gain as much from negotiations to codify the rules of collective bargaining in the 1930s as it might have gained in 1909, negotiations had evidently become less risky than legislation. At the same time, LO had less to lose by negotiations now than it had in 1909, while resort to legislation still carried some risks, even though the possibilities for favorable legislative alternatives to negotiations had evidently increased for LO. For both central organizations, then, codification of the rules for collective bargaining by negotiation could be a less risky way of meeting demands for "industrial peace" than if it were to be done through legislation. Aided by the succession of new leadership in both organizations, they accordingly entered into discussions that culminated in the famous 1938 Basic Agreement.

The Basic Agreement elaborated in detail the basic terms of the relationship between unions and management generally and more ambiguously laid down in the 1906 December Compromise, though reflecting a shift in bargaining power in favor of the unions by comparison with the first decade of the century. It prescribed the procedures for collective bargaining, including the use of sanctions such as strikes and lockouts during disputes over new contracts, and for handling disputes during the life of existing contracts, confirming the "peace obligation" while contracts were in force. A national joint council was set up to provide conciliation and, in some cases, arbitration of disputes that could not be settled at workplace or industry levels, amounting to an alternative to the Labor Court.

In those aspects of the agreement concerning managerial prerogatives, LO made limited gains. In part, those gains were negative in that SAF failed in its bid to incorporate paragraph 32 into the agreement, as it had aso sought to do in 1909. Beyond that, restrictions on management's right to fire that LO wanted were partially incorporated into the agreement. Thus, employers were required to give a week's prior notice and to consult with unions that disputed a dismissal; it was provided that in case of layoffs those with least seniority should be laid off first among those otherwise equally qualified. This was a departure from the principle of paragraph 32 in that SAF now entered into collective bargaining with LO over a major aspect of managerial prerogatives and accepted some restrictions on it. However, the restrictions were limited to the right to fire, and limited even with respect to that, obliging employers only to consult with local and national unions over specific dismissals but not to negotiate with them over the dismissals or general personnel policy. In short, firing was still largely at management's discretion, while hiring remained entirely so along with the whole range of decisions concerning the organization of work. Individual unions had already won greater rights with respect to employment security, and they as well as LO subsequently won further restrictions on management's right to fire, incorporated in revisions of the Basic Agreement. LO also gave increasing attention to work organization questions, but it concentrated on expanding the scope and effectiveness of joint consultation procedures initiated in the Basic Agreement rather than on winning negotiating rights on these questions. In other words, the principle of managerial prerogatives was left largely intact.[17]

Thus, the social democratic labor movement did not use the power it had gained in either the labor market or the political arena by the 1930s to modify the essential features of the industrial relations system initially established in the 1906 December Compromise and reinforced by the 1928 legislation. At most, it brought about some changes that marginally improved the position of unions. This was accomplished primarily through centralized negotiations rather than legislation, except for the 1936 law, despite continued Social Democratic control of the government. Admittedly, no one could have predicted at that time that that control would last as long as it did. Moreover, that control subsequently proved to be highly precarious much of the time. However, the limits to the shift in power in favor of the social democratic labor movement can hardly suffice to explain its acceptance of the industrial relations system essentially as it had developed prior to the era of Social Democratic rule, particularly in view of the movement's previous strenuous opposition to various features of that system during the course of its development. In addition, that acceptance seems to have been rooted in choices about how the movement's power was to be used. These choices would seem to have been inherent in the fundamental strategy adopted by the movement for influencing an economy that was, and was expected to remain, predominantly capitalist.

As we noted earlier, the Social Democratic party during the 1920s still had no idea of how it could use the power that political democracy had been expected to bring it to achieve the economic democracy for which its original socialist goal had come to be conceived. In this respect, the party shared the fundamental strategic dilemma typically faced by the reformist labor movement parties that had socialist roots and had become committed to gradualist, reformist, parliamentary politics. This dilemma was posed most sharply with the advent of the Great Depression. There were no viable responses to it for a reformist labor movement party either within the framework of orthodox liberalism, to which Ramsay MacDonald confined the British Labour party's options, or of orthodox Marxism, to which Rudolf Hilferding confined the German Social Democratic party's options. Either capitalism was abolished or it was necessary to conform to its requirements with balanced budgets, by tax increases and spending cuts, and pressure to lower wages and prices so as to help the business cycle go through its necessary course. Neither alternative was really acceptable to a nonrevolutionary party that nevertheless wanted to protect the interests of its working-class constituency. But given the balanced-budget assumption and the prevailing configuration of political power in the relevant countries, reformist labor movement parties that wanted to protect those interests were forced into a zero-sum game they did not have the power to win.

On the other hand, if the balanced-budget assumption is dropped, the possibilities are transformed. This is the political significance of Keynesian policy in a depression context—which others advocated independently of Keynes. Since deficit-financed government spending can expand demand and reduce unemployment, without requiring increased taxes and cuts in spending, prices, and wages, coalitions can be formed that are impossible under policies of balanced-budget contraction. While British and German union leaders urged their party counterparts to press for such expansionary budget policies, the party leaders refused, closing off any possibilities for politically viable responses. In contrast, as indicated above, the Swedish Social Democrats did break with balanced-budget orthodoxy, thereby finding a way out of the dilemma as it was defined in that context.[18]

This had decisive, lasting consequences for the evolution of the Social Democrats' subsequent strategy. In political terms, it enabled them to replace their defunct alliance with the liberals by a new coalition strategy involving the agrarians, which made it possible for the Social Democrats to hold onto office in the 1950s as well as the 1930s. In economic terms, it laid the basis for the broad pattern of policy on which the Social Democrats relied, with inventiveness but no fundamental change, through most of the 1960s.

The economic strategy was to control the overall level of activity, its allocation between public and private consumption, and the distribution of the resulting income by a combination of government and union policies, while the actual production itself was left to the operation of capitalist firms. The main task assigned to the government, according to this strategy, was to maintain full employment by the kind of Keynesian fiscal techniques introduced by the Social Democrats in 1932. In addition, the budget was to be used to allocate resources between the private sector and collective priorities such as education, housing, and the like. Finally, it was to build up a structure of taxes and transfers to provide economic security and reduce inequality. With the general pattern of economic activity shaped by government policy in these ways, the task assigned to the unions was to carry out a coordinated wage policy to improve, or at least maintain, the workers' share of a growing national income, reduce the differences in income among workers, and avoid the kind of interunion wage rivalry that could feed inflation—a concern that became more important after the Second World War.[19]

Whether it could be claimed that this interaction of government and union policies meant the establishment of "economic democracy" or not—it is yet to be established as the Social Democrats now see things—it was seen at the time as determining the economic environment in which firms operated to such an extent that the economy could be effectively subjected to democratic control even though the firms themselves remained overwhelmingly capitalist. This outlook obviously had much in common with that adopted by West European labor or social democratic parties, for which Sweden's "middle way" had indeed served as a model. However, the Swedish variant was distinctive to the extent that emphasis was placed on two conditions regarded as essential to the implementation of the strategy. One was that the government had to be continuously controlled by the Social Democrats, intermittent control by labor movement parties alternating with others being seen as insufficient to offset capitalist power in the economy. The other condition was that wage pressures should continue to squeeze profits but be coordinated by the central union federation, a government incomes policy to restrain wages being seen as a threat to the unions' distributive aims and internal cohesion, which in turn would impair their ability to provide the political resources needed to keep the Social Democrats in office. Indeed, it was a general corollary of the first condition that nothing should be done, at any level of the movement in the political arena or the labor market, that might jeopardize the Social Democrats' continued control of government. A general corollary of the second condition was that authority within the LO had to be centralized sufficiently to enable it to achieve the necessary coordination of wage bargaining.[20]

The Social Democrats did, of course, succeed in retaining control of the government for nearly four and a half decades, though often just barely and with parliamentary majorities only from 1940 to 1944, and 1968 to 1970. As for LO, while it has never been as centralized as its principal employer counterpart, it became considerably more so as a result of a major rules revision in 1941 and the growth of centralized wage bargaining since the mid-1950s. LO and SAF began then to negotiate "frame agreements," which determine the general levels and patterns of wage settlements throughout the important part of the labor market in which their memberships overlap, although the agreements only have the formal status of recommendations to their respective affiliates who actually negotiate the binding contracts, the details of which are ultimately settled at the workplace. LO has been able to coordinate wage bargaining among its affiliates this way because they recognize it as a way of achieving the "solidaristic" wage policy to which they have become generally committed. Although its interpretation varies, the solidaristic principle is usually understood to mean equal pay for equal work, regardless of a firm's ability to pay, and reduction of differences in pay for different work.[21]

The LO's approach to the problem of inflation in the postwar era attached additional importance to solidaristic wage policy. It insisted that government rather than unions bore the main responsibility for maintaining noninflationary full employment, primarily by keeping general fiscal policy restrictive enough to avoid excessive demand. Under these conditions, equal pay for equal work would force firms too inefficient to pay standard rates to modernize or go out of business. The shutdown of such firms was regarded as acceptable providing that the government also carried out an "active manpower policy"—retraining, reloca-tion assistance, and other selective measures—facilitating the transition of dis-placed workers to alternative jobs and making society as a whole bear the costs. As long as noninflationary full employment was maintained by this combination of general fiscal policy and selective manpower policy, it was expected that its disruption by interunion wage rivalry could be avoided by coordinating wage bargaining on the basis of the generally accepted solidaristic principle. Such a wage policy was also expected to contribute to an improved "trade-off" between full employment and price stability by improving the proportion of efficient, low-cost firms in the economy, precisely because it forced high-cost firms to become more efficient or shut down. This approach has been usually referred to as the "Rehn model," after the LO economist chiefly responsible for elaborating it.[22]

We must stress the acceptance of technological innovation and structural change in industry that the approach reflected. That acceptance, to a greater degree than in any other labor movement, rested on LO's confidence that Social Democratic governments would carry out the combination of general and selec-tive policies needed to prevent workers from bearing the burdens of change, and that the unions could assure workers their fair share of the benefits. In other words, it was believed that government and union actions in shaping the eco-nomic conditions under which technological change took place would assure that its social consequences would be acceptable. Given these assumptions, it was accepted that decisions about technological change itself could be left up to management, compelled by competition to seek the most efficient ways of carrying out production. Hence, there was no reason to challenge management's claim to decide unilaterally on the adoption of new technology and on the organization of work required to utilize it. Furthermore, it was believed prefer-able to leave such decisions up to management, for if unions shared responsibil-ity for a firm's efficiency by participating in decisions about how to achieve it, they might compromise the independence they needed to defend workers' interests. Thus, joint consultation was deemed sufficient to provide a channel for whatever worker participation might be desired while avoiding the risk of "dual loyalty" likely from joint determination. Accordingly, LO confined its efforts with respect to workers' participation to the negotiation of a series of Works Councils Agreements with SAF—and TCO—in 1946, 1958, and 1966.[23]

At its 1971 congress, however, LO abandoned its preference for joint consultation and adopted a policy statement on "Industrial Democracy" in which it demanded instead joint determination, through collective bargaining. The statement marked a clear shift from the strategy that had prevailed since the 1930s. Power at the national level to shape the economic conditions to which managements respond was no longer accepted as sufficient. Power at the enterprise and workplace levels was now regarded as essential to have an impact on how managements respond to those conditions. To achieve that power, the long-standing obstacle of managerial prerogatives epitomized by paragraph 32 had to be eliminated, by negotiation if possible and by legislation if necessary.[24] What had happened to bring about this major change in LO's position?

THE SOURCES OF CHANGE

The most dramatic thing that had happened was the wave of wildcat strikes that broke out in the northern state-owned iron mines in December 1969, and spread to major manufacturing firms in central Sweden. Despite Sweden's reputation for industrial peace, there had been short, unofficial, local stoppages involving relatively small numbers throughout the postwar period. While the level of such strike activity was low by international standards, there was more of it than indicated by the official statistics, which recorded only the small proportion of cases brought to the Labor Court. So what was new about the winter 1969-70 strike wave was not the resort to unofficial, and illegal, action but the strikes' duration and size, and a much higher level of smaller wildcat strikes thereafter than before. The Swedish unions' hold on their members' loyalty was evidently eroding, as elsewhere in Europe.[25]

A major factor in that erosion may well have been the very centralization of authority within the unions on which their national power depended. To the extent that this increased the labor movement's power in the political arena to protect full employment, it undoubtedly bolstered the bargaining power of workers and their local representatives. But there was far less for them to bargain about to the extent that wage issues were settled at national levels. While this might be an inescapable corollary of a solidaristic wage policy, it would tend to diminish the functions of local union organizations on which to base their claims for support. This would make it all the more important for local unions to be in a position to do something as far as nonwage issues are concerned in order to retain member support. But it was precisely over such issues that the unions' scope for action was severely limited. To be sure, the practical effect of this limitation varied considerably among industries and among firms within industries. Moreover, as noted earlier, there remained a considerable amount of bargaining to be done over wages after the national frame agreements and industrywide contracts were signed, especially because of the prevalence of piecework payments systems in Swedish industry, at least until the 1970s. By and large, however, it is still probably correct to say that Swedish unions have typically had considerably less power at the workplace level than at the national level.[26]

Weakness at the workplace is indeed fairly typical in Western Europe, in contrast with the United States where unions are much weaker as a national force, largely because of the proportion of the labor force they cover or can at least mobilize is about half the West European average and a third of the Swedish level, but where they are said to have considerably greater power at the workplace, at least in some of the sectors or firms where they have achieved a very high degree of organization and "job control." While this contrast may be overdrawn, there can be little doubt that Swedish unions have been severely limited in what they could do about workplace issues that employers claimed to be within their exclusive jurisdiction, whether invoking paragraph 32 or not. The risks to which this weakness exposed the unions were revealed by the wave of wildcat strikes, more sharply than mere rank-and-file apathy could ever have done. The obvious way to reestablish the unions' claims to their members' loyalty was therefore to increase the unions' capacity to win results on nonwage workplace issues. Accordingly, the time to remove the paragraph 32 obstacle had come.

While it took the wildcat strikes to bring some union leaders to this conclusion, others had already been driven to it by a growing conviction that the rationalization of production by technological innovation and structural change was imposing greater costs on workers than had been anticipated or that could be compensated by the kind of manpower policy being carried out, no matter how "active." By intensifying the pace of work, creating new and often unperceived physical dangers, increasing social isolation, and in other ways, the rationalization of production was now seen as hurting the workers who retained jobs in firms keeping up with technological change as well as the workers who lost jobs in firms forced to shut down for failing to keep up. Increasing labor turnover, absenteeism, and recruiting difficulties were interpreted as reactions to work that was becoming increasingly stressful. Complaints filtering up through the unions, and repeatedly expressed in motions at union congresses, pinpointed many specific sources of dissatisfaction. In addition, surveys by LO and some national unions recorded its content and widespread prevalence. The wildcat strikes could be seen as yet another expression of the dissatisfaction, regardless of whether particular stoppages were triggered by wage or nonwage issues—a matter much disputed but difficult to disentangle. If so, the strikes simply reinforced conclusions to which much else had already been pointing.[27]

At the same time, it was shown that workers displaced by change were having increasing difficulty finding alternative jobs insofar as they were older or otherwise impaired in their capacity to do what was said to be the physically or psychologically more demanding jobs being created. For growing numbers of them, reentry into industry was becoming impossible despite the retraining and relocation assistance that the vastly expanded manpower policy provided and the comparatively low overall unemployment level maintained by the macroeconomic policy. And for growing numbers of those who had kept their jobs, the insecurity of how long they could continue to do so in the face of further change was added to the stresses experienced as a result of the changes that had already occurred.[28]

All this combined to make increasingly untenable the assumptions that decisions about technological change could be left to management. To do so meant that management was free to make such decisions without taking into account workers' physical and psychological needs, leaving workers with no choice but to adapt or leave. If technology was to be adapted to the workers instead of the other way around, workers had to have the power to assure that their needs were taken into account in decisions about technology. Since their union organization was the workers' only effective resource for exercising power, it followed that unions had to gain a voice in all the decisions about technology and related questions of how and by whom it was to be utilized. Without such a voice, it was becoming increasingly clear, unions could no longer claim to be defending their members' interests.

While the worker dissatisfaction on which these arguments were based was undoubtedly growing, it is difficult to know to what extent it reflected working conditions that were in fact increasingly stressful or how much it resulted from decreasing tolerance for conditions that may have been no worse—and in some cases even better—than in the past. Particularly among new entrants to the labor force who had spent more years in less rigid schools than their predecessors had, and who had not experienced the unemployment that had made previous generations more concerned with just having a job than the kind of work it involved, there may have been much less willingness to tolerate dangerous or boring jobs. Generally rising standards outside work may have made lagging standards in work more unacceptable. This evidently extended to authority relations as well as physical conditions. Declining tolerance of hierarchical organization may well have been reinforced by the resurgence of critical ideological currents. Thus, the "new left" called into question all claims to authority based on property while putting a premium on participation not only in industry but in all institutional spheres. In an atmosphere in which industrial democracy was becoming a widely invoked ideal, the legitimacy of managerial prerogatives was becoming increasingly vulnerable to attack. That was also an atmosphere in which the unions could no longer afford to minimize the importance of power at the workplace, especially in view of management's own response to growing worker discontent.[29]

In varying degrees, of course, employers were certainly aware of worker dissatisfaction and the need to respond in some way in their own interest. Production and profits obviously stood to suffer from such symptoms of discontent as absenteeism, high turnover, and recruitment difficulties. Moreover, the erosion of rank-and-file loyalty to unions, which had in the past been able to ensure industrial peace, posed dangers for management as well as unions. But it was also necessary from the employers' standpoint to contain and channel the union response lest it undermine management's ability to manage. Already in the 1966 revision of the Works Council Agreement, SAF agreed to give "greater occupational satisfaction" equal status with "greater productivity" as the purposes of joint consultation. The agreement also provided for a new, joint Development Council for Collaboration Questions to promote new forms of worker participation. The council did not do much at first but in 1969 it began arranging work reorganization experiments. At the same time, and independently of the council, a number of firms also undertook such experiments, including the widely publicized projects at Volvo and Saab auto assembly plants. SAF's technical department was given the task of stimulating such experiments and disseminating their results.[30]

In all of these work reorganization projects, the cooperation of local union officials was accepted as indispensable. It was much too late to use such projects as a tactic for keeping unions out in Sweden, as they have apparently been used by some U.S. corporations. Nevertheless, management at the firm and association levels seemed determined to retain the initiative and ultimate authority to decide what could and could not be done. Moreover, works councils still did not prove to be much more than channels through which worker representatives were informed about decisions too late to make much difference. Even when they were informed well in advance of planned changes, as called for in the 1966 revision of the Works Council Agreement, there was nothing workers could do to compel an employer to modify the plans in any way he chose not to or even to supply more information than he wanted to. His interpretation of technological or economic imperatives could be discussed but was not negotiable, and his interpretation of agreements that had been negotiated—including the Works Council Agreement—continued to prevail in case of dispute until and unless a union could win the Labor Court's assent to an alternative view.[31]

Again, some firms involved union officials and other workers in decision making to a degree far beyond the limits implied by the formal demarcation of managerial authority in paragraph 32. By and large, however, management saw the need to alter the ways in which it used its authority but was, not surprisingly, reluctant to give up any of it. This put the unions in a difficult position. On the one hand, the proliferation of work reorganization projects could make it seem that management was more responsive to worker discontent than the unions. On the other hand, to the extent that union involvement in the projects or in other ways was confined within the limits of joint consultation, it was difficult for unions to demonstrate their own capacity to respond. Thus, the unions' legitimacy and authority was threatened by the growth of workers' participation on management's terms as well as by the eruption of wildcat strikes. In the face of this dual challenge, bringing workplace issues within the scope of collective bargaining, where unions could win results to which they could point, was a matter of organizational survival.

This is not to deny that ideological commitments—to various visions of socialism or simply the responsibility of unions to their members—played a part in the drive for industrial democracy. But these motives had been present all along. By themselves, they could hardly have altered the unions' official position if the pressure of organizational incentives had not been intensified as they were. As all these pressures to expand the scope of collective bargaining grew, so too did the conviction that the possibilities for accomplishing it through negotiations with the employers were very limited. As evidence, union sources cited their experience in various attempts to negotiate a greater voice in personnel and work organization decisions. One example was the protracted negotiations to revise a 1948 work-study agreement that took place from late 1969 to mid-1972, culminating in a broader SAF-LO rationalization agreement that nevertheless remained within the boundaries of the exchange of information and suggestions.[32] Accordingly, legislation came to be viewed as probably the only way of breaking down employer resistance on an economywide basis.

Different weights were attached to the various considerations pointing to this conclusion in different unions and at different levels, and some individuals such as two successive heads of the powerful Metalworkers Union clearly had a decisive influence. However, the cumulative effect was to establish a broad consensus within LO in favor of the new position adopted in its 1971 statement on industrial democracy. But it was not only in LO that these pressures combined to crystallize a decision that the time had come for an all-out attack on managerial prerogatives. TCO, the federation of white-collar unions, moved to essentially the same position almost simultaneously. Also a party to the Works Council Agreement with SAF, TCO was already moving beyond joint consultation by 1969, as was LO, setting up an internal group on enterprise and administration democracy (reflecting the large portion of its membership in the public sector) just a few months after LO did. These steps, it should be noted, are among the many that were taken before the wave of wildcat strikes broke out in Sweden, but after the series of much more dramatic developments elsewhere in Europe that were given massive media coverage in Sweden. Subsequently, like LO and in some instances before LO, TCO called for government commissions to review existing labor law with a view toward changing it. The establishment of these commissions was the beginning of the process resulting in the legislation described previously. TCO's representatives on these commissions, along with LO's, played important roles in shaping the content of the legislation. This was especially the case in connection with the labor-law commission (referred to informally as the paragraph 32 commission because its mandate was to consider the obstacles to collective bargaining over workplace issues), which was set up in 1971 and issued its final report in 1975. The LO and TCO representatives joined in a long statement that dissented from the report. In it, they laid out a position that served as the basis for the two organizations' drive for legislation going substantially beyond the commission majority's proposals, and which was in fact largely reflected in the legislation ultimately enacted. Above all, the fact that TCO adopted a position on industrial democracy essentially the same as that adopted by LO made the issue one of critical importance for the social democratic labor movement.[33]

INDUSTRIAL DEMOCRACY AND THE REDEFINITION OF THE SOCIAL DEMOCRATIC CONSTITUENCY

As noted earlier, TCO is not part of the social democratic labor movement, having no organizational links or ideological identification with any political party. As we also indicated, LO leaders, anxious to encourage the unionization of white-collar workers during the 1930s, believed that such a politically "neutral" union could recruit white-collar workers more easily than could the LO because of the latter's identification with blue-collar workers and the Social Democrats. In addition to supporting the 1936 law on association and collective bargaining to that same end, LO also provided the fledgling white-collar unions with an expert organizer who was TCO's general secretary for many years.[34] Both the law and separate identity, and presumably the organizing expertise, contributed to the explosive growth of TCO in the postwar decades. It now includes about a fifth of the total labor force and half as many members as LO. In effect, TCO was able to make the most of the opportunities created by technological change and the growth of the service sector, which rapidly enlarged white-collar employment while blue-collar employment almost stopped growing. While this kind of change in the labor force's composition is typical of advanced industrial societies, it may well have been accelerated by the structural change central to the social democratic labor movement's economic strategy. However, both its economic and political strategies were confronted by serious problems as a result of TCO's growth.[35]

First, LO's capacity to carry out the solidaristic wage policy essential to its approach to noninflationary full employment has been impaired. While it could inhibit wage rivalry among its own affiliates, it did not provide an institutionalized mechanism for inhibiting such rivalry between LO and TCO unions. Any possibility of generalizing a solidaristic wage policy throughout the labor market depended on the ability of LO and TCO to reach agreement on it. Yet, it has proven to be extremely difficult for them to reach agreement on wage issues.[36]

Second, the Social Democratic party's capacity to mobilize electoral support has been rendered problematical by the growing membership of unions having no formal or ideological links to the party. This is a problem typical of similar parties in Europe whose growth historically rested on their mobilization of the traditional blue-collar working class that was being steadily increased by the process of industrialization. But as the working class in this traditional, narrow sense ceases to grow and even declines as a proportion of the labor force, such parties face the possibility of stagnation or decline. The social meaning and political consequences of this transformation in the occupational structure depends on the actual differences in work done, pay systems and levels, working conditions, recruitment processes, and many other factors to which status differences can be anchored. With respect to many of these factors, the differences are being diminished in Sweden and elsewhere, though there has been much controversy over whether this is diminishing the class consciousness of nominal white-collar workers. But even as the actual differences are diminished, the distinction between blue- and white-collar workers tends to be preserved in Sweden precisely because they belong to unions in separate federations. And as the number of workers in the politically neutral TCO grows, it becomes increasingly implausible for the Social Democratic party to identify itself as the "workers' party" by virtue of its association with LO. By the same token, LO's effectiveness as an instrument of political mobilization for the party is increasingly limited by the restricted scope of its coverage.[37]

The problem posed for the party by the growing white-collar component of the labor force was made increasingly pressing by another change that was as much a part of the process of economic development, namely, the decline of the agricultural sector. It will be recalled that the Social Democrats' ability to stay in office in the 1930s and 1950s rested on a coalition strategy involving the agrarian party. But by the 1950s, time was running out on that strategy. Faced with extinction signaled by the agricultural decline, the agrarian party opted for organizational survival by reestablishing and redefining its separate identity and trying to carve out a new constituency. It left the coalition government that it had formed with the Social Democrats from 1951 to 1957 and changed it name to Center party. It then proceeded to build up a "Green Wave" to ride, articulating the discontent generated by rapid urbanization and the decline of small- and middle-sized-town society among people with very recent memories of what things had been like, and tapping widespread misgivings about bureaucratization and centralization. This proved so effective in reversing the party's decline that it became the largest of the three bourgeois parties, posing the greatest threat to the Social Democrats.[38]

Having lost the margin of support provided by the farmers (farm workers tended to belong to LO unions and vote socialist), the Social Democrats either had to find another coalition partner or try to mobilize enough support to stay in power on its own. No possibility for the former was available; one possibility for the latter was to also abandon its original class identity and follow the course of those European labor movement parties that sought to become "catch-all parties."[39] However, the Swedish Social Democrats did not do so, relying instead on more fully mobilizing their core constituency of blue-collar workers and attracting enough additional support from white-collar workers to continue in office while remaining a "workers' party."

Its initial effort to do so was highly successful. It rested on a proposal to add a universal, compulsory, earnings-related pension scheme to the flat-rate scheme enacted earlier. Partly because it included the buildup of a massive fund that could dominate the capital market, it elicited intense business opposition. The ideological polarization this produced helped the Social Democrats mobilize a higher proportion of blue-collar voters than ever before in the 1960 election. At the same time, the universality of the scheme combined with generous benefit levels for middle-income groups marginally increased while-collar support.[40] Thus began the process of blurring the distinction between blue- and white-collar workers and redefining the party constituency as wage earners generally—*löntagare*—or the employee class, rather than the working class in the traditional narrower sense of blue-collar workers—*arbetare*.

The need to carry the process further became acute in the mid-1960s. Having reversed its postwar electoral decline in 1958, the Social Democrats increased their strength during the early 1960s, and the party was suffused with complacency over its record of reform and effective management of the economy.[41] In the 1966 local government elections, however, the party sustained its sharpest setback since the advent of universal suffrage. One reason for this was that the effectiveness of its management of the economy sharply declined, frustrating the expectations its past performance and promises had aroused. But another, more far-reaching reason was the crystallization of a reaction against some inherent features of the social democratic labor movement's basic strategy for managing the economy. These were the rapid urbanization, decline of other regions, disruption of communities, and the like, which were the direct results of the structural change that the strategy was designed to accelerate, and which now were being attacked by the Center party as well as an emergent "new left."[42]

In short, just as the consequences of technological and structural change shaped by managerial decisions were arousing discontent among workers within the enterprise, they were also doing so as well in the larger society outside the enterprise. And just as the discontents within the enterprise were expressed in ways that made some response by the social democratic labor movement necessary, the discontents outside the enterprise were expressed in the electoral arena in a way that made some response imperative. If the discontents in the two different contexts indeed had a common source in the strategy that left microeconomic decisions up to the managers of capitalist firms, the solution evidently lay in a change in strategy that subjected those decisions to greater social control. In fact, the movement's response was a shift toward greater intervention in microeconomic decision making by both unions and government.

We have already seen how the LO responded in this way by its turn to industrial democracy. The Social Democratic party responded more immediately with a "new industrial policy." Early in 1967 and at a special party congress called later in the year, a program was set forth aimed at establishing control over the process of technological change and its social consequences, so as to assure both long-term economic development and a just distribution of its burdens and benefits. Implementation began in that year with the establishment of a state investment bank, followed later by a ministry of industry, a holding company for managing and expanding state enterprise, some new research and development agencies, expansion of the regional planning apparatus, and a new agency for sectoral planning.[43]

The need to build up and learn to use these instruments almost from scratch, plus the necessarily long-term character of any effects they could be expected to have, meant that there could not be any palpable results to point to in the short run. The immediate effects were primarily symbolic, stimulating ideological controversy much as the pension issue had done a decade earlier. This probably helped the Social Democrats to score a major victory in the 1968 Second Chamber election instead of the defeat foreshadowed in 1966, giving them a majority for only the second time in their history. But the mobilization effect of their policy initiatives was only part of the story. The rest of it was the atmosphere of international crisis precipitated by the Soviet invasion of Czechoslovakia, to which the Social Democrats reacted by turning the election campaign into a national protest against the suppression of Czechoslovakia's bid for "socialism with a human face." Both of these factors operating in the 1968 election were necessarily short-lived. In the 1970 election for a new unicameral parliament that was to begin operation in 1971, the Social Democrats lost their majority, while the small Communist party won just enough seats to prevent the bourgeois parties from winning a majority. Having staked their claim for support on effective management of the economy, renewed failure to live up to expectations made the Social Democrats again vulnerable on just this count. In the cold light of this reality, the new industrial policy lost whatever symbolic value it might have had. While trying to work up the capacity to cope with economic problems that were becoming genuinely more intractable, not only in Sweden but in the rest of the international economy to which it was tied, the Social Democrats needed an alternative basis for attracting the support it needed to stay in office.[44]

The issue of industrial democracy seemed to offer the most promising pospossibility. The fact that LO was in the process of deciding to press the issue and was defining it in terms of specific demands for legislation suggested that it was becoming the issue around which the party's core constituency could now be most effectively mobilized. Even if it was not clear how much interest there was in it at the time among the rank-and-file membership, the pressure for greater power from local union officials suggested that they had a sufficient stake in the issue to perform the crucial function of drumming up interest in it. Equally important, however, the fact that TCO was taking a position on this issue virtually identical with LO's suggested that it was one around which the necessary increment of white-collar support could be attracted as well.[45]

Thus, the emergence of a common LO-TCO stand on the set of demands summed up in the abolition of paragraph 32 was apparently marking out an area of interests common to the members of both federations. This established a context in which the organizationally sustained distinction between blue- and white-collar workers could be blurred as it had been by the pension issue. Indeed, it could probably be more effectively blurred than in the context of the pension issue because there were no significant differences within TCO over workplace power, whereas it had been seriously split on this during the pension controversy.[46] Under these circumstances, the translation of these common interests into a legislative program carried out by the Social Democratic government could put the party in a substantially improved position to make a credible claim to be the party of all the workers, regardless of which federation they belonged to.

Besides the prospect of a solution to the Social Democrats' electoral problem offered by a campaign against managerial prerogatives along the lines advocated by both LO and TCO, a shift of emphasis to workplace issues on which the two organizations took a common position also opened up the possibility of coping more easily with the economic policy problem posed by their disagreement over wage issues. Potentially at least, as nonwage issues assumed greater importance and unions gained more power to press them, the experience of cooperation on such issues by LO and TCO officials at all levels could be expected to improve the possibilities for agreement between the very same officials when they came to grapple with wage issues. To the extent that this turned out to be the case, a major difficulty besetting the social democratic labor movement's economic strategy could be overcome.[47]

Accordingly, the incentives that both components of that movement had for mounting a legislative attack on managerial prerogatives were very strong. The counterpart of those incentives were the risks involved in a failure to pursue the attack on paragraph 32. Some of these have already been noted, particularly the threat to organizational cohesion faced by the unions as a result of the limits on their power at the workplace. There was also the threat that the Social Democratic party would lose support to challengers on both the right and left if they failed to respond in some way to growing worker dissatisfaction and rising criticism of centralized, bureaucratic decision making in society generally. The mid-1960s resurgence of radical left ideologies mentioned earlier found political expression in the de-Stalinized Swedish Communist party—which changed its name to Left Party Communists—and a proliferation of fringe groups, all of which challenged the social democratic labor movement's commitment to advancing workers' interests, in the workplace as well as nationally. On the right, the liberal party, which had lost most of the working-class support it had enjoyed in the early postwar period, put in a bid to regain it by taking up the quest for industrial democracy at an early stage, though in an admittedly modest form. The agrarian party, which had reincarnated itself as the Center party, also adopted the slogan of industrial democracy and improvement of the work environment as part of its highly successful effort to present itself as the champion of decentalization and environmental protection generally.[48]

Whatever misgivings the more managerially minded segments of the Social Democratic leadership might have had, therefore, the party could ill afford to resist the growing union pressure for a legislative attack on managerial prerogatives. Of course, proceeding with that attack could not assure electoral success if the party was vulnerable on other issues. The Social Democrats already introduced industrial democracy and the work environment into their campaign in the 1970 election. At that time, though, these themes reflected little more than declared intentions, for not much had been accomplished, so that they made very little impact. In 1973, these themes were given much greater prominence in the Social Democrats' campaign, but with no better results. The liberals and the Center party simply put the same slogans on their posters and went on, along with the conservatives, to focus instead on the Social Democratic government's economic performance. Unemployment, higher and more persistent that at any time over a decade—though very low by U.S. standards—made it vulnerable on this issue. The Social Democrats barely managed to remain in office as the Communists won enough seats to produce an exact parliamentary tie between the two socialist parties and the three bourgeois parties.[49]

As far as both the workplace reform and unemployment issues were concerned, the Social Democrats were in a much better position by the time the 1976 election rolled around. Their claims on industrial democracy and work environment had gained much greater substance from the series of measures culminating in the Codetermination in Work Law. Their economic performance was also strikingly better, with unemployment actually falling from a rate of 2.5 percent in 1973 to 1.6 percent in 1976, in the face of the worst recession since the 1930s in the rest of the capitalist world. If the Social Democrats had indeed found in workplace reforms the issues around which they could mobilize a new employee majority, the 1976 election should have been the one in which that strategy bore fruit. But that is not the way it turned out. The Social Democrats were unable to reverse the decline in electoral support, which fell further by a small but critical 0.6 percent—from 43.5 to 42.9 percent of the total vote. The Communists also lost support, bringing the socialist bloc's share down to 47.5 percent. Its combined parliamentary strength was reduced to a minority, 169 seats, while the bourgeois parties won a total of 180 seats. Unlike previous situations when the Social Democratic party could remain in office despite a minority of seats, because one of the bourgeois parties had supported it, this time there were no potential coalition partners available among the bourgeois parties, which were united at least in their determination to form a government. Hence, the Social Democrats finally fell from office after 44 years of virtually uninterrupted rule.[50]

Until the necessary survey data are available, one cannot tell whether the industrial democracy issue brought the Social Democrats any more support in the 1976 election than it had in the previous one. However, it had been difficult to capitalize on the industrial relations reforms because the bourgeois parties had again refused to make an issue of them. Indeed, the "middle" parties, the Center party (whose leader became prime minister) and the liberals, had claimed to be in favor of industrial democracy all along. Their representatives on the labor-law commission had even managed to outflank the Social Democratic representatives by siding with the LO and TCO representatives on the question of interpretation prerogatives. Not surprisingly, the conservatives' position tended to parallel SAF's, citing the changes sought by LO and TCO as threats to efficiency, and seeking to limit the changes. Moreover, during the parliamentary proceedings, the middle parties joined with the conservatives to move amendments opposed by the unions and the government, winning in five out of six instances in which the question had to be decided by drawing lots to break the tie between the two blocs. In the end, however, the amended legislation was supported by all parties, effectively neutralizing it as a mobilizing issue for the Social Democrats. While the latter also tried to make the most of the other issue on which they were in a particularly strong position, the maintenance of full employment, it too did not serve as a powerful mobilizing issue, perhaps because it was something that had come to be taken for granted.[51]

Instead, the Social Democrats were put on the defensive on a variety of issues on which they lost support in diverse segments of the electorate. While there has not been a marked backlash against high taxes and the welfare state, widely publicized instances of inequities—including tax breaks of which the finance minister took advantage—and of apparent bureaucratic heavy-handedness in tax enforcement—including Ingmar Bergman's self-imposed exile following his brush with the tax authorities—provided targets for a vague resentment and fed the feeling that the Social Democrats had been in power too long. The Center party leader also succeeded in putting the Social Democrats in a position where they seemed insensitive to the risks involved in nuclear energy, which became the dominant issue toward the end of the campaign. Finally, the Social Democrats proved vulnerable to attack on a new proposal for some form of collective profit sharing adopted by LO at its 1976 congress.[52] However, this proposal is relevant to our concerns not simply as a factor—probably minor—contributing to the Social Democrats' defeat. LO's adoption of the proposal, and particularly the considerations leading it to do so, shed some additional light on the limitations of industrial democracy as a solution to the strategic problems to which, we have argued, it was a response. Accordingly, we shall set our conclusions about the reforms made in the name of industrial democracy against a brief discussion of LO's collective profit-sharing proposal.

UNIONS AND THE COLLECTIVIZATION OF PROFITS

In a nutshell, LO's proposal is that some percentage of profits—say, 20 percent—of all private firms above a certain size, be transferred in the form of new, directed issues of shares to a system of "wage earners' funds" set up and administered by the unions. The portion of profits allocated to the funds would constitute new equity capital, remaining at firms' disposal for the purpose of investment. But instead of accruing to private shareholders, the new wealth thereby created would become the collective property of all wage earners. Dividend income, like the shares, would not be distributed but used for a variety of services for all workers, such as education, and to provide the technical backing unions need to make the most of their enlarged voice in workplace and enterprise decisions. The voting rights as well as claims to wealth that go with share ownership would also accrue to the funds, so that in time they would gain controlling shares in the corporations.[53]

The implications of this proposal are clearly much more far-reaching than those of the industrial democracy program adopted at the 1971 LO congress. In some respects, it is true, the proposal can be seen as a further development of the policy adopted in 1971. Unions' capacity for influence through the expanded scope of collective bargaining would be reinforced financially by the income of the wage earners' funds, while the shareholder voting rights that the funds would give unions would add a new dimension to their power. The extension of industrial democracy in these terms is indeed one of the avowed aims of the proposal. However, the idea of basing union influence on ownership rights as distinct from collective bargaining rights reflects the fact that the proposal is primarily addressed to a problem different from the kind that specifically precipitated union demands for greater workplace power. Moreover, the idea of tying new investment to the growth of collective property marks the proposal as a much more fundamental departure from the pattern of policy pursued by the social democratic labor movement since the Great Depression.

The problem to which the proposal is addressed is one that LO came to see as inherent in its effort to implement its so-called solidaristic wage policy in an economy that remains predominantly capitalist—that is, where most firms continue to be privately owned, so that selection of management and appropriation of profits continue to be determined within the framework of private property institutions. LO's wage policy, it will be recalled, prescribes equal pay for equal work and a reduction of differences in pay for different work regardless of individual firms' ability to pay, understood as a function of their profitability. As we saw earlier, wide acceptance of these principles of solidaristic wage policy among

LO's affiliated unions has served as the basis on which they have agreed to coordination of wage bargaining by LO. This, as we also saw, was regarded as essential to the movement's overall approach to maintaining noninflationary full employment, both as a factor contributing to structural change and as a factor inhibiting the kind of interunion wage rivalry that can act as an autonomous source of inflationary pressure. Beyond these economic functions it is believed to perform, solidaristic wage policy is also evidently valued as a factor contributing to the movement's political cohesion. By linking the LO unions together in a joint wage policy, it gives operational expression to the norm of classwide collective action, which denies legitimacy to particularistic efforts by individual unions. To the extent that this reinforces the conception of a single, unified movement, it enhances LO's capacity to mobilize electoral support for the Social Democratic party as well as its ability to integrate union wage policy with the Social Democratic government's economic policy. In general, the ideology of solidarity probably commands wider unconditional assent throughout the movement than explicitly socialist ideology does, so that it presumably is a more effective means of symbolic mobilization. Accordingly, a great deal is at stake in LO's ability to continue implementing its solidaristic wage policy.

However, in LO's view, its ability to do so is threatened by a tendency of the policy to have unacceptable distributive consequences, a tendency inherent in it insofar as the firms to which it is applied are privately owned. To the extent that coordinated wage bargaining is successful in enforcing standard rates and raising low-paid workers' wages faster than those of others despite differences in firms' ability to pay, the policy will tend to maintain or even sharpen variations in the levels of retained profits among firms with differing profitability. The less profitable a firm, the more its profits will tend to be squeezed, increasing the pressure on it to become more efficient or shut down. On the other hand, the more profitable a firm, the more its profits will tend to remain at its disposal to finance new investment. In combination, it is these effects that contribute to the structural change on which the economic strategy relies. At the same time, however, if the profits retained by the more profitable firms are greater as a result of union compliance with LO policy than they would be if unions pressed for all that firms could pay, the unions see themselves as in the position of adding to the wealth of the firms' shareholders what they have abstained from extracting for their members. This runs counter to the broadly egalitarian ideology on which the legitimacy of solidaristic wage policy rests and to which the movement is avowedly committed. Concretely, compliance with the policy becomes very difficult for unions to justify to their members on any terms, and the unions can continue to comply only at the risk of serious internal strains and loss of support. The organizational as well as ideological basis for LO coordination of wage bargaining therefore breaks down.

Yet, whatever tendency LO's wage policy may have to redistribute income in favor of owners of more profitable firms in theory, it has been curtailed in

practice because of limitations in the effectiveness with which LO and its affiliates have been able to implement the policy through centralized wage bargaining. Variations in market conditions, payment systems, and the like affect
what happens in local bargaining, introducing substantial discrepancies between
the wage patterns established in national contracts and actual earnings. Thus,
over the whole period in which centralized bargaining has been conducted, only
about half of total increases in earnings have been accounted for by national
contract provisions. The remainder has resulted from "wage drift"—increases in
excess of contractual increases. The incidence of wage drift is uneven, however,
and this has important consequences. While easing some of the intraunion and
interunion strains that more fully effective implementation of solidaristic wage
policy might generate, wage drift tends to aggravate some of the strains the
policy was intended to reduce.

Where wage drift occurs, workers may be able to get more nearly what
firms can pay than they might have gotten if their earnings were more fully
determined by national contract terms. Consequently, profits and derivative
incomes may not rise at the expense of wages as much as they would if LO's
wage policy were more effective. The workers involved are therefore less likely
to be dissatisfied with the contracts their unions have negotiated on their behalf.
On the other hand, insofar as their earnings have been increased without the
unions' help, the workers also have less reason to give the unions their support.
But unions are also vulnerable to loss of support where wage drift does not
occur, for workers there are likely to be dissatisfied with the contracts their
unions negotiate insofar as their earnings consequently fall behind those of
workers who are in a position to benefit from wage drift. Pressures for com-
pensatory increases may then result, giving rise to precisely the interunion wage
rivalry the policy was designed to avoid. Thus, the basis for LO coordination of
wage bargaining breaks down as much because of the actual consequences of its
ineffectiveness as because of the potential consequences of its effectiveness.[54]

In the light of all this, LO finds itself in a position where it cannot continue to coordinate wage bargaining on the basis of solidaristic wage policy
unless the policy can be implemented more effectively—and the policy cannot be
implemented more effectively unless some way can be found to avoid the
unacceptable distributive consequences that would otherwise result. Since it sees
those consequences as inherent in the growth of profits and their reinvestment in
firms organized within the framework of private property institutions, it is difficult for it to find ways of avoiding those consequences as long as that framework
remains intact.

What makes it so difficult can be illustrated by the obstacles to using taxation as a solution. The techniques made available by control of the state's
budgetary mechanism—taxes and spending—are the principal ones on which the
social democratic labor movement's economic strategy has depended. Fiscal
policy has unquestionably been put to abundant and ingenious uses to influence

the levels, composition, and distributive effects of economic activity. The extent
to which it has been possible to reduce economic inequality through taxation is
doubtful, however, especially as far as the distribution of property-based wealth
is concerned.[55] Sharper taxation of capital gains and more effective constraints
on tax avoidance through the transformation of income into property could contribute to a greater reduction of inequality, and to that end, LO has called for
comprehensive reform of personal taxation. But it does not see such reform as
sufficient to meet the specific problem posed by the wealth—and power—
accruing to private shareholders as a result of high profits.

Changes in corporate taxation might seem to offer a more direct way to
diminish the distributive consequences of a more completely effective solidaristic wage policy. The higher profits of more profitable firms could be taxed away,
either proportionally, as they would be if the effective tax rate corresponded to
the nominal rate or, if this were not sufficient, by making effective corporate tax
rates progressive—as some unions have urged. But this way of dealing with the
problem is rejected because it conflicts with the other economic functions to
which corporate taxation has been increasingly adapted. One is the stabilization
of economic activity, and hence employment. Corporate taxation has been
geared to this purpose through the so-called investment reserve fund system,
which gives firms strong tax incentives to shift investment from periods of tight
demand to periods of slack demand. Another function is to keep industrial
investment at the level needed to preserve employment over the long run in the
extremely export-dependent Swedish economy. This is done especially through a
system of capital allowances that gives firms strong tax incentives to maintain a
high rate of investment in new plant and equipment.[56] As in LO's wage policy,
then, there is in the corporate tax structure a strong bias in favor of the kind of
investment believed to enhance Swedish industry's international competitive-
ness. The need for such investment is accepted as a fundamental premise underlying both wage and tax policy. But as in the case of wage policy, the proinvestment bias of tax policy tends to increase the wealth and power of the
private shareholders in whom ownership of the more profitable and consequently expanding firms has been increasingly concentrated. Given the premise
that tax as well as wage policy most continue to have this proinvestment bias,
but that it is bound to have unacceptable distributive consequences as long as
the investment takes place in privately owned firms, LO is driven to conclude
that the link between investment and individual wealth built into capital formation when it is organized within the framework of private property institutions
must be broken.[57]

How, then, is that to be done? The traditional socialist answer, of course,
is to abolish private ownership of the means of production. But there is obviously no prospect whatsoever of any direct, immediate collectivization of
Swedish industry. Everything in the social democratic labor movement's whole

history rules that out. On the other hand, piecemeal nationalization is not ruled out, although Swedish Social Democratic ideology has never given it the significance attached to it in the British Labour party's formula of gradualism. However, it fails to offer a satisfactory way of dealing with the problem immediately confronting LO. It would leave unaltered the unacceptable distributive consequences of investment in the part of the "mixed economy" in which firms are still privately owned—a part that would continue to be predominant for a long time even if it would be diminishing as a result of successive increments of nationalization. What is needed therefore is some alternative to nationalization consistent with the movement's commitment to reformist, incremental change, but which is nevertheless wide enough in scope to have some immediate impact throughout the private sector of the economy, where the problem arises. In LO's view, establishment of a system of wage earners' funds would provide just such an alternative.

Even if limited to medium-sized and large firms—having a minimum of 50 or 100 employees—the system would immediately apply to firms covering some two-third of the labor force employed in the enterprise sector (although this would include only between 1 and 2 percent of the firms because the private sector is characterized by a large number of small firms). On the assumption that 20 percent of profits in the affected firms would be allocated to the funds, there would be an immediate and continuing reduction in private shareholders' claims to wealth resulting from plowed-back profits of approximately the same magnitude or more, depending on a variety of factors. The percentage allocation rate could of course be raised. But whatever the rate, it would make possible a reduction in the inegalitarian effects of investment without a corresponding reduction in the proinvestment bias of tax and wage policies regarded as necessary for other economic goals. At the same time, there would be a cumulative growth in the proportion of shareholder rights transferred to collective ownership. The growth would be slow, not reaching 50 percent until after 35 years, on the assumption to 20 percent of profits averaging 10 percent of equity is annually allocated to the funds.[58] Nonetheless, introduction of the funds would establish alongside the private property institutions within which capital formation is now organized an alternative mechanism for capital formation in which the link between investment and individual income, of owners as well as workers, is completely severed. Over the long run, this alternative mechanism would account for a progressively larger portion of the total capital investment in the firms involved. In short, establishment of the funds would set in motion a process that would inexorably displace private ownership by collective ownership in the core of the economy.

THE STRATEGIC LIMITATIONS OF
INDUSTRIAL DEMOCRACY

The report on wage earners' funds to LO's 1976 congress concludes by defending the proposal as "reformist" in "its character, its aims, and its likely effects." Introduction of the funds would therefore not be a "departure" from "the social democratic labor movement's method . . . of step-by-step policy" but a "new step along the way toward the goal of this development: equality and economic democracy."[59] Yet, by encroaching directly on the private property basis of capitalist firms, establishment of the funds would clearly be a step that goes beyond the limits of the relationship between the movement and Swedish capitalism, within which the reformist strategy has been pursued until now. In its economic dimension, as we have emphasized, the strategy has been to use state and union power to harness economic activity to the movement's purposes without altering the capitalist basis of the firms conducting the bulk of the activity. The main features of the economic strategy, it will be recalled, were crystallized in response to the specific malfunctions of capitalism that became acute in the Great Depression of the interwar period. It was in that context that the state budget came to be seen as the principal means not only for counteracting the fluctuations in aggregate demand generated by the interaction of capitalist firms but also for allocating resources among broad types of uses and influencing the social distribution of access to resources. Particularly as far as the industrial core of the economy is concerned, the strategy was largely confined to the essentially macroeconomic forms of intervention to which budgetary policy, and also the centralization of union wage policy, lent themselves. These continued to be the characteristic features of the movement's economic strategy throughout most of the long era of Social Democratic rule.

In this light, the turn toward microeconomic intervention beginning in the late 1960s, first in the form of industrial policy and then increased union influence in managerial decision making, was a definite modification of the strategy. Nevertheless, like almost all of the industrial policy measures, expanding the scope of collective bargaining to increase union influence does not alter the role of private property institutions as the framework within which the selection of management and appropriation of profits is determined. Hence, it is hardly surprising that the reforms made in the name of industrial democracy did not arouse the kind of opposition that could turn industrial democracy into an ideologically polarizing issue around which the Social Democrats could mobilize support. In contrast, the pension reform in the late 1950s could serve as that kind of issue because the vast increase in public sector savings it provided for evoked intense, ideologically charged resistance on the part of those who saw it as a threat to the role of private power in the capital market. Even the party's relatively modest industrial policy initiatives in the late 1960s could serve as an issue for mobilizing support because the establishment of a state investment bank and more general revival of public enterprise as a policy instrument seemed to some as a threat to private property. Since the industrial democracy reforms carried no such threat, they aroused no such opposition. This, perhaps as much as anything else, kept industrial democracy from having much efficacy as a solution to the social democratic labor movement's problem of redefining and mobilizing its working-class constituency—one of the two fundamental strategic problems to which, we suggested, industrial democracy was a response.

In view of the analysis underlying LO's collective profit-sharing proposal, the fact that industrial democracy leaves the private property basis of capitalist firms intact also seems to limit its efficacy as a solution to the other fundamental strategic problem—the one arising out of the movement's relationship to capitalism or, somewhat more precisely, its effort to manage an economy that remains predominantly capitalist at the level of the firm. To be sure, with respect to the particular aspect of the problem to which industrial democracy was addressed, it was undoubtedly a necessary and possibly a reasonably effective response. The economic strategy's viability was clearly threatened unless state and union power could be used to provide workers with greater protection than they had in the face of the technological and structural change inherent in the strategy. As long as management's claim to virtually exclusive authority over microeconomic decisions was left unchallenged, it appeared inevitable that unions would lose support. This, in turn, would necessarily impair their capacity to comply with the wage policy requirements of the strategy and to mobilize electoral support for the Social Democratic party, thereby jeopardizing the control of the state, on which the whole strategy depended. Even if industrial democracy ultimately did not turn out to be an issue around which sufficient support to retain control of the state could be mobilized, expanding the scope of collective bargaining was undoubtedly crucial to the movement's cohesion. Failure by the movement to respond as it did to the increased salience of workplace issues would certainly have rendered it much more vulnerable to attack on those issues.

On the other hand, the extension of collective bargaining to workplace issues was essentially irrelevant to the aspect of the problem to which LO's proposal for wage earners' funds is addressed. According to LO's analysis, as we saw, this aspect of the problem arises because the proinvestment bias of the tax and wage policies called for by the movement's economic strategy necessarily has unacceptable distributive consequences as long as investment takes place in privately owned firms; these consequences are believed to threaten the viability of the strategy as surely as did the direct impact of technological and structural change on workers. Hence, it is as necessary to find some way of dealing with these distributive consequences as it was to strengthen union power to deal with workplace issues. Since there is no way of avoiding the consequences of investment within the framework of private property institutions, as LO sees it, the only acceptable option is the establishment of an alternative framework that would permit an increasing portion of the claims to wealth and power resulting from investment to be transferred to collective ownership. In short, a solution to this aspect of the fundamental strategic problem growing out of the movement's relationship to capitalism is to be found only by transcending the limits of that relationship and finally beginning the process of replacing capitalism with socialism. This seems to be what introduction of a system of wage earners' funds would do, more directly and unequivocally than any other institutional changes carried out during the nearly four and a half decades of Social Democratic rule.

Thus, while the introduction of the funds would admittedly be a "reformist" step, in the sense that it would be taken through normal parliamentary rather than revolutionary politics and that the ensuing changes would be gradual, it must surely be seen as a "nonreformist reform," in Andre Gorz's sense of the term. For as long as the funds continue to operate—that is, as long as the political conditions for that are met—they are certainly "system transforming" rather than "system maintaining" in their cumulative effects.[60] It is in such a perspective of fundamental transformation that the idea of collective profit sharing is placed in the new program adopted by the Social Democratic party at its 1975 congress. Considerably more radical than the previous program, dating from 1960, the new program declares that the movement is embarking on a third stage in its struggle to develop a democratic socialist alternative to both capitalism and communism. The "democratization of political life" is specified as the achievement of the first of the two preceding stages, while establishment of the welfare state was the outcome of the second. Now, in the third stage, the task is the "democratization of economic life." Expansion of "collective influence and ownership" through the workers' "right to codetermination" and "participation in the firm's capital formation" is cited among the means for achieving economic democracy, as LO was to claim in 1976.[61]

Not only at the most recent congresses of the two organizational components of the movement but in the movement more generally, a fascinating discussion has broken out about just how a system of wage earners' funds would function in relation to a broader "democratization of economic life." A wide range of issues has been raised—for example, whether the firms involved would be transformed into "social enterprises without owners," how comparable they might be with Yugoslavian firms, the extent to which they might foster particularistic rather than solidaristic identifications, what the possible consequences for political alignments might be, and so on.[62] All that seems reasonably clear so far is that the firms involved would cease to be capitalist in any meaningful sense, and would become part of some kind of socialist political economy.

There is little doubt that this would be the case as far as the business community generally is concerned, and it has been actively opposing LO's funds proposal. The reactions run the gamut from strident condemnation of the idea as "the biggest confiscation ever seen in the Western world" to the solidly reasonable and highly technical critique and counterproposal issued by a joint committee set up by SAF and the Federation of Swedish Industries–*Industriförbundet* (IF).[63] The gist of the counterproposal is a scheme to give individual workers ordinary shares that would become negotiable after some waiting period. This, of course, is the kind of individual profit-sharing approach adopted by business in many countries. Variously heralded as "people's capitalism," "property-owning democracy," and the like, such schemes are presumably designed to bolster the legitimacy of the property institutions on which capitalism is based without in any way altering them. Quite expectedly, the bourgeois parties advocate roughly comparable approaches, stressing the income and participation benefits they would supposedly bring to individuals, in contrast with the concentration of power in union bureaucracies that would allegedly result from collective profit sharing along the lines urged by LO. Once the 1976 election campaign began in earnest, the opposition parties intensified their attack, warning that if the Social Democrats remained in power they would proceed to impose "collectivistic socialism." This, the Center party leader insinuated, meant socialism of the "East European" variety, while the Liberal leader predicted that LO's funds system would lead to "an increased concentration of power" that would be "a threat to freedom."[64]

Clearly, then, the opposition evoked by LO's collective profit-sharing proposal makes it the kind of ideologically polarizing issue around which the Social Democratic party can mobilize its core constituency most successfully. Indeed, it would seem capable of serving as that kind of issue even more effectively than the pension issue did in the 1950s, and certainly more effectively than the industrial democracy issue. In addition, in at least some respects, it seems to offer the prospect of attracting the needed margin of support beyond the party's core constituency. As indicated earlier, much of that margin is to be found among members of TCO unions.

So far, admittedly, TCO has not adopted a position on wage earners' funds parallel to that taken by LO, as it had with respect to the issue of union workplace power. In fact, the 1976 TCO congress accepted the recommendation of a report on the subject that it take no position on it but give it further consideration. Noncommittal though the report was, its analysis of the main aspects of the question was nevertheless very similar to LO's, pointing toward similar conclusions. What is particularly significant is that it virtually ruled out the individual profit-sharing approach advocated by organized business and the bourgeois parties. This is hardly surprising since such an approach has little to commend it to the more than 60 percent of TCO members who are in the public sector. For them, LO's approach is bound to be more attractive. For one thing, whatever services the funds would finance out of their income would be available to all workers regardless of where they work. For another, the public sector members' position would be improved relative to those in the private sector who are more likely to be able to benefit from wage drift insofar as the funds system would siphon off some of the more profitable firms' ability to finance wage drift. To a lesser extent, this also is true of TCO private sector members who are typically on fixed weekly or monthly salaries. But it is apparent that many of the latter take an opposing view concerning the individual shares approach.[65] Such conflicts within TCO will undoubtedly make it difficult for it to settle on a definite policy. But this obviously need not prevent the Social Democrats from bidding for the support of those TCO members whose interests are consistent with the kind of scheme put forth by LO. A reasonable measure of success in doing so is all the Social Democrats would need.

To both of the fundamental strategic problems to which industrial democracy was apparently a response, then, collective profit sharing in the form proposed by LO seems to offer a considerably more effective response. On these grounds, the Social Democratic party might be expected to embrace and promote the LO proposal as enthusiastically and vigorously as it did the unions' demands for greater workplace power. Moreover, the sympathetic ideological terms in which the new party program anticipated LO's proposal suggests that the party was ready to make the most of the possibilities it offered to again draw sharp the lines dividing it from the bourgeois parties. Nothing of the sort happened, however.

CONCLUSION: STRATEGIC OPTIONS AND TACTICAL CHOICES

If the party leadership regarded ideological radicalization as necessary or irresistible within the party, it evidently did not believe that such radicalization was needed in the electoral arena. On the contrary, the emphasis in its 1976 campaign was not on new initiatives to achieve "economic democracy" but on preserving what had been accomplished, including the very substantial feat of lowering unemployment in the face of severe world recession. Ideas about the collectivization of profits obviously did not fit in with this cautious, conservative stance.

Quite apart from considerations of electoral tactics, there were genuine doubts and differences within the party concerning the substance of LO's proposal. Many aspects of it were unclear or undeveloped and there were many uncertainties about the economic effects the funds were likely to have, not only in the long run but in the short run as well. As far as their cumulative impact on the structure of the economy is concerned, one of the most important questions concerned the amount of power the funds would give unions over firms and how that power might affect the implementation of national economic policy decided in the political process. That there remain many serious unresolved questions like these that require much further discussion is widely recognized, within LO as well as the party, regardless of how radical the perspective in which the funds are viewed. This by itself, though, does not necessarily mean that the party cannot seize the ideological offensive and mount a campaign for the "democratization of economic life," in which collective profit sharing would play a part at least in principle.

However, it is precisely the principle embodied in LO's proposal that puts socialism back onto the Swedish political agenda, more explicitly than at any time since the Social Democrats came into office in 1932, with the possible exception of the movement's 1944 Postwar Program. The party leadership clearly did not think that the chances of coming out ahead in a direct confrontation over socialism were any better than they apparently had been in the past. In 1920, and again in 1928, such confrontations were followed by sharp electoral setbacks. So too, in 1948, if the course of events culminating in that election are viewed as a similar kind of confrontation.[66] If socialism were to become the salient issue again in 1976, similar results were expected to follow. There could be no doubt that the bourgeois parties would resort to scare tactics, as in fact they did. The potential such tactics had for success was newly suggested by a poll done for the leading Swedish conservative daily in June 1976. Asked whether they were "for or against the socialization of Sweden," 65 percent of the respondents said they were against. An even larger majority, 69 percent, said no when asked whether they were "for or against unions taking over the ownership of all firms."[67] In the light of our previous discussion, these questions will be recognized as more than a little misleading. The first implied wholesale nationalization, which was farthest from the Social Democrats' intentions, while the second implied that the LO scheme would apply to all firms, when in fact it left out the overwhelming majority of firms. It was hardly likely that such qualifications would be observed in campaign propaganda, however, and there was plainly a reservoir of fear to be tapped.

In addition to the electoral risks with which the party leadership apparently believed the LO proposal was laden, it was likely to be an obstacle to the political course the leadership seemed to be pursuing in the parliamentary arena since the 1973 election. As noted earlier, that election was the second in a row in which support for the Social Democrats declined, resulting in an exact tie between the socialist and bourgeois blocs in parliament. The likelihood of reversing the decline in the 1976 election was judged to be uncertain at best, even without a confrontation over socialism. In the face of the real possibility that the Social Democrats, even together with the communists, would not win a parliamentary majority in 1976, the leadership seemed to be trying to lay the basis for staying in power with the support of the liberals, either in a formal or informal coalition. There were many indications that the Social Democrats were, at the very least, concerned with leaving that option open. Among these signs were the agreements over tax policy negotiated in 1974 and 1975 between the Social Democrats and liberals (and the Center party as well in 1975), and which the LO and TCO said they would "take into account" in the forthcoming wage bargaining rounds. There was also the care which Olof Palme took to exempt the liberals from some of his attacks on the bourgeois parties. He especially singled the liberals out for praise for being "constructive" in connection with the industrial democracy issue.[68] But it was a lot easier for the Social Democrats to respond favorably to LO's demands and still find common ground with the liberals with respect to industrial democracy than on collective profit sharing, given the fundamentally different systemic implications of LO's positions on the two issues. Accordingly, if our conjectures concerning the Social Democratic leadership's tactical outlook is correct, it was bound to view a commitment to collective profit sharing along the lines advocated by LO as a serious liability in the parliamentary as well as the electoral arena.

At the same time, there could not be any outright disavowal of a policy officially adopted by an LO congress. To do so would severely strain the party's links with the unions. Unlike the British Labour party, which has repeatedly displayed a willingness to subject its relationship with the unions to such strains, this is something the Swedish Social Democratic party has consistently tried to avoid. The priority it has placed on working out policies compatible with LO's perceived interests—which of course include the cohesion of the labor movement as well—has undoubtedly been crucial to the party's success in staying in power so much longer than its British counterpart.[69] Whatever risks the party leadership may have seen in going along with LO's position on wage earners' funds, it undoubtedly considered the risks involved in an open breach with the unions as far greater. Of course, repudiation of the idea of wage earners' funds would also inevitably arouse intense opposition within the party itself, given the symbolic importance that had come to be attached to them as a token of the party program's radicalization.

Unable to take a stand either for or against the LO proposal, the party leadership seemed to fall back on trying to avoid taking any stand on it at all. It was rather clear that it would have preferred not having the idea of wage earners' funds come up, or at least delaying it from coming up until after the 1976 election. However, once the 1971 LO congress had decided that a proposal on the question should be prepared for consideration at the next congress, scheduled for just a few months prior to the 1976 election, nothing could have headed off the proposal that was ultimately accepted except strong pressure against it from powerful elements in the union leadership. There was no such pressure, presumably because most union leaders perceived the problem pretty much as it was described in the report to the congress. While there was remarkably little communication between LO and the party concerning the preparation of the proposal, it was apparent that it was proceeding according to its preordained timetable long before a preliminary version was issued for discussion in August 1975. Knowing that it would inevitably be confronted with the issue, the party took the opportunity to give it a plausible basis for postponing the time when it had to take a definite stand on it. In January 1975, the finance minister, Gunnar Sträng, set up an official commission of inquiry to study the matter of wage

earners' funds, in accordance with the standard Swedish procedure. The commission was not to begin working on it seriously until after LO came up with a
specific proposal, and the commission was not expected to report its findings
until 1978 or 1979. Consequently, when Prime Minister Palme was repeatedly
pressed for his view of LO's proposal, he was in a position to say that it was too
soon to make any decision, pointing out that a commission had been appointed
to consider the matter and that in the normal course of events it could not be
expected to provide the basis for a government decision until after the 1979
election. This, in turn, meant that there was really no possibility of introducing
wage earners' funds, even if it were decided to do so, until the 1980s.[70] It was
quite true that the procedure could not be expected to run any faster than that,
especially in so complex and far-reaching a matter. The labor-law commission set
up some months after LO adopted its industrial democracy program in mid-1971
did not report until four years later. On the other hand, the party leadership did
not wait until the labor-law commission had reported to declare its commitment
to abolishing paragraph 32. And when a government wants to act quickly, it can
entirely short-circuit the standard commission procedure, as the Social Democratic government did when it reached and implemented its decision to establish
a state investment bank in a matter of months. So, the fact that there was a commission looking into the question of wage earners' funds was not a very con-
vincing argument that they ought not to be an issue in the 1976 election. Under
the circumstances, the party's unwillingness to take a clear stand on the issue
had the appearance of evasiveness, which could hardly help dispel whatever fears
the bourgeois parties' scare tactics might have aroused.

In retrospect, it looks as if the party may have lost more by allowing itself
to be put on the defensive on this issue than it would have if it had gone on the
ideological offensive. As it turned out, there was not much potential for any
kind of coalition with the liberals to be lost. The liberals, as the smallest and
most vulnerable party, with a stake in certifying its claim to being a party of
reform, may have had some incentives to enter such a coalition. However, they
retained the alternative of joining with the other bourgeois parties, and a change
in leadership gave control of the party to those who favored that option.

As for the risks attached to a confrontation over socialism in the electoral
arena, they may have been a good deal less than the Social Democratic leaders
seemed to believe. The extent to which the issue of socialism was by itself decisive in the party's setbacks in the 1920s and 1940s is by no means unambigu-
ously established. Whether it would necessarily be such a liability in 1976 is in
any case a separate question. As noted earlier, and contrary to the conventional
wisdom concerning the moderation of Swedish politics generally and the Social
Democrats particularly, the latter have opted for sharply ideological confrontation tactics on previous occasions and come out ahead. Admittedly, the reforms
that were the focus of conflict on those occasions—deficit spending in 1932,
pensions in the late 1950s, industrial policy in 1968—may have been so patently

consistent with the preservation of the existing political economy that exaggerated efforts to tar them with the socialist brush may have defeated themselves by their own implausibility.[71] This time, on the other hand, it would have been difficult for the Social Democrats to launch a campaign for "economic democracy" that was not understood as a campaign for democratic socialism in at least the sense in which the two are identified in the party's own program. But it does not follow that this would have scared away more votes than it would have attracted. Evidence of the kind provided by the June 1976 poll referred to earlier might simply demonstrate the effects of the Social Democrats' failure to make an unequivocal case for doing certain specific things—and not others—to end what its own program refers to as the "present concentration of economic power in private hands." What can be accomplished by making a strong case was demonstrated in 1960 when the Social Democrats succeeded in transforming a majority among its own supporters that was against a sales tax into a majority in favor of the tax, using the argument that it was essential for the welfare state.[72] Their reticence concerning the collectivization of profits in 1976, motivated presumably by the fear of arousing fear, may have been the main reason for their vulnerability to the mobilization of fear. In this way, the Swedish Social Democrats may have fallen victim to a kind of self-fulfilling prophecy to which, as Richard Hamilton has pointed out, reformist labor movement parties seem to have been particularly prone in the postwar period.[73]

Even so, the damage done may have been minimal. Some evidence that could be read this way is provided by a poll taken two months after the 1976 election. It showed support for the bourgeois and socialist blocs split evenly at 49.5 percent for each, in contrast with 50.8 percent and 47.5 percent, respectively, recorded in the election. The two-percentage-point gain by the parties that lost the election was directly contrary to the tendency for support for the winning parties to go up immediately after each past election.[74] The Social Democrats were obviously not permanently damaged by being accused of being socialists, although it is admittedly impossible to say whether they would have suffered more or less if they had made an open virtue of it.

Whatever the immediate electoral costs, or gains, of avoiding a clear public position on collective profit sharing, the LO proposal for it defines for the Social Democratic party a critical issue on which it cannot avoid a choice much longer. As the LO report puts it, when the Metalworkers Union motion to the 1971 congress called for a method for allocating "increased resources to investment" that would not have "negative effects on the distribution of wealth," it was addressing itself to a "central problem in the process of capital formation that cannot be solved with the help of either wage or tax policy."[75] That problem will not go away. The party will accordingly have to find a solution that is both economically effective, in the technical sense, and politically viable, in the tactical sense—that is, one that is both consistent with the perceived stakes of the LO unions comprising its core constituency and capable of attracting the necessary margin of additional support. Otherwise, there can be no effective response to the fundamental strategic problems that began to confront the Swedish social democratic labor movement with increasing urgency in the late 1960s. As far as the reforms made in the name of industrial democracy are concerned, we can only conclude that they were a necessary but not sufficient response to those problems.

NOTES

1. Speech during parliamentary debate, June 2, 1976. *Snabbprotokoll från riksdagsdebatterna* no. 151 (1975/76), p. 139.

2. Arbetarskyddslagen, SFS 1972: 829. English translation in *Workers Protection Act*, Ministry of Labour, Stockholm, May 1974. Proposals for the new law are presented in the report of the Commission on the Work Environment, *Arbetsmiljölag*, SOU 1976: 1 (with summary in English).

3. The 1971 laws and proposals for subsequent legislation are spelled out in the report of the Commission on Employment Security, *Trygghet i anställningen*, SOU 1973: 7 (with English summary). Lag om anställningsskydd, SFS 1974: 12; Lag om vissa anställningsfrämjande åtgärder, SFS 1974: 13; Lag om facklig förtroendemans ställning på arbetsplatsen, SFS 1974: 358. English summaries are provided in *New Labour Laws*, Ministry of Labor, 1974.

4. Lag om styrelserepresentation för de anställda i aktiebolag och ekononomiska föreningar, SFS 1972: 829, and SFS 1976: 351. The text of the 1972 law, a survey of experience under it, and recommendations for the new legislation are available in English in *Board Representation of Employees in Industry*, The National Swedish Industrial Board, 1976.

5. Lag om medbestämmande i arbetslivet, SFS 1976: 580. English translation in *European Industrial Relations Review*, July 1976.

6. Lag om offentlig anställning, SFA 1976: 600. Discussion and text of draft agreement in *Inrikesutskottets betänkande* 1975/76: 45, pp. 54–65, and Bilagor, pp. 57–61.

7. Bernt Schiller, "Years of Crisis, 1906–1914," in Steven Koblik, ed., *Sweden's Development from Poverty to Affluence, 1750-1970*, trans Joanne Johnson (Minneapolis; University of Minnesota Press, 1975), p. 199. In the following discussion, I also rely heavily on Schiller's excellent work in this essay, his book, *Storstrejken 1909* (Göteborg: Akademiförlaget-Gumperts, 1967), and his monograph, "LO, paragraf 32 och företagsdemokratin," in *Tvärsnitt* (Stockholm: Bokförlaget Prisma, 1973). Early party-union relationships are summarized in Donald J. Blake, "Swedish Trade Unions and the Social Democratic Party: The Formative Years," *The Scandinavian Economic History Review* 8, no. 1 (1960): 19–44. The standard work on Swedish unions in English is T. L. Johnston, *Collective Bargaining in Sweden* (London: George Allen & Unwin, 1962). A survey of later developments, including those discussed in this chapter, is presented in Casten von Otter, "Sweden: Labor Reformism Reshapes the System," in Solomon Barkin, ed., *Worker Militancy and its Consequences, 1965-75* (New York: Praeger Publishers, 1975).

8. Stig Hadenius, Hans Wieslander, and Björn Molin, *Sverige efter 1900* (Stockholm: Bokförlaget Aldus/Bonniers, 1969), pp. 38–39; Yngve Myrman, *Maktkampen på arbetsmarknaden 1905-1907* (Stockholm: Stockholms Universitet, 1973), pp. 20–22.

9. Quoted in *Industrial Democracy: Program Adopted by the 1971 Congress of the Swedish Trade Union Confederation* (Stockholm: Swedish Confederation of Trade Unions, 1972), p. 50.

10. Ibid., pp. 51–52. See also Schiller, in *Tvärsnitt*, op. cit., pp. 304–05.

11. Schiller, "Years of Crisis," in op. cit., pp. 210–17.

12. The standard work on Swedish labor law in English is Folke Schmidt, *The Law of Labour Relations in Sweden* (Cambridge: Harvard University Press, 1962). A more critical view from a labor standpoint is presented in Per Eklund, "Rätten i klasskampen—en studie i rättens funktioner," and Sten Edlund, "Perspektiv på arbetsdomstolen," in *Tvärsnitt*, op. cit. Edlund was LO's representative on the Labor Law Commission, which laid the basis for the Law on Codetermination in Work.

13. Sven Anders Söderpalm, *Wallenberg och Branting* (Lund: Gleerups, 1970).

14. Sven-Ola Lindeberg, *Nödhjälp och samhällsneutralitet: Svensk arbetslöshetspolitik 1920-1923* (Lund: Uniskol, 1968); Hadenius et al., *Sverige efter 1900*, pp. 97–116; Ragnar Casparsson, *Saltsjöbadsavtalet i historisk belysning* (Stockholm: Tidens förlag, 1966), pp. 29–44.

15. Swedish economic policy during the Great Depression is surveyed in H. W. Arndt, *The Economic Lessons of the Nineteen-Thirties* (London: Oxford University Press, 1944), pp. 207–20; and Erik Lundberg, *Business Cycles and Economic Policy* (Cambridge: Harvard University Press, 1957), pp. 54–55. Controversies over the origins and extent of innovation in economic policy by the Social Democrats are reviewed in Bo Gustafsson, "A Perennial of Doctrinal History: Keynes and the Stockholm School," *Economy and History* 17 (1973): 114–28, and Carl G. Uhr, "The Emergence of the 'New Economics' in Sweden," *History of Political Economy* 5 (1973): 243–60. Political developments during the period are summarized in Dankwart A. Rustow, *The Politics of Compromise* (Princeton: Princeton University Press, 1955), pp. 90–110.

16. T. L. Johnston, op. cit., pp. 129–31.

17. Ibid., pp. 169–90; Schiller, in *Tvärsnitt*, op. cit., pp. 333–43.

18. This view of the Swedish case is stressed in Leif Lewin, *Planhushållningsdebatten* (Stockholm: Almqvist & Wiksell, 1967). For the British case, Alan Bullock, *The Life and Times of Ernest Bevin*, vol. 1 (London: Heinemann, 1960), chaps. 16–18, is essential. See also Dennis Kavanaugh, "Crisis Management and Incremental Adaptation in British Politics: The 1931 Crisis of the British Party System," in *Crisis, Choice and Change*, ed. Gabriel A. Almond et al. (Boston: Little, Brown, 1973). Especially illuminating on the German case is W. S. Woytinsky, *Stormy Passage* (New York: Vanguard, 1961), pp. 458–72.

19. For a general discussion, see Andrew Martin, "Is Democratic Control of Capitalist Economies Possible?" in *Stress and Contradiction in Modern Capitalism*, ed. Leon N. Lindberg, et al. (Lexington, Mass.: D.C. Heath, 1975).

20. Ibid. On LO centralization, see T. L. Johnston, op. cit., pp. 31–44.

21. For brief discussions, see Derek Robinson, *Solidaristic Wage Policy in Sweden* (Paris: Organization for Economic Cooperation and Development, 1974); and Rudolf Meidner, "Samordning och solidarisk lönepolitik under tre decennier," in *Tvärsnitt*, op. cit.

22. Gösta Rehn, "The Problem of Stability: An Analysis and Some Policy Proposals," in *Wages Policy Under Full Employment*, ed. Ralph Turvey (London: William Hodge, 1952). Rehn's views were embodied in a policy statement adopted by the 1951 LO Congress and translated as *Trade Unions and Full Employment* (Stockholm: Swedish Confederation of Trade Unions, 1953).

23. T.L. Johnston, op. cit., pp. 216–31; Schiller, in *Tvärsnitt*, op. cit., pp. 344–62.

24. Swedish Confederation of Trade Unions, *Industrial Democracy* (Stockholm: Swedish Confederation of Trade Unions, 1971).

25. A comprehensive but controversial account of the iron miners' strike is Edmund Dahlström et al., *LKAB och demokratin* (Stockholm: Wahlström & Widstrand, 1971). Walter Korpi, *Varför strejkar arbetarna?* (Stockholm: Tidens förlag, 1970) is a study of unofficial strikes in the metal industry.

26. The prevailing view is set forth in Everett M. Kassalow, *Trade Unions and Industrial Relations* (New York: Random House, 1969), chaps. 7, 8, and 11. The principal study of Swedish unions at plant level is Horst Hart and Casten von Otter, *Lönebildningen på arbetsplatsen* (Stockholm: Prisma, 1973).

27. The argument is summarized in the 1971 LO report, *Industrial Democracy*, op. cit., chap. 2. Similar views were expressed at the LO congress discussion of the report, Landsorganisationen i Sverige, in *Kongressprotokoll 1971*, pp. 431–501 and 518–601. See also discussions at the metalworkers' union's 1969 and 1973 congresses, Svenska Metall-industriarbetareförbundets kongress *Kongressprotokoll, 1969*, pp. 258–93, and *Kongressprotokoll, 1973*, pp. 233–318. An influential survey of research is Edmund Dahlström, et al., *Teknisk förändring och arbetsanpassning* (Stockholm: Prisma, 1966). Bertil Gardell, *Produktionsteknik och arbetsglädje* (Stockholm: Personaladministrativa rådet, 1971) is one of the most substantial pieces of research done. Among the studies conducted directly under union auspices is Bo Ohlström, *Kockumsrapporten* (Stockholm: Prisma, 1970), a survey of discontents among shipyard workers.

28. See the study of geographical mobility in *Att utvärdera arbetsmarknadspolitik* SOU 1974: 29, chap. 7 (summary in English); also *Report on Labour Market Policy* (Stockholm: LO, 1975), especially pp. 17–21.

29. The paragraph summarizes widely encountered views. On changes in the educational system, see Jarl Bengtsson and Kjell Härnqvist, "La politique de l'education en Suede," in *Sociologie de l'education*, ed. Alain Gras (Paris: Librairie Larousse, 1974). Olof Palme has repeatedly stressed the alleged implications of educational change on expectations about work, as in a 1970 speech, "Företageren och industriarbetet," in Olof Palme, *At vilja gå vidare* (Stockholm: Tidens förlag, 1974). New left and other challenges are summarized in M. Donald Hancock, *Sweden: The Politics of Postindustrial Change* (Hinsdale, Ill.: Dryden Press, 1972), pp. 76–88.

30. Eric Rhenman, *Företagsdemokrati och företagsorganisation* (Stockholm: SAF, 1964) was a path-breaking effort to define the issues confronting employers. See Schiller, in *Tvärsnitt*, op. cit., pp. 355–62 on the 1966 agreement. The Development Council is discussed in two papers by Karl-Olof Faxen, "Development of Collaboration in Firms," (mimeographed, SAF, January 1971), and "Research on Self-Developing Forms of Organization" (Presented to the International Economic Association, August 1971). In addition to many reports in Swedish on individual projects, SAF has published a summary analysis in English, *Job Reform in Sweden* (Stockholm: Swedish Employers' Confederation, 1975).

31. *Industrial Democracy*, op. cit., pp. 23–24; Schiller, in *Tvärsnitt*, op. cit., pp. 375–78; *Landssekretariatets berättelse för år 1968* (Stockholm: LO, 1969), p. 119.

32. Metallindustriarbetareförbundet, *Kongressprotokoll, 1973*, pp. 263–64; *Landssekretariatets berättelse för år 1972* (Stockholm: LO, 1973), pp. 52–64. SAF's general position can be seen in its comments on the Labor Law Commission's report and especially the LO-TCO dissenting opinion, which was eventually largely incorporated in the Law on Co-determination in Work, Svenska Arbetsgivareföreningen, Remissytrande till Arbetsmark-nadsdepartementet, mimeographed (Stockholm, July 11, 1975).

33. Christopher Wheeler, *White Collar Power: Changing Patterns of Interest Group Behavior in Sweden* (Urbana: University of Illinois Press, 1975), provides a readable general view of TCO and case studies of TCO efforts to influence policy outcomes on several issues, unfortunately not including union workplace power.

34. LO's position is described in T. L. Johnston, op. cit., pp. 125–31. The LO official who became TCO's general secretary was Valter Åman, who was a leading Social Democratic member of parliament. He headed the Commission on Employment Security, which drafted the legislation cited in Note 3 and which is referred to as "Åmanlagarna."

35. Since the merger bringing the present TCO into being in 1944, it has grown from

180,427 members to 880,589 in 1975. *TCO Verksamhetsåret 1972* (Stockholm: TCO, 1973), p. B-329, and *1976 års kongresstruck*, no. 19 (Stockholm: TCO, 1976), p. 10. Over the same period LO grew from 1,069,287 members to 1,863,481. *Statistisk årsbok 1975* (Stockholm: Statistiska centralbyrån, 1975), p. 244.

36. A brief survey of successive efforts at coordination between LO and TCO is provided in a report to the 1976 LO Congress, *Löner, Priser, Skatter* (Stockholm: Prisma, 1976), pp. 198-227.

37. John D. Stephens, "The Consequences of Social Structural Change for the Development of Socialism in Sweden" (Ph.D. diss., Department of Sociology, Yale University, 1976), provides an excellent analysis. Stephens concludes that "changes in the occupational structure alone are not likely to keep the Social Democrats out of office in the future" (p. 590). He argues that the party's prospects depend largely on whether it makes the strategic choices that make the most of the changing opportunities that are opened up. The industrial democracy legislation is a clear case in point.

38. The Center party's development is analyzed in David A. Swickard, "The New Opposition in the Welfare State: The Case of the Swedish Center Party" (Ph.D. diss., Government Department, Harvard University, 1976).

39. The term is used in the classic analysis of the phenomenon by Otto Kirchheimer, "The Transformation of the Western European Party Systems," in *Political Parties and Political Development*, ed. Joseph LaPolombara and Myron Weiner (Princeton: Princeton University Press, 1966).

40. Bo Särlvik, "Party Politics and Electoral Opinion Formation: A Study of Issues in Swedish Politics 1956-1960," *Scandinavian Political Studies* 2 (1967).

41. See "Resultat och reformer: riktlinjer för socialdemokratisk politik" (Document presented to the Social Democratic party's 1964 congress).

42. On the 1966 election and Social Democratic response, see Hancock, op. cit., pp. 137-40.

43. Briefly summarized in Martin, op. cit., pp. 48-51.

44. Ibid.

45. TCO positions on industrial democracy issues are presented in "Demokratisering av arbetslivet" (Reports presented to TCO's 1970 and 1973 congresses). A joint LO-TCO position is given in "Report on the Workplace Environment" (Presented to the European Trade Union Conference, Geneva, February 28-March 1, 1975). The joint LO-TCO dissent to the majority report of the Labor Law Commission is on pp. 930-61 of the report, *Demokrati på arbetsplatsen*, SOU 1975: 1. It may be noted that the TCO representative on the Commission, Stig Gustafsson, had previously served on the LO staff and is an active Social Democratic member of parliament.

46. Wheeler, op. cit., pp. 66-91.

47. Increasing possibilities for cooperation between LO and TCO on wage policy are suggested by a succession of three understandings between the two union organizations and the Social Democratic government (and with the liberals in the first instance, and the liberals and Center party in the second), to the effect that union wage demands would be moderated in view of income tax reductions that would increase take-home pay, while the revenue loss would be made up by increasing a payroll tax the employers pay—the so-called "Haga" agreements of 1974, 1975, and 1976; the 1976 agreement is described in *Från Riksdag & Departement*, April 1, 1976, pp. 1-2.

48. See Bengtsson and Härnqvist, op. cit., Palme, op. cit., Hancock, op. cit., and Swickard, op. cit.

49. A poll by SIFO (Swedish Institute of Public Opinion) a few months before the 1973 election showed that only 4 percent of the electorate thought that industrial democracy was one of the three most important issues, whereas 41 percent thought that employ-

ment and labor market issues were among the most important; cited in Stephens, op. cit., p. 304. The election is reviewed in Olof Petersson, "The 1973 General Election in Sweden," *Scandinavian Political Studies* 9 (1974).

50. The election results are presented with an illuminating commentary in Sven Svensson, "A New Regime After 44 Years," *Current Sweden* (January 1977), published by the Swedish Institute, Stockholm, and available from the Swedish Information Service.

51. *Demokrati på arbetsplatsen*, op. cit., pp. 917–18; *Snabbprotokoll från riksdags-debatterna*, no. 151 (1975/76); and *Från Riksdag & Departement*, June 10, 1976.

52. Well-informed accounts of the campaign in English are–despite its ill-informed title–Hendrik Hertzberg, "Sweden's Unassailable Socialism," *New Republic*, October 9, 1976; and Steven Kelman, "Letter From Stockholm," *The New Yorker*, November 1, 1976.

53. The proposal adopted by LO is presented in a report to its 1976 congress, *Kollektiv kapitalbildning genom löntagarfonder* (Stockholm: Prisma, 1976). The proposal is frequently referred to as the Meidner proposal, after the chief author of the report, Rudolf Meidner, the senior economic adviser to the LO. He and his coauthors, Anna Hedborg and Gunnar Fond, prepared a preliminary version, *Löntagarfonder* (Stockholm: Tidens förlag, 1975). It was distributed along with a variety of substantial study materials for discussion in study groups set up in the affiliated unions. The study groups returned questionnaires on a number of the issues involved, which were summarized in the final report.

54. *Kollektiv kapitalibildning genom löntagarfonder*, op. cit., pp. 29–34, 118–21.

55. Roland Spånt, *Förmögenhetsfördelningen i Sverige* (Stockholm: Prisma, 1975).

56. A convenient English summary of these tax provisions is Martin Norr, Claes Sandels, and Nils G. Hornhammar, *The Tax System in Sweden* (Stockholm: Skandinaviska Enskilda Banken, 1972).

57. *Kollektiv kapitalbildning genom löntagarfonder*, op. cit., pp. 23–28.

58. Ibid., pp. 77–86, 63–66.

59. Ibid., p. 136.

60. Andre Gorz, *Strategy for Labor: A Radical Proposal* (Boston: Beacon Press, 1968), pp. 6–8. The concepts of system-maintaining and system-transforming change are discussed briefly in Hancock, op. cit., pp. 8–11. An especially careful and interesting effort to work out the same kind of distinction in terms of "reproductive" and "nonreproductive" politics is Gosta Esping-Andersen, Roger Friedland, and Erik Olin Wright, "Modes of Class Struggle and the Capitalist State," *Kapitalistate* 4/5 (Summer 1976).

61. Sveriges Socialdemokratiska Arbetareparti, *Reviderat förslag till nytt parti program* (Stockholm: Tiden, 1975), pp. 17, 20–21.

62. The first major contribution to the discussion was Villy Bergström, *Kapitalbildning och industriell demokrati* (Stockholm: Tidens förlag, 1973), originally prepared for the party's program committee. The idea of "social enterprises without owners" was put forth by Ernst Wigforss, former Social Democratic finance minister who was responsible for the introduction of expansionary budget policy in Sweden and is probably the Swedish social democratic labor movement's most substantial theorist. See his "Samhällsföretag utan agäre," in Ernst Wigforss, *Vision och verklighet* (Stockholm: Prisma, 1971). A special edition of the Swedish Economic Association's publication, *Ekonomisk debatt*, 1976: 1, is devoted to views on wage earners' funds ranging across a wide political spectrum. See also, Sten Johansson, *Når är tiden mogen?* (Stockholm: Tidens förlag, 1974).

63. Sveriges Industriförbundooch Svenska Arbetsgivareföreningen, *Företagsvinster, kapitalförsörjning, löntagarfonder* (Stockholm: Näringslivets förlagsdistribution, 1976). A summary of various positions from the point of view of organized business available in English is Per-Martin Meyerson, *Company Profits, Sources of Investment Finance, Wage Earners' Investment Funds in Sweden* (Stockholm: Federation of Swedish Industries, 1976). The remark about "confiscation" is by Hans Werthen, head of Electrolux, quoted in *Fortune*, March 1976, p. 156.

64. Boston *Globe*, September 20, 1976; Kelman, op. cit.

65. *Löntagarkapital* (Stockholm: TCO, 1976); *TCOs kongress, 1976: Snabb proto-koll 3*, pp. 141-55.

66. Hadenius et al., op. cit., pp. 99-102, 116-117, 191-210. A brief summary of the 1940s case is provided by Hancock, op. cit., pp. 208-14.

67. *Svenska Dagbladet*, June 24, 1976.

68. Palme refers to the increased "respect" for the Liberals in a long interview in *Dagens Nyheter*, April 19, 1975. This Stockholm newspaper is the principal national daily which, though "independent," tends to be sympathetic to the Liberals. In the parliamentary debate on the Codetermination in Work Law, Palme anticipated that the Liberals will join with the Social Democrats rather than the bourgeois parties to achieve future reforms. He observed that "social liberalism is a tender plant that thrives best in the shelter of a strong social democracy." *Snabbprotokoll från riksdagsdebatterna* 1975/76, Nr. 151, p. 144.

69. For a fuller discussion, see Martin, op. cit., pp. 22-44.

70. On the institution of inquiry commissions as they are used in Sweden, see Hancock, op. cit., pp. 156-59, 202-05. An illustration of Palme's approach is provided in an interview in the business weekly, *Affärsvärlden* 1/2, 1976, pp. 20-21. *Skånska Dagbladet*, a Center-oriented daily, is quoted as saying, "Olof Palme has a great many times criticized the plan to gradually give workers control of their companies. But he has never exactly said what position a Social Democratic government would take on the issue." *News From Sweden*, October 1976 (Swedish Information Service).

71. Hancock, whose work has been frequently cited here, is among the exceptions among writers on Sweden who recognize that all is not consensus and compromise in Swedish politics. On class structure and conflict, see James Fulcher, "Class Conflict in Sweden," *Sociology* 7, no. 1 (January 1973); and, at a theoretical level, Walter Korpi, "Conflict, Power and Relative Deprivation," *American Political Science Review* 68, no. 4 (December 1974).

72. Särlvik, op. cit., pp. 176-80.

73. Richard Hamilton, *Affluence and the French Worker in the Fourth Republic* (Princeton: Princeton University Press, 1967), p. 292; quoted in John H. Goldthorpe, et al., *The Affluent Worker in the Class Structure* (Cambridge: Cambridge University Press, 1971), p. 192.

74. *Dagens Nyheter*, November 28, 1976.

75. *Kollektiv kapitalbildning genom löntagarfonder*, op. cit., p. 35.

4

WORKER PARTICIPATION IN MANAGEMENT IN BRITAIN: EVALUATION, CURRENT DEVELOPMENTS, AND PROSPECTS
Derek C. Jones

INTRODUCTION

Much of the current debate on workers' participation in management in Britain is concerned with workers' participation in strategic decision making.* The debate is proceeding in three main areas. Dominating the debate are the discussions evoked by the deliberations of the Bullock Committee on Industrial Democracy and the recommendations in its report (published in January 1977) for the introduction of worker representatives on the boards of directors of large companies (more than 2,000 employees) in the private sector. At the same time consideration is being given to the extension of workers' participation in management of public sector organizations, and the government has requested a series of reports to be prepared that will examine this question. Thirdly, the Industrial Common Ownership Act, passed in 1976, for the first time makes funds available on a regular basis for the express purpose of assisting the

---

*No precise listing of strategic issues is attempted; most lists will include matters like deciding the location of a new plant and whether (and how) to finance major capital expenditure, but the specific nature of such lists will vary from one interested party to another.

This was written while I was on sabbatical leave from Hamilton College and a Visiting Fellow at the Industrial Relations Research Unit, University of Warwick. I am indebted to the former institution for its financial support, and I wish to thank the latter for its hospitality and support. I have benefited from conversations with Eric Batstone and Frans Leijnse.

development of worker cooperatives. Examining and evaluating these current developments is a principal objective of this chapter.

Before examining current developments in more detail, it is instructive to evaluate some of the diverse forms that workers' participation in management has assumed in Britain. Such an account is potentially of use in helping to understand the context in which current developments are taking place in Britain. Three main classes of schemes providing for workers' participation in management in Britain are distinguished according to degree and scope of worker power.* First there are worker cooperatives, that provide the potential for workers' control over all decision making. Second are schemes that essentially provide for consultation on most issues and certainly only do so on strategic issues. These include traditional methods of joint consultation and more elaborate plans like that of Glacier Metal. Last are schemes that provide for worker influence on strategic issues via worker directors. Hence this is not a comprehensive survey. The two most important omissions are traditional collective bargaining and the unilateral regulation of workplace activities by shop-floor groups centered on shop stewards, the principal features of both of which are well known (see Clegg [1976] and Batstone et al. [1977] on collective bargaining and shop-steward organization, respectively). Also omitted are those essentially task-based schemes such as job enrichment, job enlargement, and autonomous work groups. Though these schemes often provide for workers' control, they seldom do so for more than a limited range of issues and by definition exclude workers from bringing influence to bear on strategic issues. Furthermore, in the main these schemes appear to constitute a participatory form that is neither much different from the well-documented experience elsewhere† nor commanding as much attention among British participatory forms as do those schemes with which this chapter is concerned.‡

---

*These attributes are selected as being most relevant to the development of a typology of participatory forms suitable for this survey. By so doing, the importance of factors stressed in other typologies is often downplayed. Those aspects include the distinction between representative and direct forms of workers' participation in management (see Walker and Crombie in Pritchard 1976); the distinction between legal and voluntary schemes (Sorge 1976); the principles of self-management that enable it to be distinguished from other forms of industrial democracy (Markovic, in Horvat et al. 1975; Vanek 1975, Introduction); and who initiates particular schemes (Poole 1975). Yet in the absence of a well-developed or generally accepted paradigm (see Dachler and Wilpert 1976) that might include most of these factors, no other way of proceeding is obvious.

†Gang systems, however, are forms of task-based participation possibly peculiar to the United Kingdom (see Melman 1958; Rayton 1972; and Wright 1961).

‡However, much British literature has focused on such schemes (see Guest and Fatchett 1974; Daniel and McIntosh 1972). Moreover they do seem to be becoming increasingly popular with studies of pertinent experiments that usually have been only newly

The chapter has three main divisions reflecting the main classes of participation schemes noted above. For each category the principal features of the main forms of past and contemporary kinds of participation are briefly described and evaluated. Following the example of Walker (1974), the general experience is evaluated from three main perspectives—power sharing, personal fulfillment of workers, and economic efficiency and industrial peace. The results of existing studies are recalled, though these are integrated with the fruits of some original research.* Some of the more interesting current developments in the three categories are described and their implications briefly discussed.† In a shorter and more speculative final section some of the factors likely to promote and retard the extension of workers' participation in management in Britain are identified, and the possible forms such developments might assume are discussed.

WORKER COOPERATIVES

Today in Britain there exist three types of worker cooperatives—situations where in principle there is provision for at least potential control over all decision making by employees. The oldest examples are the long-established industrial

---

introduced, including those of Emcar (in *Industrial Relations Review and Report (IRRR)*, no. 123, March 1976), Baxi Heating, Seaboard, United Biscuits and Canadian Transport Terminal (in *European Industrial Relations Review*, no. 31, July 1976) and Scottish and Newcastle (Industrial Participation Association, 1975).

*There are important problems in implementing this approach. Studies differ radically as to definitions, objective, and empirical methods. Much research seems overly colored by authors' preconceptions, reinforced by pressures to demonstrate success, and produces what Klein (1976 , p. 47) calls "Hallelujah stories"; in other cases the "better known experiments become busy centers of scientific tourism" (1976, p. 43) and lead to shallow and glib accounts. There has been virtually no interdisciplinary inquiry and few longitudinal studies. Evaluation is complicated by the problem of trying to control for environmental influences, especially in view of continuing changes in this context and the dynamic nature of most participatory schemes. Finally, there are often problems with the quality of the available data, in part because of data-gathering techniques employed (usually survey methods) and the gulf that frequently exists between concepts and the attempt to operationalize these concepts.

†Much other legislation has implications for worker participation in management. For example, both the Employment Protection Act (1975) and the Industrial Relations Act (1971) provide for workers to have rights of access to information. The Health and Safety at Work Act (1974) provides for rights of access to information and enables union safety representatives to make inspections. Such developments are not examined here because usually they are not concerned with giving workers power over strategic decision making and seldom involve the development of participation structures above and beyond existing collective bargaining arrangements.

producer cooperatives (PCs) registered under the Industrial and Provident Societies Act (1852). The postwar era has witnessed the growth of many common-ownership firms that are members of the Industrial Common Ownership Movement (ICOM). And since 1975 three new worker cooperatives have been formed. Each of these will be looked at in some detail but first it is instructive to look at three of the historical antecedents of these schemes: workingmen's associations formed by the Christian Socialists; the early PCs, established mainly between 1860 and 1880; and the guilds established by Guild Socialists.

Past Forms

Workingmen's Associations

Good accounts of the events leading up to the formation of workingmen's associations, their structure, and their functioning are provided by Potter (1891) and later by Boggis (in Balfour 1973). The associations were promoted in activities including weaving and baking. They were short-lived, with most not surviving more than two years. Yet as Boggis (in Balfour 1975, pp. 34–36) makes quite clear, the conditions under which the associations were formed should hardly have led anyone to entertain any other expectations. In most cases the promoters did not respond to any discernible demand for self-management by workers but instead imposed their ideas on, if not unwilling, most certainly uninformed workers who had known nothing else but autocratic relationships all their lives and now were expected to be willing and able to self-manage. Little forethought was given to making technical resources available to workers, or to trying to find managers flexible enough to attempt a participatory leadership style, and many schemes were very hurriedly promoted.

Early, Unstable PCs

Following the demise of the workingmen's associations and until the establishment of a form of PC that in some cases has shown a powerful resilience, numerous early PCs were formed, mainly between 1860 and 1880. Most of them were short-lived.*

These early and usually unstable PCs were a mixed bag. Sometimes their origins lay in a strike or lockout; less frequently a strong desire for self-

---

*See Potter (1891), S. and B. Webb (1914), B. Jones (1894), and a later account by Boggis (in Balfour 1973).

employment was the prime moving force. More often wealthy businessmen were involved in the scheme (for example, Rutherford and Ouseburn Engineering), or trade unions (for example, Amalgamatical Societies of Engineers) assisted in supplying a substantial amount of initial capital. It is clear, however, from the investigations of B. Jones (1894), Potter (1891), and S. and B. Webb (1914) that many of these early societies were not genuine PCs, and if they did initially provide for substantial employee participation in decision making, they mostly soon degenerated into nonparticipatory institutions or associations of small capitalists. Unlike the case with subsequent PCs, no federation existed to act as a central coordinating institution, to provide certain technical services and exercise an overviewing role to see that existing societies continued to observe PC principles, as well as to assist new societies with their initial organization. Little information is available on the comparative economic performance of these early PCs. Most information, particularly lists of failures and attempts to derive PC mortality rates, proceeds in a vacuum. As C. Webb (1904) and others argue, there is reason to believe that such procedures tend to distort the true position, particularly since such pessimistic pronouncements can often be shown to be based on ideological preconceptions hostile to the PC form (D.C. Jones 1975a).

Guilds

While much has been written on the doctrines of guild socialism, much less literature has been concerned with the actual structure and functioning of guilds and there are even fewer descriptions and evaluations of the total British experience. Even as basic a statistic as the number of guilds established is uncertain. Most accounts argue that the first operational guild was the Manchester building guild in 1920, but estimates of the number existing in that industry in 1922 range up to 200, with indications that by that year guilds had been established in industries as diverse as musical instrument making, dairying, and manufacturing packing cases. But accounts of guild practice tend to be confined to the experience in the building industry and it is on these sources that this discussion must rely.

The authoritative account of the building guilds is by Mathews (in Briggs and Saville 1971); earlier useful reports are given by Joslyn (1922) and Hewes (1922). There were about 100 guild committees in the building industry, many of which raised some initial finances by selling non-interest-bearing shares through trade union branches. Soon a national guild was formed. This national body acted as a central agency through which finances, at a fixed interest rate, for initial plant supplies, and the underwriting of guild contracts, via the Cooperative Wholesale Society (CWS) and the Cooperative Insurance Society (CIS) were channeled. But while financial responsibility was largely centralized, day-to-day control was by and large decentralized. For example, authority to conclude contracts lay with regional councils, which were elected partly by regional craft organizations and partly by local guild committees. Each regional council appointed a manager and headquarters staff. The foreman on the job was appointed by the local committee, which in some cases (Hobson 1938, pp. 224–25) was tantamount to direct employee election. Surplus funds were distributed between consumers and guilds, the latter using such funds for general improvement. Individual guildsmen did not receive any bonus; instead they worked under a system of continuous pay with guaranteed money during unemployment, harsh weather, illness, and accidents.

In evaluating guild performance, little published information exists that usefully bears on the matters of power sharing and personal fulfillment. It is clear, however, from the more influential guild doctrines that the guilds did not aspire to complete self-management but saw the need for representation of consumer interests in ultimate policy-making bodies; in practice it is quite probable that the relationship with the CWS and the CIS constrained the building guild's freedom of action. It is also clear that the structure of the building guild provided little if any direct democracy but was essentially a representative system. At the work-group level, Joslyn's (1922, pp. 124-25) account of foremen's exercise of power suggests that they were hardly inhibited by the existence of democratic machinery, even when appeals systems existed for grieved employees. Harder information exists in the area of economic efficiency and industrial peace, though again mainly for the building guilds and only for the 1920-22 period. Investigations led Joslyn (1922, p. 121) to conclude, "The evidence is overwhelming . . . that the efficiency of guild labor is much superior to that of labor employed by the average private builders." An array of evidence of matters including return on capital, costs of guild-built houses compared to those built under private contract, and the efficiency of labor was produced to support this conclusion. Hewes (1922, pp. 232-34) arrives at a similar finding. It is also clear that good industrial relations prevailed in the building guilds during the early years. There was little labor turnover, good discipline, and little abuse of the system of continuous pay.

Despite this apparently stable and successful picture, by the beginning of 1923 most building guilds had collapsed and many of the remainder were floundering. In explaining this dramatic turnabout it would seem that both structural and contextual factors are important. The change in government policy over the provision of basic-sum contracts, to a large extent a result of pressure from the Master Builders Association (Joslyn 1923, p. 524; Hobson 1938, pp. 227-29; National Federation of Building Trade Operatives 1922, p. 5), severely undermined guild markets. Partly because they lacked technical expertise, they were unable to take up the slack elsewhere. The need for professional assistance is also reflected in the numerous instances of maladministration, particularly by the inexperienced guild committees (National Federation of Building Trade Operatives 1922, p. 56). Working capital was always scarce, though acutely so after the change in policies by the CWS and the CIS precipitated by the government's own change in policy on basic-sum contracts; alternative capital supplies were not forthcoming either from building trade unions or individual workers. The organization structure left much to be desired. Under conditions of duress, a system combining central responsibility with decentralized control first creaked—note the abuse of local autonomy reported by Joslyn (1923, p. 528)—and then collapsed. Analogously, the relationship of the guilds to building unions was never satisfactorily developed, always gave rise to jurisdictional problems (Hewes 1922, p. 235), and deteriorated rapidly during tough times.

Contemporary Forms

Long-Established PCs

The oldest surviving form of worker cooperative in Britain is the long-established PC—many PCs have been established for more than 70 years. The oldest, Walsall Lock, was formed in 1874; no new PCs have been formed since 1950.* While most belong to the official organ of the British cooperative movement, the Cooperative Union, today only about seven are members of the Cooperative Production Federation (CPF), a body founded in 1882 to help promote and defend the interests of PCs.†

Most societies began for one of two principal reasons. Many were formed by retail societies (sometimes with the assistance of a trade union, sometimes by only the trade union) to provide a particular service or product for the retailers. Often this was the case in the printing industry and sometimes with clothing PCs. In footwear, however, many PCs were formed at the initiative of workers in times of economic distress. Some were formed following the lockout of 1895 in the boot and shoe trade. In other cases the impetus for foundation came during or following a strike. Most British PCs continue to be concentrated in the Midlands region of England.

Long-established PCs are registered as industrial and provident societies. For membership in a PC, ownership of a minimum (and ordinarily a nominal)

---

*For overviews see Boggis (in Balfour 1973) and Fletcher (in Coates 1976). For basic statistical information and doctrinal surveys see the author's work cited later (1975a, 1976). For economic analysis see D.C. Jones and Backus (1977).

†Not all PCs registered under the Industrial and Provident Societies Legislation are necessarily members of either the Cooperative Union or the CPF. Many societies exist that might be classified as PCs if coordinated information were available. They exist particularly in building (East Midlands Housing Association) and printing (Blackfriars Press). Obviously some of these societies might have been formed since 1950.

number of shares is legally required. Typically there are three classes of members: employees, other individuals (particularly former employees), and other societies (particularly retail societies, other PCs, and trade unions). Only in exceptional cases do current employees own a majority of the share capital. In many cases, though, the vast majority of employees are members, and often a majority of members are employees. Most importantly, adherence to the cooperative principle of "one member, one vote" means that in many cases, particularly in the footwear industry, a majority of the committee of management are employees. In some cases all of the members of this single-tier policy-making board are employees. In other cases, though, especially in printing and clothing, there are few (perhaps no) worker representatives on the management board. But in nearly all cases it appears that provision exists for direct employee participation in nondirective decisions through works committees of various kinds. An interesting feature in the British context is the existence of courts of appeals, which consist mainly of employees and are principally concerned with claims against unfair dismissal.

Financial characteristics of PCs differ substantially from those of capitalist firms. A PC is constrained by law to paying a limited interest on share capital. Shares remain at their nominal or par value such that substantial collective ownership of assets exists. There are legal restrictions inhibiting a PC's ability to raise outside financing; for example, preference shares cannot be issued. Relatively little use is made of permissable external capital courses, such as bank overdrafts. In practice most PCs rely on internal financing from retained earnings that cannot be recovered by individual employees, except upon dissolution of the society.

Most PCs distribute part of their net income (surplus) to employees as an annual bonus; other shares often go to customers as a form of rebate and to capital owners. A union shop frequently exists in PCs with employees' incomes at least equal to prevailing union rates. PCs do not appear to have specific egalitarian policies concerning relative wages of their members.

Four periods in the history of long-established PCs have been discerned (D.C. Jones 1974). The first sees the emergence of a strong and organized general cooperative movement in Britain dominated by the retailers and consumer cooperative principles. The establishment of the Cooperative Productive Federation in 1882 represented a formal recognition by PC devoteees that the battle to structure a movement around the central importance of PC principles had been lost. From 1882 until 1893 the number of PCs increased more than sixfold. While the movement was to lose a little ground before the beginning of World War I, it was still vigorous, and 1928 is chosen as the obvious watershed rather than 1905, the year when the number of PCs peaked. The interwar years constitute the third period. The unifying feature of this phase is that the expansionary momentum generated during the second period was not sustained; the movement was on the defensive. The final period, during and after the Second

World War, has not been a good one for long-established PCs. The number of societies has fallen to almost a third of its postwar high of 48 in 1948—in 1965 there were 35 societies and ten years later only 17. Moreover no new PCs that are members of the Cooperative Union and registered under the Industrial and Provident Societies Act have been formed since 1950. For the traditional PC industries—printing, footwear, and clothing—no new societies have been formed since the 1930s.

Seven of the 17 societies existing in 1975 are in printing, four in footwear, and three in clothing. Five societies had over 100 employees, but only one, Ideal Clothing, employed more than 500. All printing societies are small, with all but two providing employment for fewer than 30. Sales tend to show a similar size distribution: Ideal Clothing had an annual turnover in excess of £1.5 million, and Equity Shoe had sales of more than £1.1 million. But only six other PCs had sales in excess of £400,000, and six societies recorded sales of less than about £150,000.

In evaluating the experience of long-established British PCs with respect to employee power, an important aim is to determine to what extent the industrial relations reality corresponds to formal structures that provide for substantial (sometimes complete) worker participation in strategic decision making. In what is perhaps the most careful and relevant study, Kirkham (1973) examines the experience of Equity Shoe and Leicester Printers and finds a marked difference between the actual processes of decision making and formal structures. A detailed account is given of how at Equity Shoe, power was transferred first from workers in different departments to the committee of management and how that committee relinquished power to the manager. The latter process was in large part caused by the inability of the committee to agree on basic issues and the subsequent referral of these matters to the manager for resolution. At the same time the frequency with which meetings of major components of the participation machinery were held has diminished; for example, general meetings were initially held weekly, subsequently monthly, then quarterly, beginning in 1959 only every six months, and now are held annually. Attendance at meetings has also fallen quite markedly. Sawtell (1968) takes a less jaundiced view of the situation at Equity and concludes that Equity (firm E in his survey) has a high level of participation. Furthermore, additional analysis of Sawtell's results shows that some decisions, which are normally considered to be exclusively management prerogatives, including "possible dismissal of departmental manager for inefficiency," were issues that were determined jointly with employees. More mundane matters, such as deciding sanctions for absenteeism and determining smoking regulations, were also shared decisions. In a study dealing exclusively with PCs, D.C. Jones (1974, pp. 286-92) found that in a quarter of PCs examined, employees exercised some influence on what might be called a strategic decision "to raise new capital." In all such cases at least one-half of the management board were employees. When the results were contrasted with a comparable study of capitalist firms (Clarke, Fatchett, and Roberts 1972, chap. 4), in no capitalist firms did employees exercise any influence on this kind of decision making. On nonstrategic matters—including introducing new working methods and changing starting and stopping times—the commitee of management was perceived by senior management to exercise substantial power, significantly more than in comparable capitalist firms. It was particularly powerful in those PCs with at least parity representation of workers on management boards. Also, Ostergaard (1957) has shown that average attendance at general membership meetings of PCs was significantly higher than average attendance at retail coop-erative society meetings and trade union meetings; furthermore "of the various classes of membership, workers constituted by far the largest proportion of attendance." At Leicester Printers, the constitution provides for potentially less direct employee influence on policy decisions than at Equity—only one-third of the board of management are allowed to be employees whereas at Equity no such restriction exists and all of the board in fact tend to be employees. Yet as Kirkham (1973) shows, there is active interest in the election of worker repre-sentatives to the board at Leicester and there is evidence of employees being actively involved in the democratic machinery of the PC.

On the matter of job satisfaction in PCs, few robust and systematic investigations appear to have been made. The meager evidence available is impressionistic, mainly of an anecdotal kind, and largely confined to workers' job satisfaction; it appears to show that workers generally are satisfied with work in PCs. There is, however, a snippet of evidence on the matter of management's views on this question. Further analysis of Sawtell's (1968) study of Equity (firm E) shows that in assessing the effects of participation, senior management had "more satisfaction from personal relationships with colleagues and other employees . . . [and] more sense of purpose in [their] work."

On the broad questions of performance and industrial peace, the most important preliminary conclusions of an earlier study by the author (1974) are that (1) PCs can undertake technical change; (2) while comparisons with capi-talist firms suggest that labor productivity is poorer in PCs, unit labor cost com-parisons do not point firmly one way or the other; (3) labor practices and strikes were much less prevalent in PCs than in comparable capitalist firms; (4) on average, workers in PCs received lower money income than employees in com-parable capitalist firms; but in those PCs where workers had either parity or majority representation on management committees, on average, workers received higher money income than both employees in comparable capitalist firms and workers in PCs with less than parity representation on the board; (5) though individual PCs can survive for long periods of time (perhaps on aver-age even longer than for comparable capitalist firms), on the whole the long-established British PC movement has been of diminishing importance since the 1920s; (6) in general, the average PC is smaller and undercapitalized compared to capitalist firms; over time these differences tend to become more marked, with

PCs often having shrinking labor forces. In the main these conclusions tend to be buttressed by the usually firm-specific and short-time-period studies of Sawtell (1968) and Edelstein (1975, p. 17) for Equity Shoe. They also tend to undermine the less optimistic beliefs of S. and B. Webb (1914) and B. Jones (1894).

In reconciling these apparently contradictory phenomena—despite their sometimes superior performance, PCs appear to be self-strangulating—D.C. Jones and Backus (1977) have presented preliminary evidence on the thesis that the failure to charge a scarcity price for the use of collectively owned assets constitutes the primary reason why most PCs self-destruct. For example, collective ownership implies that the individual worker-member can never recoup the principal of an investment. In order to recoup their equity, the existence of collective ownership provides founder-members with an incentive to try to force the PC into liquidation. Since capital rents primarily accrue to labor (share capital remains at par and usually receives less than the market rate of return) as the PC grows, capital rents per worker will be growing, and if members aim to maximize their individual incomes (and workers control the societies), they will be increasingly reluctant to admit new members. The number of working members would be expected to decline. The demise of the CPF and the consequent absence of a nerve and educational center for the movement have also undoubtedly played a part in this process. Furthermore, the growth of bureaucracy in PCs, which Kirkham (1973) emphasizes, or, as Boggis (in Balfour 1972, pp. 36-38) suggests, the difficulties of developing technically competent managers with effective "participative" leadership styles, plus the failure to develop mechanisms to sustain ideological commitment toward producer cooperation (Edelstein 1975, p. 27; Fletcher, in Coates 1976, p. 184) have undoubtedly interacted with these aspects of the economic structure to contribute to the CPF's demise.

Members of ICOM

The second contemporary type of worker cooperative is represented by member firms of ICOM, a body established to promote, help, and coordinate firms that are exclusively owned and controlled by all those who work within them. In September 1976 there were 13 member companies in ICOM and more than 70 associate members (which are planning to move toward full membership).*

About half the ICOM member firms were originally conventional capitalist enterprises that later converted to common ownership. For example, Scott Bader Commonwealth, the founder-firm of ICOM, was established when Ernest

---

*For descriptions of ICOM firms, see ICOM (1975); Derrick and Phipps (1969); Blum (1968); Sawtell (1968); and accounts in Vanek (1975).

Bader and his family gave their shares in Scott Bader and Company Limited to a company limited by guarantee (Commonwealth) and invited Scott Bader employees to join Commonwealth. Some firms, including Fakenham, originated from a work-in or a redundancy of owners. The remaining (and usually the smaller) firms have been established with a common-ownership structure from the start.

Members of ICOM are characterized by various forms of legal structure, three of which involve registration under the Companies Acts: (1) a two-tier structure where all shares are held in common by a democratically controlled holding company which is limited by guarantee—only employees in the operating company are eligible for membership in the holding company; (2) single-tier "loan-stock"-based companies which are limited by guarantee and have no share capital; (3) a single-tier company limited by shares where new shares are issued to all employees each year from the trading surplus, such that the longest-serving employees have most shares and most votes. A fourth possible legal structure is provided by societies registering under the Industrial and Provident Societies Legislation. Most ICOM firms favor the first form, only two firms have adopted the second and fourth forms, and only a single firm has adopted the third form.

Diverse types of formal machinery for participation characterize ICOM firms. In some, including Rowen South Wales and Sunderlandia, the firm's constitution provides, and size permits, direct and frequent sharing in decision making, on a basis of one member, one vote on all issues, by the whole workforce. In others, various types of representative systems exist. In some cases (including Michael Jones and Scott Bader, as reported respectively by Thomasen in Balfour 1972, p. 159, and by Pateman 1970, p. 81) an element of outside control persists with final authority on certain matters remaining in the hands of trustees who are not employees in the operating company. Sometimes founders have devised institutional arrangements that ensure themselves or their heirs continued involvement in major policy making for a prolonged period. While all firms encourage employees to become members and to participate in decision making, not all employees have availed themselves of this opportunity. (For example, at Scott Bader in 1975 less than 70 percent of the workers were members, and of the nonmembers about 20 percent had worked long enough at Scott Bader so that they were eligible for membership.) Not all ICOM firms insist on equal voting rights; Landsman's, for example, allows plural voting based upon differential share holdings.

All firms have a "social purpose" written into their constitutions, to which part of their trading surplus is devoted, and some holding companies are registered as charities. Several have a "peace provision" in their constitutions and do not make goods that could be used in war.* Many believe that the quality of working life will suffer unduly if the firm grows too big, and consequently express an intention to remain small. Rowen Glasgow, one of two defunct ICOM societies, aimed to limit firm size to 25 members in order to preserve grassroots democracy. Beyond this, growth was to be achieved by initiating similar units.

ICOM firms limit the return paid on capital to the minimum necessary to attract capital in prevailing market conditions. In most cases (with the single exception of Landsman's) individual share capital is viewed with disdain; capital is principally provided via retained earnings, though some use is made of loan capital and bank loans. Except in the case of Sunderlandia, would-be members are not required to subscribe a capital-entrance fee. Often there is provision for mandatory accumulation from trading surplus; in the case of Scott Bader, for example, 60 percent of surplus must be retained for taxation and plowback. Except to some extent with Landsman's, retained earnings are collectively owned and cannot be recouped by individual employees, even upon dissolution of the society.

Enterprises often limit the maximum differences that can arise in the internal wage structure to differences narrower than in comparable capitalist firms. In Scott Bader the limit between top and bottom is 1:7, Rowen Glasgow began with 1:1.5 permissible wage range, and Sunderlandia has a maximum differential of 2:1 for all except apprentices. Most firms sympathize with the objectives of trade unions and encourage members to join unions. But only Sunderlandia has a union shop. Processes for determining payments as well as patterns of payment differ. At Trylon all members are paid a monthly salary but at Rowen Glasgow hour time rates are applied to shop-floor workers. At Scott Bader a system of job evaluation has been employed.

ICOM firms operate in various industries. The two largest firms,† Scott Bader and Bewley Cafes (each with about 400 employees), manufacture chemical and plastic intermediaries, and operate shops with cafes, repectively. Other enterprises include a jewelry retail and repair firm (Michael Jones), a building and contracting enterprise (Sunderlandia) and a builder of industrial mobile units (Landman's).

The 13 member companies employ about 1,100 employees. If Scott Bader and Bewley Cafes are excluded, though, most ICOM members are tiny, with

---

*This is in sharp contrast with the practice of long-established PCs, many of whom supplied, under public-authority contracts, goods to be used during the First World War. (See Board of Trade, 1896, sec. 1.)

† The largest common-ownership company, the John Lewis Partnership, with a workforce of about 25,000 and a turnover of more than £250 million, is neither a member nor an associate member of ICOM.

none employing more than 50 and five employing fewer than 20. A similar picture prevails with sales. Excluding Bewley Cafes, in 1976 aggregate sales were estimated at £18 million. But Scott Bader accounts for about £15 million of this.

Though small in absolute size, ICOM has grown quite rapidly. Started in 1958 by Ernest Bader and originally called the Society for Democratic Integration in Industry (Demistry), by 1965 ICOM had added three member companies, with ICOM members employing about 400. Two more firms joined before 1970 but the most rapid growth has taken place since then, during which time nine new member companies have been added. Only two ICOM firms have failed. In assisting this process of growth, the establishment of Industrial Common Ownership Finance Ltd., a revolving loan fund that receives loans from companies and individuals and makes loans to prospective and existing common-ownership ventures in need of capital, has played an important part. More than £50,000 in loan capital is available and more than ten loans have been made to new and existing member companies.

As with long-established PCs, evaluation of the experience of ICOM firms is made difficult by the limited availability of empirically oriented accounts of member firms. Further, the better-known accounts including those by Blum (1968) and Hadley (in Vanek 1975) tend to be individual case studies (though Sawtell [1968] investigated four ICOM firms) that stress the importance of firm-specific factors and the dangers and difficulties of making inferences applicable to all ICOM firms. Bearing these important considerations in mind, the first problem area evaluated is that of worker power.

For each of the four ICOM firms existing in 1967 Sawtell (1968) concluded that each was characterized by a high level of worker participation. For two small firms, Rowen Glasgow (firm B) and Rowen South Wales (firm A), there was shared decision making on all issues, including strategic matters. Further analysis of the returns of the other firms, Scott Bader (firm F) and Landsman's (firm C), shows that in both cases, of the many issues that were jointly decided, directive and nonstrategic matters were included in this process. The reports on Rowen Glasgow by Jarvie (1968) and on Rowen South Wales by Hadley (in Vanek 1975) further support the view that the actuality in both instances was workers' self-management. Visits by the author to Rowen South Wales and Trylon in 1971, with unstructured interviews with workers and managers, access to firm's minutes, and attendance at the November meeting of the firm's Advisory Council at Rowen South Wales, yielded similar impressions. But in visits to Rowen Glasgow in late 1971 (merely three years after Jarvie's studies), the situation was found to be one where all members of the firm acknowledged that senior management unilaterally made all major decisions. This was reflected in part by the General Council—in principle the basic decision-making body of the firm—meeting less frequently from about 1968 onward than during the firm's first five years (1963-68). Also, the practice of a rotating chairman at these meetings, reported by Jarvie (1968, p. 5), had been abandoned, with the manager now permantently occupying the chair. There is also some measure of disagreement between Pateman (1970) and Sawtell (1968) over actual practices at Scott Bader, with Pateman drawing on Blum's study (1968) to characterize Scott Bader as a case of "partial" (and not full) participation. Moreover, since these studies, there have been inportant changes in the organization's structure, reported in part by Bader (in Vanek 1975), which were designed to devolve more power to workers and away from the firm's founder and his family. It is quite possible that a more current study would yield a differing picture on the extent of workers' power at Scott Bader. Similarly, Thomasen's harsh appraisal (in Balfour 1972, p. 159) of the situation at Michael Jones might now be obsolete because of the continuing evolution of the democratic machinery at that firm.

Information on the matter of job satisfaction of members of ICOM firms is spotty at best. Hadley (in Vanek 1975) records statements by both managers and workers, all of whom testify that working at Rowen South Wales was a rewarding experience. Managers of the four ICOM firms participating in Sawtell's survey (1968) were similarly well pleased with their lot. But Blum (1968) is hard put to find reliable support for his premise that worker satisfaction is higher at Scott Bader than in comparable firms.*

On economic efficiency and matters of industrial peace, some information is available but much is of an uneven nature. In general, ICOM firms appear to enjoy industrial peace. But Rowen Glasgow was a notable exception to this general pattern. Beginning in about 1966 signs of overt conflict are frequently recorded in the firm's minutes (April 4, 1966, June 8, 1966, and June 1968) on matters including the suspension and eventual dismissal of a founder member, differential access of different skill groups to overtime work, which was paid at a premium rate (May 1966); and divided views on the necessity and wisdom of the frequent travels of the firm's first manager, ostensibly undertaken to solicit additional capital by donations and to promote a wider understanding of the broad objective of the "Factory for Peace" (Derrick and Phipps 1969, pp. 104–106), yet frequently perceived by workers as a thinly disguised management perquisite (April 4, 1966). Perhaps the experience of Rowen Glasgow illustrates the potential importance of contextual factors: whereas most ICOM firms are located in areas and/or industries that have good industrial relations reputations, Rowen Glasgow was located in an area with a history of bitter industrial relations. Many shop-floor workers had spent long periods in local shipyards with particularly virulent industrial relations and long-established hierarchical attitudes; such

---

*Comprehensive research on job satisfaction at selected ICOM firms is currently being undertaken by a research team headed by R. Paton and M. Lockett of the Open University. Their findings have not yet been made public.

inherited attitudes probably persisted and proved difficult to adjust to the directly democratic machinery at Rowen Glasgow.

It is also noteworthy that in a questionnaire survey of ICOM firms administered by the author in 1971 (covering five existing ICOM firms, that is, all except Scott Bader), only one firm had more than 50 percent union membership, two had no union members, and the average density was about 10 percent. Not that unionism was discouraged. On the contrary, senior management has sometimes encouraged union membership. In fact the minutes for the February 27th, 1970 meeting of the Community Council at Michael Jones record the comment rejecting the idea of union membership that had been suggested by the managing director. In addition to the size factor it is clear that many workers did not join because they neither saw much scope for the traditional collective bargaining role of unions within an ICOM framework nor were particularly concerned to have unions develop a new role in this situation, with a watchdog function and perhaps responsibility for matters like education in industrial democracy. Responses to the author's questionnaire survey also showed that ICOM firms had much job flexibility and no recent strikes or noticeable restrictive labor practices.

Both Rowen firms had suffered at one time or another from undercapitalization. Hadley (in Vanek 1975) documents the South Wales experience; interviews by the author with the chief executive at Glasgow and his predecessor led to similar concerns being voiced. No similar problems seem to have affected ICOM firms that converted to a common ownership, and the establishment of Industrial Common Ownership Finance Ltd. seems to have gone some way toward alleviating problems of securing adequate foundation and working capital for ventures beginning life as common-ownership firms. In some cases the processes used to determine relative incomes of members have caused strains. During the early days at Michael Jones some paternalism persisted, with relative earnings determined unilaterally by the managing director; the information was also kept confidential.* A commitment to egalitarianism and the resultant compressed internal payment structures has also caused dissent in some instances. Thus at Rowen Glasgow maximum differentials, which were initially 1:1.5, were widened to 1:2.5 in response to white-collar resentment that they were being badly treated. While little information exists on incomes compared to those received by employees in capitalist enterprises, earnings surveys suggest that ICOM workers receive at least the local average rate. For example, a survey for 1970-71 by the National Association of Goldsmiths showed that for both years, average earnings and salaries of workers at Michael Jones were in the top quartile, and a

---

*Information on salaries is now available to all members at Michael Jones.

survey by Constable (1974) showed remuneration for employees at Scott Bader to be on average higher than at four other chemical companies. Fringe benefits also appear in general to be good (see ICOM 1975). In his survey Constable (1974) calculated partial productivity measures including return on capital; by this measure Scott Bader consistently outperformed other chemical companies.

New Worker Cooperatives

Since 1975 a third wing has been added to the British worker cooperative movement with the establishment of three new industrial cooperatives—Kirby Manufacturing and Engineering (KME), Meriden Motorcycle, and the Scottish Daily News (SDN).* In each case the cooperative was established by employees after the proposed closure of the productive unit, with union activists, usually shop stewards, at the forefront in the fight against unemployment. Long delays occurred in the formation of these cooperatives. Complications arise for various reasons including difficulties in finding lawyers with experience in PCs, problems in obtaining foundation financing, negotiation delays as former owners sought to secure favorable selling prices for factories and capital assets, and difficulties in obtaining credit from suppliers.†

The most novel feature of these developments is the partial initial funding of the enterprises by the government. In the case of Meriden this included a grant of £750,000 and a loan of £1.2 million for 15 years at 10 percent interest. KME received a grant of £3.9 million and the SDN a loan of £1.2 million. Some individual share capital was also provided by workers at the SDN (£100,000), and additional shares were bought by trade unions and the general public (£175,000), in particular by Robert Maxwell (£100,000).

At both Meriden and KME the legal structure resembles that of two-tier ICOM firms: each has a holding and an operating company and is registered under the Company Acts. Shares of the holding company are held by trustees. But the trustees are required to act in accord with the wishes of the members of the cooperatives and real power rests with the operating company. It appears that the legal structure at the SDN was that of a conventional company—single tier and limited by shares.

---

*The SDN collapsed in November 1975. At least five worker cooperatives have also been established in Northern Ireland. But even the largest of these—Foyle Cooperative and Millmark Engineering—do not provide employment for more than 20.

†As yet there is little literature on these new cooperatives. Most useful are the accounts in Coates (1976), though most attention is paid to descriptions of the development period. See also Briston (1976), Edelstein (1976), and Carnoy and Levin (1976). Some of the points made in this section are derived from talks with members of cooperatives, sometimes during visits to the cooperatives by the author.

The formal organizational structure of each cooperative has been rather fluid, with workers never having complete control, though provision usually exists for majority control by employees; in reality power normally resides with shop stewards who were active during the formative period. In all cases, basic policy as well as routine production decisions are determined by a management board that consists primarily of elected worker representatives. At Meriden the eight full-time directors are the eight shop-steward conveners representing the eight unions in the cooperative; in addition there are two outside part-time advisors. At the SDN, six of the ten members of the board were elected shop-floor representatives, Two other members—the general manager and the editors—represented management, while the two remaining members represented outside shareholders and included Maxwell. In addition the Fathers of the Chapel Committee (the joint shop-steward committee) was to continue to play an important advisory role. At KME the structure is more elaborate. The sole directors are the two shop-steward conveners, and an Advisory Council advises the managers and directors on policy and is essentially a shop-steward committee consisting of more than 25 shop stewards chosen from all departments; this committee is also led by the two conveners. The third level in the structure at KME is a works council comprising one representative from each union. Finally, all new industrial cooperatives have provisions for regular general meetings. At these, workers—on the basis of one adult member, one vote—exercise ultimate control except in the case of Meriden, where Carnoy and Levin (1976, p. 49) report that a system of plural voting to reflect length of service has been introduced. Most constitutions lay down procedures for the calling of extraordinary general meetings. These are held at the place of work and perhaps during normal worktime, though usually at the end of the workday.

Each of the cooperatives introduced simplified wage structures and policies that provided for a more egalitarian distribution of income. Most radical is Meriden where all, except the most senior executives, receive identical pay. At KME sex differentials have been eliminated by the introduction of a policy of equal pay for equal work, and the pay structure has been revamped such that adult production workers have been assigned to three broad classes (skilled, semiskilled, and unskilled) with a basic pay differential between skilled and unskilled of about £11 per week. Substantial changes have also taken place in other facets of industrial relations. At all new worker cooperatives there is more job flexibility and most restrictive labor practices have been eliminated. At KME for example, all shop-floor workers do any job consistent with their grade, even if the new job is in another department. Whereas undermanning of a particular task in pre-cooperative days would usually bring that job to a standstill, now production workers at KME will continue to work an undermanned task for one hour, thus allowing management the opportunity to find a replacement worker. The occupational structure of the labor force has usually witnessed a marked reduction in the proportion of supervisory personnel. Yet except at Meriden there does not appear as yet to have been much direct concern with the quality of working life as affected by job enlargement, autonomous work groups, and the like. All new cooperatives actively support trade unionism and have closed shops—at KME this now extends to all staff workers too, including the general works manager.

Both of the surviving cooperatives have grown quite rapidly. At KME, 300 workers have been added and the workforce now stands at 770. Similarly with Meriden, from its conception in March 1975 the labor force has more than quadrupled in growing from 162 to more than 700 in October 1976. During its six-month life the SDN provided employment for more than 300. No formal links exist as yet either between the new worker cooperatives or between them and long-established PCs or members of ICOM. In both cases the new worker cooperatives' principal concern is with survival and consolidation; no evangelical role in assisting the establishment of more worker cooperative is foreseen.

The recentness of the new worker cooperatives obviously inhibits any in-depth examination of their experience, and only tentative comments can usefully be made. Evaluation of the two surviving cases is made more difficult because of the fluidity of the two situations. As regards power sharing it is clear that in principle structures exist that provide for workers' control over all basic decision making. Formal structures notwithstanding, it appears (see articles in Coates 1976) that in each case prominent, perhaps dominant, leaders have emerged. At KME for example, Eccles (in Coates 1976, p. 163) argues that "day to day power . . . rested on four people." But other shop stewards at KME argue that the democratic machinery does provide for substantial and continuing employee influence on decision making. Turnover of shop stewards on the shop-stewards committee and high attendance at the various meetings suggest sustained interest by the workforce in influencing policy; indeed, though most mass meetings quickly approve the committee's wishes, there have been instances of the general assembly registering their disagreement by voting not to accept the committee's recommendations. In the case of SDN, Briston (1976) had no doubts of the ability of the workforce, or segments thereof, to exercise its power within the cooperative structure. Indeed he argues that the democratic machinery was abused, with extraordinary general meetings being frequently and unnecessarily held. It is clear that this is an area particularly deserving of careful analysis. It is not clear that the workforce will continue (if it does now) to be satisfied with participating in decision making mainly indirectly via the established machinery. The failure to make minutes of the meetings of the shop-stewards committee and the works council freely available to the workforce at KME under the pretext of preserving confidentiality probably inhibits the ability of the workforce to influence decision making as effectively as they might otherwise do so. At Meriden, the system of plural voting may serve to undermine the egalitarian power-sharing ethic.

On the matter of personal fulfillment not even much qualitative data are available. In each case, however, it is clear that such objectives were distinctly secondary considerations of the workforce. Somewhat more fragmentary information is available concerning economic efficiency and industrial peace. All cooperatives began badly, with the SDN soon going into liquidation and Meriden losing £1.3 million during its first 13 months (N.V.T. Annual Report) and KME losing £1.5 million during the first 15 months (KME Annual Report). But since then KME has begun to break even and Meriden may too have turned the corner; each has expanded its labor force. It is clear that in all cases there have been substantial improvements in the efficiency of labor. In the case of the SDN, Briston (1976) and Mackie (in Coates 1976) record the remarkable flexibility and enthusiasm of the labor force shown particularly by the ability to begin production of a newspaper within three weeks of being established. At KME there are several specific instances of productivity improvements. In the radiator shop the output quota for a four-man team in the pre-cooperative days was 64; since KME was established the quota is now 72. All cases are replete with accounts of savings in wastage. Each cooperative has been able to introduce new products. At KME the Arcadiair heater was developed and marketed during the first year, at SDN the original newspaper was converted to a tabloid, and at Meriden they have begun to assemble a new Italian motor bicycle. Substantial savings have been made at both Meriden and KME in the payroll departments because of the simplified wage structures. All suffered (and the two remaining continue to do so) from problems of capital shortage. The position has been alleviated to some extent at KME because the government now permits KME to borrow against its assets. Meriden's plight in this respect has been highlighted by a desperate (and so far unsuccessful) attempt to find an additional £1 million, which is required as working capital and to secure marketing rights. All have at one stage or another been troubled by marketing problems, with KME currently in the healthier position, and SDN proving unable to develop an editorial policy that appealed broadly and generated sufficient advertising revenue quickly enough. None have been troubled seriously by industrial relations problems, though conflict has hardly been eliminated. All cooperatives have enjoyed only muted support from relevant unions, with Meriden (Carnoy and Levin 1976, p. 49) and SDN (Mackie, in Coates 1976) sometimes experiencing hostility from individual unions. Yet many members of the new cooperatives remain active trade unionists, convinced that their activities constitute an important model for the new unionists.

Current Developments

Of most potential significance to British worker cooperatives is the November 1976 Industrial Common Ownership Act. The act has two major parts. The financial section provides for grants totaling £30,000 during each of the next five years to an (or any) agency that exists to give advice about the organization of common-ownership enterprises and cooperative enterprises. The agency (or agencies) is also empowered to make loans to such enterprises up to a maximum of £250,000 during the next five years. The other section spells out definitions of the two classes of firms that are eligible for assistance under the terms of the act, that is, common-ownership firms and cooperative enterprises. The significance of the act lies not so much in the amount of financial assistance provided but in the precedent-setting legal presumption that the problems facing worker cooperatives in a capitalist economy are such that provision for any special dispensation is needed. In commenting on the act, the underlying premises deserve attention. First, the act assumes that self-governing enterprises are unable to obtain adequate financing by conventional channels without surrendering their autonomy. The experience of British PCs, particularly during their early years and particularly those which, like Rowen South Wales, begin as worker-managed firms, from the start testifies to the need for a special institution in the capital market that will provide loans for worker-managed firms. Second, it is assumed, and again the historical record bears witness, that the viability of a collection of self-managed firms is assisted when individual firms—both prospective as well as actual—have access to diverse services that are provided via central coordinating institutions. It would be more effective if a single organization representing all workers cooperatives was to do this job, rather than the disparate entities that currently exist (CPF, ICOM, and the two surviving new worker cooperatives). Perhaps the differences that have precluded such a development in the past, at least between the CPF and ICOM, will be smoothed over, prompted by the new law and the probable urging of the Department of Industry (Small Firms Division), which is in charge of supervising the new law. But any such suprafederation seems unlikely to include the new worker cooperatives and the latter show no signs of promoting a rival umbrella organization. Consequently since ICOM is clearly the most dynamic of the existing agencies,* with ICOM members playing an important part in securing passage of the new law, it is likely that ICOM or Industrial Common Ownership Finance will emerge as the principal agency involved in administering the money made available under the terms of the law. If the historical record is any guide it also seems that in addition to providing technical services, agencies should play a watchdog role by ensuring that worker cooperatives continue to be self-managed and actively assisting with educational work within and without individual firms concerning both techniques for administering self-managed firms and the general concepts and purposes of self-management. Third, though the act is intended "to further the development of enterprises controlled by people working in them," legislative

---

*The position of the CPF is further complicated by the death of the long-serving secretary, James Leonard.

support is given to a particular type of workers' self-management, namely, that based upon common ownership. But the history of long-established British PCs suggests that the failure to charge a scarcity price for the use of collectively owned assets constitutes a primary reason why most PCs must self-destruct. Various methods exist that enable the difficulties associated with major reliance on collective ownership to be avoided; all involve designing legal structures that "separate the functional roles of workers as capital suppliers and workers while avoiding a misallocation of capital and stimulating savings by assuring that the investing firm pays and the savers (workers) receive a price approximating one which reflects the scarcity of productive resources in the economy" (Knight, in *Newsletter*, no. 18, 1976, p. 9, of the Association for Self-Management). Without an overseeing agency ensuring that individual worker cooperatives comply with this requirement, the long-term outlook for many British worker cooperatives will probably be bleak. Even firms that require mandatory reinvestment of a large part of their surplus may experience slow rates of growth of their labor forces (since the opportunity cost of collectively owned capital is zero). More importantly in the future, pressure may grow from aging workers to relax this reinvestment requirement in order that they may enjoy more current income via higher rates of remuneration and so obtain the implicit equity they have built up in the firms.

There are other less important comments that can be made on the act. The definitions used for eligible firms are somewhat imprecise. Furthermore, if strictly applied they could lead (intentionally or otherwise) to cooperatives like Meriden and Landsman's being excluded from receiving assistance, because in the first case the company is limited by shares and not by guarantee while at Meriden provision apparently exists for weighted voting. In addition the existence of nonworking members at most PCs might lead to their exclusion. The problem is how to judge when a "body is controlled by a majority of the people working for the body" (as stipulated in the act). These comments notwithstanding, the act represents a legal milestone in the history of British workers' participation in management.

Three other events are of interest to students of British worker cooperatives; each helps to reinforce the expectation that in the immediate future there is likely to be continuing growth in the extent of the British PC sector. First, interest by local authorities in encouraging the development of worker cooperatives is growing. Diverse advantages are seen by local authorities in assisting this process. Most often stressed are job creation and job security, local control, and retention of wealth created within the local community. In 1975 the local authority of Cumbria appointed, for the first time in Britain, a local government official whose job is specifically to help the development of worker cooperatives (D.C. Jones 1975b, p. 337). In October 1976 the Policy Review Subcommittee of the London Borough of Wandsworth (D.C. Jones 1976, pp. 16–20) advised that the local council should support workers' cooperatives. Furthermore, it was recommended that £100,000 of the local taxes be used to provide financial assistance for embryonic worker cooperatives. This is probably the first time that Section 137 of the 1972 Local Government Act has been used in this way. Applications for additional financial assistance under the provisions of various pieces of national legislation was also recommended. The subcommittee's report also indicates that other local authorities were active in similar ways.

The second matter is the continuing consideration that the government is giving to the establishment of a Cooperative Development Agency. (In the Lords debate on July 27, 1976 following the second reading of the Industrial Common Ownership Bill, Lord Melchett made it clear that that measure is not regarded as a substitute for a Cooperative Development Agency.) This agency would aid established and proposed cooperatives of all kinds in several ways including providing a central pool of technical expertise for professional services such as legal and accountancy skills, and acting as a funding agency or a cooperative bank. Indications, however, are that such an agency would be largely concerned with retail cooperatives, rather than worker cooperatives.

Thirdly, the 1976 Finance Act makes it simpler and financially easier to convert conventional capitalist companies into PCs or common-ownership firms; henceforth such conversions are to be exempt from both capital gains tax and capital transfer tax. Undoubtedly this will lead to many such conversions particularly by owners of companies sympathetic to their employees' aspirations for participation in management, yet who wish to safeguard their heirs' financial interests, but more so by family-owned firms contemplating conversions (sometimes associate members of ICOM) mainly because of the absence of heirs.

SCHEMES FOR JOINT CONSULTATION

Diverse schemes of various complexity exist where the form of participation on strategic issues is essentially a process of joint consultation, though this form of participation may be integrated with other forms allowing for greater degrees of worker power in decision making at other levels in the organization. These schemes come under the category of classical joint consultation. Before examining some of these schemes it is useful to briefly recap some of the essential aspects of traditional joint consultation, which has often been an historical forerunner of classical joint consultation.

Traditional Joint Consultation

Traditional joint consultation is a form of indirect or representative participation by workers in management. Its history is well known. In the private sector schemes have usually been initiated by employers and at a level in the organization structure that did not involve strategic matters. Traditional joint consultation has been kept distinct from collective bargaining machinery. Details of individual schemes have been provided by Renold (1950) while overviews and accounts of the main stages in the ebb and flow of joint consultation have been provided by the National Institute of Industrial Psychology (1952) and later by McCarthy (1966) Thomasen (in Balfour 1973, pp. 144–46), Guest and Fatchett (1974, pp. 33–36), and Horvat (in Horvat, Markovic, and Supek 1975, vol. 1, pp. 40–56). Joint consultative machinery has often been introduced as a device to contain the aspirations of workers and to ensure that no basic changes took place in the status quo; this was the case during the 1920s following the shop-steward movement (see Pribicevic 1959) and the recommendations of the Whitley Committee. During the Second World War the need for increased and smoother war production led to the development of joint production committees. Both periods of rapid growth of joint consultation were followed by almost as rapid and extensive contractionary phases (Horvat, Markovic, and Supek 1975, vol. 1, p. 42; Clarke, Fatchett, and Roberts 1972, chap. 3). In the public sector many organizations and industries, including nationalized industries, have usually had a legal obligation to introduce some form of joint consultation. Though this machinery frequently exists at more than one level in the organizational structure—in the coal industry, it exists at the national, divisional, area, and colliery levels—the form of participation does not differ in substance between levels. At different times it has been especially popular in the electricity supply industry (Sallis 1959) and the coal industry (Anthony, in Balfour 1973).

The nature, scope, and extent of the machinery have seldom differed markedly between the public and the private sectors, usually being perceived by management as a means of achieving unity of purpose or assisting communications and being concerned largely with noncontroversial and, most certainly, nonstrategic issues. This finding is confirmed by nearly all available studies, including those already cited. Here, as was the intended purpose, the introduction of joint consultation has never led to any significant increase in worker power. On the matter of job satisfaction, the little available evidence indicates, as might be expected with a system of indirect democracy, that joint consultation has not been accompanied by any marked improvement in worker job satisfaction in general. Sustained beneficial effects on worker representatives do not seem evident. With regard to economic efficiency, though, joint consultation does not seem to have deleterious effects and may have led to improved performance. For example, see the testimonies by employers reported by Horvat (in Horvat, Markovic, and Supek 1975, vol. 1, p. 52) and the observations of Robertson (1923, pp. 153–56).

Classical Joint Consultation

While most examples of classical joint consultation are in large firms (employing more than 2,000 employees) in the private sector, some small private firms have such schemes, as do enterprises involving important, sometimes total, degrees of public ownership. Despite the existence of many well-known studies of individual instances of this kind, including the studies of Glacier Metal by Brown (1960) and Jaques (1951), and of the John Lewis Partnership by Flanders, Pomeranz, and Woodward (1968) it seems that comprehensive accounts of the number, scope, and extent of these participatory types have never been published. Studies by Sawtell (1968), Derrick and Phipps (1969), Gordon-Brown (1972), and numerous contributions to journals like *Industrial Participation* offer descriptions of the workings of selected schemes, yet none of these claim complete coverage. More importantly, most accounts are long on description yet comparatively short on systematic evaluation. A particularly important neglected dimension is the economic aspect that often constitutes an important form of participation within the overall scheme. Consequently any brief overview and evaluation of these schemes must be particularly eclectic.

On the basis of published accounts of such schemes it seems that the underlying philosophies enable two types of classical joint consultation to be distinguished—those developed in enterprises dominated by a unitary or organic conception of the firm and those based upon a pluralist perspective. Certain common attributes can usually be distinguished for both categories. The unitary approaches of various firms, together with their multilevel structures, have been described and analyzed in a number of studies, as follows: Glacier Metal (Brown 1960; Jaques 1951); the John Lewis Partnership (Flanders, Pomeranz, and Woodward 1968); Best and Lloyd (Best 1964); Computer Management Group (Industrial Participation Association 1975); Cadbury-Schweppes (Cadbury-Schweppes 1976); and Woodward Governor (company D in Sawtell 1968). The unitary conception of the firm has usually been introduced by an individual, often the owner and normally without serious participation by other parties in the design of the scheme. Structures are designed to reflect those organic beliefs and to promote a sense of community; enterprise newspapers constitute an important element in the participation process and are intended to be something more than merely a vehicle for communication. Emphasis is also given to creating the right climate and the correct conditions as well as to designing the appropriate structure. Furthermore, "the idea that 'industrial democracy must consist in giving the workers the right to appoint their bosses' is rejected as prejudicing the economic viability of the enterprise and the interests of all its members" (Flanders, Pomeranz, and Woodward 1968, p. 182). Membership in unions is not prohibited but, since such membership could clearly constitute a threat to the unitary spirit, it is not usually encouraged. Finally there is frequently an important economic dimension to these schemes. They often provide for participation in profits (and sometimes in ownership) and restrict the return on capital. Most, though Computer Management Group, with its commitment to high wages and narrow differentials, is an exception, accept the market-determined pattern of income differentials.

Not unexpectedly then, when the power-sharing aspects of such schemes are investigated, the picture that emerges is typically one of little employee participation in strategic decision making. After examining the activities of the various elected bodies with decision-making powers at the John Lewis Partnership and the composition of the membership of these councils, Flanders, Pomeranz, and Woodward (1968, chap. 3) conclude that the reality of the situation was not one of significant worker power in big decisions. The data in Table 1 show that since that study, which dealt with the period 1957-67, the percentage of rank and file elected to the Central Council (the partnership's principal elective body) has improved a little but is still less than one-quarter representation on the council. Likewise, most assessments of the Glacier Metal experiment conclude that the theoretically wide scope of powers of the four-tier participation system in practice is not fulfilled; in particular, workers do not share in strategic decision making. Thomasen (in Balfour 1973, p. 48) points out that "the requirement in Glacier that any decision of the Works Council should command a *unanimous* vote is of paramount importance . . . [and] the machinery of Glacier's representative system . . . allows representatives of employees to challenge the rule setting process only, as it were, by grace and favour of the top management . . . [while] the real power must yet remain with the top management." But Sawtell (1968, firm I) judged that the system of Glacier provided for a high level of participation by workers in decision making. Further analysis of his results, though, reveals that all of the issues that might be considered strategic, such as deciding the location of a new plant, were decided by a process involving other-than-shared decision making by employees, usually consultation. At Best and Lloyd, after an extensive investigation of their system of participation, Ross (in Best and Lloyd, 1966) reported that he had found no "conclusive evidence that the workers at Best and Lloyd . . . had effectively participated in the management of the firm." Even at Computer Management Group, with its emphasis on open information and delegation of responsibility, major decisions are made by the directors (Industrial Participation Association 1975, p. 12). So far as personal fulfillment is concerned, the balance of evidence available on schemes of this type suggests that there has been no discernible impact on worker job satisfaction. At the John Lewis Partnership, Flander, Pomeranz, and Woodward (1968, p. 190) show "that in general job satisfaction in the partnership reaches much the same level as that recorded in a national sample of the working population." Sawtell (1968, p. 16) reports senior executives at Glacier Metal, Cadbury-Schweppes, and the John Lewis Partnership (respectively firms I,

TABLE 1

Status Composition of the Central Council
at the John Lewis Partnership

Council Year	Ex Officio and Nominated Managerial Councillors		Elected Managerial Councillors		Elected Rank-and-File Councillors		Total Council Membership	
	No.	%	No.	%	No.	%	No.	%
1957-58	27	24	75	66	12	10	114	100
1961-62	31	23	90	67	13	10	134	100
1965-66	29	21	87	63	22	16	138	100
1966-67	29	21	94	68	15	11	138	100
1968-69	30	22	81	59	26	19	137	100
1969-70	30	22	79	57	29	21	138	100
1970-71	20	15	82	63	28	22	120	100
1971-72	20	15	90	67	25	18	135	100

Sources: Data for 1957-67 from Flanders, Pomeranz, and Woodward (1968, p. 60); information for the remaining years supplied by the John Lewis Partnership.

M, and O) as believing that their own satisfaction from personal relationships with colleagues and employees had increased because of the existence of the participation scheme. On the economic front no hard data exist for any of the firms. Again Sawtell (1968, p. 16) records statements by senior management that they believed the scheme to have had beneficial effects on productivity and the extent of "damaging" conflict, though the speed of decision making may have been slowed. It also seems that many of these companies have not been irretrievably damaged commercially by the introduction of these schemes, with many recording high growth rates. But no information, which uses generally accepted economic criteris, exists on questions such as the economic perform-ance of these firms compared with firms without such schemes or the per-formance of the firm itself before the introduction of the participation struc-ture. Furthermore, the attribution of any such difference in economic per-formance—whether it exists because, or in spite, of the democratic machinery—remains a controversial question in many cases.

Unlike unitary approaches, pluralist participation schemes coexist with collective bargaining machinery established by strong unions; joint shop-steward committees and, in multiestablishment companies, combine committees, may also exist. Many multilevel pluralist participation schemes are looked at by Sawtell (1968), including Hay's Wharf (firm H), ICI agricultural Division Bill-ingham (firm N) in the private sector, and Samuel Fox (firm L), a steelmaking firm in the public sector. The best known experiment involving a degree of public ownership was at Fairfields (see Alexander and Jenkins 1970). Pluralist schemes also differ from unitary schemes in that they are seldom inspired by one strongly ideologically motivated individual, attach less importance to the role of company newspapers, do not attempt to promote a sense of community, and seldom have provisions for profit sharing or restrictions on the return to capital. Many pluralist schemes had adopted a single (union) channel of representation.

So far as power sharing is concerned, all of the available evidence supports the expectation that in practice there is extremely little employee influence on strategic matters, though often there is substantial worker influence on non-strategic matters via the collective bargaining machinery and the participation structure. Thus Sawtell (1968) found that all four enterprises mentioned could be categorized as having a medium level of participation. Yet, further breakdown of his results reveals that in no cases did workers exercise substantial influence on vital policy matters: medium levels of worker power were achieved by worker influence over what many have long accepted as appropriate subjects for collective bargaining. At Fairfields, Alexander and Jenkins (1970, p. 212) report that though the crisis situation there provided scope for the transfer of much power, in practice full-time union officials and shop stewards failed to capitalize on all of their opportunities for increased participation. Concerning personal fulfillment, no published work appears to be available on the impact of these schemes on employees or middle-level management. Sawtell (1968, p. 16), however, finds that each of the senior executives responding to his questionnaire in firms H, K, L, and N replied that their experience with participation had had a beneficial impact on personal relationships with colleagues and other employees. On efficiency, Sawtell's results (responses to questions a, c, and d) again indicate that senior managerial perceptions of such effects were usually positive. Klein (1976, pp. 48–49) reports that most firms examined in his survey, some of which probably use multilevel pluralist approaches, believed that productivity had improved since the introduction of the participation scheme. In the most careful available evaluation of this question for schemes of this type, Alexander and Jenkins (1970, pp. 199–210) report large gains in labor productivity, on the order of 16 percent compared with similar periods before the scheme began. Labor productivity improved till it was almost as high as the best ever achieved in the industry. In part these gains were achieved by the elimination of numerous restrictive labor practices.

Current Developments

Many studies have shown that there has been a marked reduction in the frequency of joint consultation (compare National Institute for Industrial Psychology 1951 with Clarke, Fatchett, and Roberts 1972, pp. 72–74). Some authorities seem to go so far as to suggest the tolling of the death knell for joint consultation, believing its usefulness to be outlived and displaced by the growth of workplace bargaining. But it may be that joint consultation is a more resilient institution. Particularly for larger firms there is some evidence of a rebirth in interest in joint consultation, especially classical joint consultation of a plural-ist kind, and it also seems that there are qualitative changes afoot in the charac-ter of schemes in unitary frameworks. For example, note the change in the long-established participation structure at what is now Cadbury-Schweppes, as reported in their 1976 evidence presented to the Committee of Inquiry on Industrial Democracy, and the changes in the ICI scheme (reported in Brit-ish Broadcasting Corporation 1976). Both expand the area of employee in-volvement into issues previously considered to be exclusively management prerogatives, though stop far short of giving workers formal powers in mak-ing strategic decisions. Other schemes probably have already been introduced, and no doubt others will be, that are stimulated at least in part by the threat of legislative action in this area. Potentially important implications are ap-parent for organizations adopting such schemes. For plans within pluralist frameworks the increasingly frequent use of single (union) channels of repre-sentation, particularly shop stewards, both recognizes and fosters the further development of the power informally held by shop stewards. In some ostensibly unitary structures, the pressure for change has in large part been prompted by internal developments that threaten to rupture the unitary framework. At Cadbury-Schweppes, for example, unionization has steadily increased, such that 90 percent of employees are currently represented for the purposes of collec-tive bargaining. The strain produced between the rapid development of this system and the long-established and slowly evolving consultative machinery is reflected in the antipathetic response of employees in major factories to a change in the participation program at Cadbury-Schweppes and their refusal to be directly represented in newly created elements in this structure (see Cadbury-Schweppes 1976, sec. 4).

In the public sector an elaborate (three-tier) scheme for worker partici-pation has also been implemented at British Leyland (*IRRR*, no. 117, December 1975). It essentially follows the major recommendation of the Ryder report, which argued that provision for worker participation in management should be expanded as an aid to efficiency. Though the intricate apparatus established by the scheme basically provides for little more than consultation and provides for no representation in any shape or form in the area of basic policy making, it is clear that the trend is in that direction. Again, certain basic principles charac-erize the scheme: a single (trade union) channel—exists governing eligibility for voting and candidacy, the machinery for participation is separate from the col-lective bargaining apparatus, and shop stewards play a key role in the scheme. Legislation is also expected to be introduced during early 1977 to enable a greater degree of worker participation in the management of the Post Office

Corporation. Tripartite discussions (between unions, corporation management, and officials at the Department of Industry) are underway to determine the specifics of the participation system. There are also provisions, in the bills relating to the nationalization of aircraft, shipbuilding, and ship-repairing, that under state ownership the corporations must introduce a form of worker participation in management that is acceptable to concerned unions.

Hence in the foreseeable future, with or without the introduction of legislation enabling the introduction of worker representatives on boards, it is likely that elaborate consultative schemes will continue to flourish and to develop. But as many have argued (see McCarthy 1966, pp. 35–36), in its attempt to separate subjects that are allegedly properly jointly determined via collective bargaining from those that remain exclusive managerial prerogatives, joint consultation is an inherently unstable system. The upward drift in the scope and extent of joint consultation evident in new changes in some famous schemes are manifestations of this instability. In turn, since such schemes are increasingly based on single (union) channels of representation, with key employee representatives being shop stewards whose degree of power at the shop-floor level far outdistances that provided via these more elaborate consultative schemes at other levels, this generates pressure for further change and expansion of the scope and extent of workers' participation in management.

WORKER DIRECTORS

Past and Contemporary Examples

Schemes for worker representation on boards of directors have long existed in Britain. The earliest recorded examples are the South Metropolitan Gas Company and South Suburban Gas Company schemes, which, respectively, provided for three and two employee representatives on the board of directors as well as for a system of profit sharing (see *Co-operators Yearbook* for 1906). Current examples include the worker-director scheme at Bonser Engineering, which since 1975 provides for one employee to be appointed to a nine-person supervisory management board (see evidence submitted by Bonser to the Committee of Inquiry on Industrial Democracy, and *IRRR*, no. 142, December 1976). But most famous is the scheme for worker directors in the British Steel Corporation (BSC). It is also the experiment about which most is known and, accordingly, to which attention shall be directed below.

The scheme may be looked at as encompassing three phases. Brannen et al. (1976, p. 96) describe the main phase of the scheme, which began operating in early 1968, as follows: "There would be three part-time worker directors on each of the four group boards; they would work at their normal jobs when not undertaking board duties; they would be drawn from the group in which they

worked; they would be appointed by the chairman of the corporation, preferably from trade union nominees, and on appointment would have to relinquish any
union posts they might hold." After a review of the scheme there were some
minor changes in it partly in response to complaints made by worker directors.
The second phase began in 1969 when more detailed job descriptions were provided and it was made clear that worker directors could attend meetings that
helped to shape and form policy before it reached the board, including those of
study groups, advisory committees, and working parties. A little later (in 1970)
the product division structure replaced the group boards structure and thereby
permitted the addition of four worker directors, making a total of 16. The
scheme entered its third phase when it was decided that it should become
permanent, with several minor changes to be implemented in 1973. D.C. Jones
(in Balfour 1973, pp. 87–88) describes these changes. Most important were those
prompted by the recognition that to require worker directors to relinquish union
offices they might hold was an undesirable feature and that some procedure
needed to be devised to permit worker representatives to report back on a regular and systematic basis to their constituents.

In evaluating this experiment, the most comprehensive study available is
that by Brannen et al. (1976), which focuses on the operation of the scheme
during the first four years. The authors argue that if the intention of the scheme
was to increase the influence of employees on decision making, the basic structural design of the scheme would hardly permit this objective to be achieved.
The worker directors were part-time minority members of advisory boards. Also
it was extremely likely that whatever formal powers the boards possessed, real
power lay at other-than-board level. Moreover, the already limited influence
employees would be able to exercise on decision making, imposed by the realities of the formal structure, was to be further circumscribed by various
processes, described by Brannen et al. (1976, chaps. 6-7). These include the way
in which influence was brought to bear on the orientation of worker directors
toward their role, the selection process, and the training process; each, it is
argued, helped to produce and shape worker directors with unitary perspectives
and with viewpoints that regarded efficiency (as compared with, say, social)
considerations as paramount. Detailed observation and analysis of the operation
of the scheme during these early years leads Brannen et al. to conclude that their
expectations were substantially fulfilled; D.C. Jones (in Balfour 1973, pp. 93–
101) agrees that the influence of worker directors on policy formation during
the early years in general was negligible. But whereas Brannen et al. (1976, pp.
237-43) are not persuaded that the most recent changes made in the scheme will
make any dramatic difference in the area of power sharing, D.C. Jones (in
Balfour 1973, pp. 101-03) is of a different opinion. He believes that the ability
of employees to attend meetings of policy-forming bodies will lead to a substantial increase in employee influence on decision making.

In other areas of interest somewhat less information is available. It is apparent, however, that improving personal fulfillment in general was not a major objective of the scheme; it is equally clear that in general no great changes did take place in this regard. But for those groups most directly affected there were discernible changes. Evidence is presented by Brannen et al. to show that during the early stage of the experiment, worker directors felt not only isolated because no machinery existed to enable them to report back to the shop floor, but frustrated because of their inability to participate in policy formation outside of the boardroom. It is also evident that there were some managers, usually those supervising worker directors during non-worker director activity, who experienced status loss and were uncomfortable with the implications of the scheme as it concerned their own authority. So far as the economic effects of the scheme are concerned, if the influence on decision making by employee directors had indeed been negligible, then no great economic impact of the scheme is to be expected. Yet the discussion by Brannen et al. (1976, chap. 10) of the role of worker directors in redundancy situations is an interesting and illuminating application of the thesis of Brannen et al. that "pressure to accept Board-room rationality made it difficult to put forward and represent worker rationality" (pp. 190–91). Rationalization and industrial peace may well have been aided by the existence of workers on the board.

Current Developments—The Private Sector and the Bullock Committee on Industrial Democracy

In August 1975 it was announced that an independent committee of inquiry was to be set up to consider ways of extending industrial democracy in the private sector; the committee was given the following terms of reference: "Accepting the need for a radical extension of industrial democracy in the control of companies by means of representation on boards of directors and accepting the essential role of trade union organizations in this process, to consider how such an extension can best be achieved, taking into account in particular the proposals of the Trades Union Congress [TUC] report on industrial democracy as well as experience in Britain, the EEC [European Economic Community] and other countries. Having regard to the interests of the national economy, employees, investors and consumers, to analyze the implications of such representation for the efficient management of companies and for company law." Since then discussion about the deliberations of the committee have been the fulcrum of the debate on British industrial democracy.

Much initial reaction was highly critical of the allegedly restrictive terms of reference. Not everyone accepted the need for a radical extension of industrial democracy (nor agreed on the definition of "radical"). If they did, the reasons for favoring such a change often differed markedly, with arguments stemming from the three problem areas of work organization distinguished by Walker

(1974)–the need to formally redistribute power from capital to labor, to aid personal fulfillment of workers, and to help industrial peace and economic efficiency–being especially frequently voiced, though with varying emphasis, and with others stressing arguments resembling those used in Pateman's (1970) theory of democracy. Many sympathetic to a radical extension of industrial democracy did not agree that special attention should be given to the TUC plan: they variously argued that this gave excessive emphasis to worker directors and ignored the merits of schemes that might include board members representing interests other than those of workers and shareholders and/or provide for simultaneous participation in decision making at other levels in the organization; that while the notion of workers directors was appealing, the idea of parity representation was a mistake; that a single-tier board system (rather than representation on supervisory boards) was preferable and that election to and candidacy for positions of worker directors should not be confined to union members. Many failed to see the wisdom in separately considering the extension of industrial democracy in private and public sectors and by differing procedures.* Other adverse comment followed when the composition of the committee, under the chairmanship of Lord Bullock, was announced. It was frequently argued that it would be virtually impossible to secure agreement among a group including leaders and representatives of major union organizations (Jack Jones, of the Transport and General Workers Union [TGWU]; Jenkins, of the Association of Supervisory, Technical, and Managerial Staff [ASTMS]; and Lea, of TUC) and chairmen or past chairmen of important corporations (Heath, of Guest, Keen, and Nettlefolds, Ltd. [GKN]; Biggs, formerly of Esso; and Williams, Glyn, and Callard, of ICI). In view of the concern expressed, regarding the committee's terms of reference, for the "efficient management of companies," the failure to include an economist in the team was also criticized. Finally, the need for the committee to report before the end of 1976 was queried: it was believed it would prove highly problematical to investigate all available evidence from relevant perspectives so as to enable a majority opinion to be formed within the allotted time.

Since late 1975 diverse groups and individuals have submitted evidence to the committee and two reports for the committee on the European experience of industrial democracy have been published.† Though the committee's report has not been published at the time of this writing (December 1976), the

---

*The role employees should play in decision making in the public sector was to be examined in a series of confidential inquiries.

†Much of this evidence is reviewed in various editions of *IRRR* between September 1974 (no. 87) and July 1976 (no. 131). A good overview of the early evidence is contained in Industrial Partnership Association (1976). For the two reports prepared for the committee, see Batstone and Davies (1976).

considerable public debate aroused thus far allows what are probably going to be some of the issues with which the report will be concerned to be distinguished. Three sets of issues are readily apparent, and on each of these there will likely be disagreement in the report, reflected in a majority and a minority report, with the likely signatories of the latter the three employer members.

The first set of issues concerns the shape and scope of representation at the board level. Recommendations will undoubtedly be designed to fit in with the British system of industrial relations yet take into account the experience with the scheme for worker directors at the BSC and the German experience with codetermination. Both of these schemes, though, will likely be criticized as generally being inappropriate for British industrial relations at this juncture in time, with proposals taking cognizance of the limitations in the scope and form of those schemes, distinguished in the committee's research reports (Batstone and Davies 1976). It is likely that all members will accept the motion to have worker representatives (no longer called worker directors) on the board. It is believed the majority report will favor the $2X + Y$ formula whereby on a single-tier board, two groups of equal numbers of directors would represent shareholders and the company's employees, with a third, smaller slice being nominated and approved by the two equal sides. The scheme may be described as one of "minority parity," with the third, smaller slice holding the balance of power and with the chairman coming from the shareholder side. If the majority report was cast in these terms it would mean a change from the original TUC proposals. These called for parity representation for worker representatives and shareholder representatives on the supervisory board of a two-tier board structure, with no other representatives at this level.* The original TUC scheme may be described as one of "equality parity." On these matters it is probable that the minority report will reluctantly acquiesce, though probably expressing a preference for worker representation on the supervisory board of a two-tier board structure, rather than on a single-tier board. The possibility of a different formula emerging, which reduces the relative power of the worker representatives, perhaps a $3X$ formula (three equal slices), should not be discounted. Moreover, it is likely that the three minority members of the committee will forcefully argue that they felt bound by the terms of reference to report on how (rather than whether) worker directors should be introduced, and that they do not necessarily think the basic concept to be a good one.

---

*In its later evidence to the committee (*IRRR* no. 126, April 1976) however, the TUC softened its 1974 position and opened the door to a unitary rather than a two-tier board. It is interesting to note that the CBI opinion has firmly tilted in the other direction, with it originally favoring a single-tier company structure (with the possible introduction of two nonexecutive directors who might be employees of the company) and now preferring instead experimentation of this kind at a supervisory-board level.

The second set of issues concerns the role of trade union organizations. It is likely that the majority report will include a provision that permits unions to trigger worker representative systems; where unions are weak or many unions exist in a company and are in disagreement concerning the desirability of worker directors, procedures will be devised perhaps stressing the role of the Advisory Council and Arbitration Service (ACAS) to determine whether or not the trigger shall be pressed. This triggering will probably entail that all company employees be polled secretly to see whether or not they are in favor of a system of worker representation at the board level along the lines previously described. If approved it is probable that only members of unions recognized by the company will be eligible to vote in the elections and be candidates for worker representatives, though conditions for eligibility for candidacy may include a minimum period of employment at the company. Thus workers who are not union members will be disfranchised from all but the triggering elections, and the only way in which union officials who are not employed by the company could gain membership to the board would be by being jointly nominated by worker and shareholder representatives. It is likely that the minority report will criticize the concept of a single (union) channel of representation, preferring a more broadly based constituency that enables all employees and not just union members to be eligible to vote in all elections and for candidacy. To buttress the argument for an alternative nonunion channel of representation (works councils?), it is argued that unions are not necessarily representative of the general workforce and that this disinterest is reflected in low attendance figures at union meetings, entrenched union leadership, and so on.

Much of the report will probably be concerned with the legal implications of these proposals. It is probable the committee will recommend the introduction of enabling legislation that would allow (and not mandate as in Germany) unions in large private companies, as described above, to request that the triggering vote be put to all employees and, only if that is favorable, that worker representatives be eventually introduced. Initially the trigger will probably not have to be pulled before a certain date, though procedures regulating any subsequent kicking-off of opportunities for the introduction of worker representatives are likely to be included. There will be important changes in company law. The legal definition of a company will probably be changed so that there is a statutory obligation for companies to respond to the interests of workpeople as well as shareholders. Yet in codifying the duties of directors, it is unlikely that the proposed law would differentiate between varied groups of workers but rather would indicate that the legal responsibility of all directors lay with the company as redefined. This would not, of course, prevent worker and shareholder representatives from being accountable and able to report back to those who elected them. But such a recommendation would mean that at least the majority of the committee disagreed with the TUC Report of 1974 and its proposal to separate worker power in decision making from responsibility for its use. Despite the fears felt by many over possible leakages of confidential information by worker representatives,* the proposal is unlikely to recommend that the legal limits on the right of employee representatives to disclose information to their constituents should either differ from the existing position regarding shareholder representatives or vary among industries. But the minority report will likely favor more stringent legal limits governing disclosure of information by employee representatives in industries including the financial sector.

Minimum and maximum sizes for boards may be recommended. Some tidying up of existing legislation will be needed particularly where statutes (as in Life Assurance, for example) prohibit employee membership on the board. Likely to prove most troublesome from a technical angle is exactly how the need to devise procedures that enable all interest groups to effectively participate in the election of worker representatives can be translated into law. This problem will be particularly acute in situations where a British company operates abroad (and thus has an overseas workforce), where the company has several plants, and where holding companies exist that operate through subsidiary companies.

In commenting on these matters, it is most important to stress that none of this, if implemented, would dislodge collective bargaining from the center of the British industrial relations stage. The changes, by allowing workers, should they wish, to elect worker representatives to the board, would serve to augment existing collective bargaining arrangements. Indeed it is quite likely that the committee will recommend that collective bargaining be extended (100 percent trade union membership?) partly in order to back up the scheme for worker representatives on the board. The adoption of a $2X + Y$ formula apparently suggests that the TUC will have lost its battle for "equality parity" representation. Yet this is not at all clear and depending upon the nature of the third, smaller slice—which might well vary considerably in different situations—and its susceptibility to influence from worker representatives, the worker faction, if they operate in unison, might well emerge as the more powerful of the two basic groupings on the board. It appears that there is some merit in the observation that it is a strange form of industrial democracy that disfranchises a section of the potential electorate. Yet existing practice in Britain (though not on a legal

---

*These fears are particularly strongly felt by firms in the financial sector. See Stock Exchange (1976, pp. 7–8) and City Company Law Committee (1976). Such fears are also of a long-standing nature. For example, Marhall (1919, p. 855) observed: "A business which has special methods of production, or special knowledge as to favourable markets, may fear that working men directors will be drawn on, without evil purpose, to communicate to comrades information, apparently unimportant, but yet likely to help any rival business that it may reach by indirect routes. And if the working man director is reticent, his comrades may suspect him of want of loyalty to the collective interests of his class."

bargaining-unit basis as in the United States) is that unions via collective bargaining generally determine the terms and conditions of employment for all
workers in a particular skill level. To exclude nonunion members from such
coverage would probably be viewed by employers as highly disruptive. It seems
that a preferable remedy to this problem is for employees to join recognized
unions—and for employers to encourage this rather than to encourage the establishment of an alternative and competing channel to a union channel of representation. There are several additional reasons for this viewpoint. First, the
continuing growth of union membership bears witness to the continuing relevance that the majority of the workforce see in unions as the vehicle for representing their workplace interests.* Union penetration in large private companies
is particularly high. The argument that most union members are disinterested in
union processes is countered by the observation that this is hardly equivalent to
antipathy toward the consequences of such processes (Eccles 1977b). It seems
likely that if new workplace structures were introduced, the workplace industrial
relations problems would be compounded by the divisiveness this would cause
among the workforce. Lastly, in the British system of strong workplace organization the introduction of new institutions would lead only to their decay unless
union support were forthcoming; the history of traditional joint consultation
schemes lends support to this belief.

At the risk of oversimplification, if the probable substance of the report is
ever introduced via enabling legislation, the major implications of the legislation
as they affect major parties can be examined in terms of three categories of
firms: large companies that are highly unionized and where workers favor the
introduction of worker representatives on the board; large companies that are
highly unionized and where workers reject the introduction of worker representatives on the board; and large companies that are not highly unionized and
where workers are unlikely to opt for the new scheme. The number of companies likely to fall within each of these groups is difficult to estimate, with
uncertainties surrounding the number of large companies, the extent of average
unionization within these, and worker attitudes concerning worker representatives on the board. Estimates range up to 750 British companies with more than
2,000 employees, though many of these are holding and subsidiary companies so
that there may be more than 1,500 separate companies to which the recommendations may be applicable. Most speculate that, in about one-quarter of
these, fewer than half of the workforce is unionized, though such estimates are
little better than guesses because of the unavailability of data on union density
on a company basis. While many major unions have favored the idea of worker
directors in their evidence presented to the committee (though there are notable

---

*This has principally taken place among sections of the British labor force tradition-
ally considered to be areas of low union density, which also tend to be benefiting most by
structural change in industry (see Price and Bain 1976).

exceptions, particularly the Amalgamated Union of Engineering Workers [AEW] and the Electrical, Electronic, and Telecommunication Union [EETU], and perhaps the General Municipal Workers Union [GMWU]), this does not mean that the workforce in which these unions have membership will think and vote similarly,* and even if they did the multiunion nature of most large employers generates additional uncertainty. Consequently, it is quite feasible that the majority of affected companies might belong to the second category and that no radical change would be forthcoming following the passage of the legislation. Nevertheless it is the implications that any such legislation might hold for companies in the first category that are most novel and of most interest and it is to them that the bulk of attention is directed.

In these cases there are several other matters that need clarifying if a system involving worker representatives on the board is to be effective. Batstone and Davies (1976, pp. 18, 62), drawing in part from the experience with worker directors at the BSC, show that in order for worker representatives to be effective, they must be able to participate in policy formation before matters come to the board. Furthermore, representatives must be able to report back to their constituents. This, in turn, requires the existence of some companywide machinery that could serve this purpose. A dual function could be served by such machinery if the introduction of worker representatives were to be taken as the signal to devise plans to integrate this with either new or strengthened machinery for participation at other levels in the company's organization. In many of these cases a multilevel approach is vital for success, with worker representatives at the top of the organizational pyramid likely to prove ineffective without lower-level supportive machinery.

It is from these perspectives that the postwar growth in workplace organization—in particular the growth of joint shop-steward committees and combine committees—assume great significance and that their growth in general receives an added stimulus. Such plant- and/or company-based institutions will be the natural organizations to satisfy these corollary requirements attending the introduction of worker representatives on the board.† They would also probably have

---

*Most opinion on this suggests that shop-floor workers in general are either apathetic or antipathetic toward schemes for worker directors and that they would most prefer increases in control at the shop-floor level. Surveys tend to support these beliefs (see Ramsay 1976). Much less information is available on the general attitude of shop-stewards' committees and combine committees toward the introduction of worker directors, even on a basis of equality parity. Available evidence does, however, suggest the existence of a deep cleavage of opinion, with the Lucas Aerospace Combine Shop Stewards Committee opposing the introduction of worker directors (see *IRRR* no. 124, March 1976), while the Vickers Northeast Shop Stewards Combine Committee favors the idea (Vickers Northeast Combine Committee 1975).

†Depending on the specifics of Bullock's recommendations (and this translation into law), in some cases there may have to be changes in the nature of these and related

a key part to play in devising schemes governing the way in which it was ensured that all relevant interest groups would be represented, and act as a clearing house for the list of union nominees for positions as worker representatives and positions on other participation machinery. Thus the growth in power of the shop floor and their representatives (and further reductions in the relative power of full-time officials, particularly those at branch level) would be aided by recommendations of this sort. The formal recognition given to, and strengthening of, these shop-floor representative bodies by these developments would soon lead to a supplementary kind of union organization, which would be company (and in some cases industry) based and in addition to existing unions such as those of a craft or general nature. Though in the short term, existing forms of collective bargaining would be strengthened by the introduction of worker representatives, soon the character of these unions would probably have to change in response to these company-based developments, though the suggestion by one authority (Eccles 1977b, p. 13) of the possible breakup or disappearance of general unions is unconvincing. It is also interesting to speculate on the probable loci of power in these hypothetical company-based unions. With the continuing change in the structure of the labor force in favor of white-collar occupational groups, it is quite probable that in many of these companies the representative machinery that would emerge would reflect white-collar dominance. Conceivably this could help accelerate the qualitative changes afoot in the character of the whole organized labor movement in Britain. Yet the drive for general unionization that will probably accompany these changes could still lead to an overall increase in the level of absolute power enjoyed by existing unions, though the implications for union power of their being required to accept responsibility for decisions they will have helped to make on what may be less than an equality-parity basis are uncertain and variable. On many of these counts it is clear that much can be gained by examining the way in which the problems of devising and implementing representative machinery and responses to the implications of those developments have been handled in worker cooperatives, particularly the newer and larger union-based cooperatives.

Major implications follow from the need to make resources available so that worker representatives will have sufficient and appropriate training, information, and other backup services and be in a position to adequately discharge their responsibilities. Currently available facilities are woefully inadequate. For the experiment to succeed, experience with previous schemes such as worker directors at the BSC suggests that basic control in these areas, as well as control over the broader-based educational effort that will aim at explaining the new

---

organizations (such as delegate committees) in order to comply with the recommendations.

system to the whole workforce, must remain in union hands. Financing for these programs would probably, in the main, have to come from union sources, though government and perhaps even company support could assist in channeling funds to an independent body, such as the Resource Center established at Harland and Wolff.

Implications for management may not be as forbidding as many suggest. If decisions are seen to be codetermined at the board level, management's task in executing these policies might be easier since it will be based on authority that is recognized in many workers'eyes as more legitimate than formerly. Most studies of genuinely democratized companies find that managers' freedom to manage is not adversely affected and may even be improved. A body of economic theory (see Vanek, 1970) and some experience with workers' cooperatives suggests that in these cooperative situations, diverse economic advantages, particularly concerning labor use and minor technical innovations, can ensue. But it is much less certain that these economic benefits will occur in an enterprise where partnership prevails and neither capital nor labor controls. Indeed, the raison d'etre of such an enterprise (and all that that implies for efficiency) is not apparent, although simple objective functions customarily assumed in analyzing nonpartnership firms (such as profit maximization for capitalist firms, income per worker maximization for self-managed firms, and sales or growth maximization, subject to a profit constaint for managerial capitalist firms) seem inappropriate. Furthermore, the realization of any gains may depend in part (see Eccles 1977b, pp. 15–18) on the clear separation of the functions of policy making and policy execution and on the development of management skills and styles appropriate to the special needs of democratized enterprises. So far as the government is concerned, apart from the possible direct budgetary implications connected with education, there will be a need to either expand the resources of an existing agency (ACAS) or to create a new agency. To recap, its functions would include arbitration in disputes over the wisdom of holding triggering elections, overseeing such elections, assisting when necessary in the determination of specific participation agreements, keeping a register of agreements, and possibly acting as a training and resource center.

Many of the unions in the second category of companies have indicated that, instead of the introduction of worker representatives at board level, they prefer an approach that gives mandatory backing to the right to negotiate on major issues, with such rights being confined to existing collective bargaining machinery. It is extremely unlikely that the committee or new legislation would provide support for this position, not only because of the terms of reference of the committee, but also because the granting of such powers without the concomitant acceptance of direct responsibility for such decisions is likely to be viewed with great distaste. But whether or not an enabling law governing the introduction of worker directors is introduced, there is nothing to prevent unions, especially those with strong decentralized organizations, from encouraging these bodies to use their economic muscle to bargain collectively over strategic decisions at the company level, albeit within a voluntary framework. It is these situations, where roughly equal power between capital and labor, and yet unequal responsibility might emerge, that management might view as most forbidding and where conflict might be most acute.

In remaining companies where unions are not strong, unions will clearly try to step up their recruiting campaigns. In the face of such prospects employers, fearing the day when unions might trigger the procedure leading to the introduction of legally enforceable schemes for worker representatives on the board or simply the growth of collective bargaining, might promote or revamp their own multilevel participation schemes, some instances of which have already been discussed previously.

It must be reiterated that the possibility of radical changes introduced by the probable substance of the Bullock *Report* is highly unlikely and that any changes will only take place after some years. If the history of the Donovan *Report* is any guide, the recommendations of the Bullock *Report* will not necessarily constitute the framework of a government bill. Moreover, the tenuous position of the present government and its heavy legislative program will not help expedite matters. The likely inclusion of a minority report in the Bullock *Report* will reflect the continuing division of opinion on the matter in the country, a division reflected in the voluminous evidence submitted to Bullock and also noticeable, though to a markedly lesser extent, within labor ranks. Further disagreement and delay may occur if the government attempts to deal with nationalized industries in a way similar to that proposed in Bullock's recommendations. All things considered, it would seem that the earliest time legislation could be introduced is toward the end of 1977 and that this could not be enacted until the following year, so that with the length of time for preparation and negotiation (provisions for which would be included in a bill) the earliest time by which worker representatives would begin to take their places on the company board on the basis of the Bullock formula (and then only if most workers so favor) would be about 1979. Of course, during the course of this protracted debate, it is quite likely that the positions currently held by major parties might change, as has already happened in several cases.

Current Developments—The Public Sector

The history of what today constitutes the public sector is replete with plans designed to provide for workers' participation in decision making, often for workers' participation in strategic decision making. Some of the more famous schemes are reported in Coates and Topham (1968, sec. 3). In practice, the establishment of nationalized industries, as was described in the previous section, has not resulted in the realization of many of these aspirations.

Collective bargaining has continued to be the major vehicle for representation of worker interests, with provision for direct participation being limited to joint consultation. As as been indicated, though, the 1960s and 1970s have seen concrete signs of a new approach, with important experiments including the one at Fairfields and worker directors at the BSC.

The pace of change in the public sector seems to have been accelerating, with a particularly important scheme announced at Harland and Wolff, a state-owned Belfast shipbuilding firm, employing about 10,000, where there is to be a multilevel (four-tier) participation structure with provision for direct worker participation in strategic decision making (see *IRRR*, no. 135, September 1976; *IRRR*, no. 102, April 1975; Compen 1976). Seats on the board of directors will be allocated on a 3X formula, with five trade union representatives holding seats along with equal numbers of government appointees and managers from Harland and Wolff. The chairman will also be a government appointee. The democratic machinery at each of the three remaining levels will be characterized by parity representation between management representatives and union representatives. A Joint Implementation Council will be charged with implementing general policy decisions determined by the board, while departmental councils will handle issues applying to particular departments and productivity committees will be concerned with shop-floor matters. Binding the whole structure together will be a Chairmen and Secretaries Committee, which will consist of union representatives from all elements of the participation system. Another distinctive and novel feature of the scheme is the establishment of a union Resource Center, a concept develped by Compen, a local consultancy group.

Compen (1976, pp. 3–18) sees the role of the Resource Center as twofold: "a provider of new skills and a source of interpreted data which gives confidence to the workers' side [and] an objective resource for all trade unionists within an organization which, while having clear loyalty to the trade union movement on a whole, has not involvement in union sectional interests." Thus the center will try to provide those informational and educational (via training courses) resources that are believed to be necessary for union representatives to effectively carry out their functions. The center will be independent of management, staffed by people paid for by Harland and Wolff, and at least during the early days of the scheme Compen will be available to give general advice to the unions through the Resource Center. Finally, a selection procedure for the worker directors has been developed; it has four main aspects. To be eligible to vote, workers must be members of a union recognized at Harland and Wolff. The form of voting will be via selective alternative voting, a characteristics system in the political sphere in Northern Ireland. However, "the selective alternative voting scheme has been modified to ensure that one member will be elected to represent each of the major interest groups: ancillary workers, staff, steelworkers, and other craftsmen" (*IRRR*, no. 135, September 1976, p. 3). Only workers who have been employed by Harland and Wolff for five years, are union members, and have been nominated by procedures approved by concerned unions are eligible candidates. The first elections are expected at the end of 1976 or in early 1977.

This scheme is a fascinating one and contains much that is of considerable interest to other large multiunion British firms. It provides an important example of how the major problem areas in such schemes can begin to be reasonably resolved. The reality of worker power in Britain suggests that many of the principles enshrined in the solutions adopted are likely to be central to other schemes that might emerge elsewhere. Most important among these are the key role that shop stewards will play in the nominations procedure for candidates for worker representatives on the board; the separation of the machinery for participation from the collective bargaining apparatus; the adoption of a single (trade union) channel of representation; workers' insistence on at least parity representation with other recognized groups; recognition of the central role of a mechanism to coordinate participation at all levels; and the equally important need for augmenting existing facilities that worker representatives will be able to call upon. It is also noteworthy that there seems to have been an effort to involve all parties in the process of determining the preferred participation structure (Compen 1976, Annexes). At the same time there remain several loose ends. The specific functions and objectives of the different pieces in the system have not been determined in any detail and the number of lower-level committees has yet to be decided. It would seem that the questions of machinery for reporting back to constituents also needs elaboration (complete reliance on informal methods?) and the way in which a permanent Resource Center would be controlled also needs amplification; an efficient communications system and an organization that facilitates the free dissemination of knowledge and permits the acquisition of effective skills are probably necessary features of healthy participation systems. It is also clear that in situations where collective bargaining is already well established, the introduction of multi-level participation systems can only take place when the new machinery is seen not to pose a threat. At Harland and Wolff this has been acknowledged, and since those issues where agreement cannot be reached at the Joint Implementation Committee stage are then to be the subject of negotiation via the collective bargaining machinery, if anything, the established system of collective bargaining is enhanced by this arrangement (*IRRR*, no. 135, September 1976, p. 3). Yet while such arrangements are probably required in the short term, it is not at all clear that they could continue to exist for very long. The prediction by Compen (1976, p. 6.35) that the collective bargaining functions would eventually be peacefully absorbed within the new participation structures perhaps contains an element of wishful thinking; the established union officials are unlikely to want to encourage those processes whereby their usefulness withers away. Furthermore, consideration of such possibilities also requires that thought be given to the logically prior question of what the objectives of an enterprise with parity worker representation should be. If interest in improving (perhaps maximizing?) earnings per worker enter explicitly into the objective (perhaps displacing, perhaps in addition to considerations of a fair return on capital), then control over the processes whereby income differentials are determined and all income remaining after costs is distributed, should be proper functions for the participation machinery.

Of potentially wider significance than this scheme is the consideration currently being given to the general extension of worker participation in the nationalized industries, the civil service, local government, and other "fringe area" activities where there is substantial government involvement. In this connection it is understood that a series of private inquiries are being conducted and that, parallel to the Bullock report, a report will be published containing recommentations on which legislation will be based. While the proceedings of these inquiries remain as yet unpublished, concerned unions have been actively working to determine their own positions and, where appropriate, in multiunion situations attempting to develop common positions. Such preliminary discussions make it abundantly clear that disagreement within unions (for example, the National and Local Government Officers Association [NALGO] and between unions (for example, mining, British Airways) continues to run deep. In many cases resolution of these differences involves the use of newly established machinery or the setting up of machinery in which shop stewards play an important role. Thus, in establishing a trade union council at British Airways in order to work out a common position on industrial democracy, the majority of places on this body are for rank-and-file workers. Other common elements, though mainly for the nationalized industries and concerning private sector industrial workers, and industrial workers in the civil service and local government, also seem to be emerging. Thus, the probable way in which disagreement among mining unions over the method of representation on the proposed pit committees will be resolved is by adopting a method that ensures representation of all interest groups and not only the National Union of Mineworkers (NUM). All union proposals will likely insist on the separation of the collective bargaining machinery from the participation structure, require single (union) channels of representation and as a corollary press for 100 percent trade union representation. In highly centralized bargaining situations the opportunity for introducing a measure of decentralization will not likely be missed (see TGWU proposals concerning industrial civil service workers, in *IRRR*, no. 135, September 1976). The need for training and support facilities is also widely recognized, though schemes differ over who would control (and how) such arrangements and how they would be financed. The publication of the Bullock report will undoubtedly give additional momentum to the debate in the public sector and it is quite conceivable that the Bullock recommendations could be adopted by nationalized industries.

Unions recognize that special problems are created by trying to introduce any form of worker participation in management into local government and the civil service because of the political roles of ministers and local government councillors. It is not yet clear what unions' positions will be on this matter, particularly insofar as worker representation on the board is concerned. Already, however, some concrete changes have been introduced, with the Greater London Council, the largest local authority in Britain, apparently having taken the lead over other local authorities in rescinding the rules that traditionally have disbarred local government employees from being elected to local authority committees; and it is probable that unions like NALGO will press for the direct election of worker representatives to such committees.

CONCLUSIONS AND PROSPECTS

Important forms of the British experience of workers' participation in management have been reviewed and separately evaluated in this chapter. It is clear that drawing broad generalizations from that experience is a hazardous exercise: at best, inferences must be tentative since they rest on largely fragmentary and most qualitative information collected for what often turn out to be organizations that differ substantially in character. There is an obvious need for careful interdisciplinary and preferably longitudinal case studies to be undertaken by impartial investigators, with potentially much to be gained from the study of long-neglected and little-publicized participatory schemes.* The available evidence, however, does permit some well-established and influential elements of previous doctrine to be overturned. The views of the Webbs (1914) and B. Jones (1894) on the inability of PCs to survive with formal structures that permit substantial workers' participation in management are clearly refuted. Equally, the pessimistic views of other authorities on the limited potential for the scope and extent of the PC sector (Clegg 1960, p. 7; Blumberg 1968, p. 3) are based on overly hasty generalizations that might be overturned as knowledge of the functioning of these institutions improves. That body of economic theory that argues persuasively for the ability of a large self-managed sector in a capitalist

---

*Much literature has been published by consultants and individuals personally concerned with ventures, and relatively few studies have been undertaken by academics. Few of the latter have been interdisciplinary, though Flanders, Pomeranz, and Woodward (1968), and Brannen et al. (1976) are important exceptions; but even they tend to pay relatively little attention to economic aspects. In view of the model implications of the new worker cooperatives, it would seem that careful study of those experiments, and perhaps the little-examined French, Italian, and Spanish counterparts, would likely produce substantial dividends.

economy to be self-sustaining (see Vanek 1975) receives some support from the obvious economic success of ICOM firms like Scott Bader and from the preliminary evidence on the performance of long-established PCs compared with capitalist firms. The contention that employees are apathetic toward participation in general and participation by them or their representatives on strategic issues in particular is often based on survey techniques with obvious defects, without adequate consideration given to the role that the socialization process plays in explaining such apparently negative attitudes.* Judgments about worker attitudes toward such schemes (and similarly, assessments of their propensity to participate) can be reasonably made only when workers have personally experienced a multilevel participation scheme over an extended period. At the same time much of the current proselytizing literature on workers' participation in management tends to ignore the fact that the economic landscape is dotted with instances of failed ventures of this sort. It is clear that some of the more optimistic notions prevalent in the literature have been too readily stated. For example, little British data exist to support Pateman's claim that workplace participation encourages the general development of political efficacy beyond the workplace,† and Blumberg's contention that job satisfaction depends upon the amount of workers' decision-making power (1968, p. 123) ignores other studies that contain no such conclusions. The strictures of many, including Walker (1974), Jay (1976), and Dachler and Wilpert (1976), regarding the need for better theory and more careful empirical work are well taken. But this process should assist and not obscure efforts to establish what the necessary elements for effective and sustained worker participation in decision making are and what forms such participation should assume in different cultures and at different times, as Bernstein (1976), Markovic (in Horvat, Markovic, and Supek 1976, pp. 344-501) and Vanek (1975, pp. 33-36) attempt to do.

Not only is there need for a comprehensive and coherent approach to research in general in this area, but in Britain all parties interested in participation need to consider the question of participation coherently. Radice and Lewis (1976, p. 3) show how different forms of participation are currently considered to be the responsibility of different government agencies. The Department of Industry provides assistance to the new worker cooperatives under the 1972 Industry Act, the Department of Employment has responsibility for encouraging programs of job enrichment, while the Department of Trade will be concerned with systems that include worker representatives on the board. Clearly this

---

*See Brannen et al. (1976, chap. 3) on some of the dangers of vocabularies of participation.

†There is apparently heavy reliance on the Rowen Glasgow experiment, which, in view of its disintegration, is not too reliable.

facilitates fragmentary and uncoordinated thinking about participation in Britain and inhibits the development of overall sensible strategies for extending workers' participation. An integral part of assuming this comprehensive perspective would be the development of an all-inclusive data bank on the number and characteristics of participatory forms in Britain. This would permit the nature, scope, and extent of such schemes to be monitored, and provide a reliable bedrock of data to aid additional investigation.

In considering the likely nature, scope, and extent of workers' participation in management during the next few years, it is worthwhile to briefly return to some past studies in order to try to identify major socioeconomic factors affecting past patterns of and interest in participation. Considerations of this question—including Brannen et al. (1976, Postscript); Clarke, Fatchett, and Roberts (1972, chap. 2); and Poole (1975)—are primarily from a sociological perspective. Usually waves of participation are distinguished. There is, however, disagreement over both the dating of the cycles and what constitutes their principal explanatory factors. The latter include workers' latent power, values held by major social actors, economic factors (particularly the industrial structure and the level of unemployment), government action, technological factors (which include firm size), education, and extent of unionization. With the exception of Poole's treatment, no formal models appear to have been constructed to examine this question. Though all treatments recognize the enormous complexity of the question and essentially identify sets of interdependent and interacting relationships, judgment on their comparative merits is likely to persist long after conceptual developments allow for formal and full specification of these relationships. Not only will definitional problems continue to bedevil, but even then, measures of many carefully defined variables will continue to prove troublesome if not impossible to find and questionable proxies will sometimes be used. For example, Poole's surrogate for his key latent power variable is based on manifestations of power that are hardly equivalent. Even if satisfactory measures can be defined, reliable data may not be available. For example, should an acceptable and operational way of measuring workers' participation in management become available, it is trite to remark that no general historical series would exist.* Furthermore, understanding is often complicated by failing to clearly distinguish between times of unusual interest in participation and times when there apparently was an unusual amount of action concerning participation. Thus the revolutionary fervor of the period 1910-21, a period which is sometimes distinguished as marking the crest of a wave of participation, does not appear to have been accompanied by an unusual degree of generalized

---

*For some of the difficulties in compiling a time series on one participatory form, the long-established PC, see D.C. Jones (1975b).

activity on the participation front. Indeed it appears that except for shop-steward committees and perhaps for guilds too, there was more activity concerning participation both immediately preceding and following the 1910–21 period. Thus the period 1890–1910 witnessed a great upsurge in the number of PCs being formed, while 1910–21 was characterized by stability (D.C. Jones 1975b) and the mid- and late 1920s saw the emergence of joint consultative machinery on a wide scale. Perhaps a more manageable way of approaching the general question of the explanation of particular patterns of participation is to try to explain why the principal forms of each major type of participation broadly corresponds to different historical periods. Concerning worker cooperatives, for example, the reasons behind the changes in the character of typical worker cooperatives in the postwar era (and particularly the 1960s and 1970s) compared with their prewar predecessors is deserving of more careful inquiry. But it is clear that the description, but particularly the explanation, of past patterns and interest in participation will continue to be controversial questions.

Similar, though perhaps not so acute, problems apply when trying to predict the future scope and extent of workers' participation in management in Britain. While it is clear that there is considerable real potential for the extension of workers' participation in management in the near future, it is equally apparent that no uniform pattern will emerge, but rather a patchwork quilt, and change is likely to continue on a gradual basis. Diverse factors can be adduced to suggest that the coming years will see gradual growth in the number of such schemes and expansion in their average scope, perhaps to frequently include participation in strategic issues. It is generally recognized that the pace of institutional change in general in Britain has lagged behind the needs and demands of present times. Most relevant to the general area of participation has been the growth in the power of organized labor and its increasing readiness to exercise that power to support bargaining demands. These changes have occurred in part because, compared to the pre-Second World War period, the economy has become increasingly technologically integrated with much higher capital-labor ratios, and there are political commitments to sustain a lower rate of unemployment and provide for more generous levels of welfare benefits, all of which have served to reduce the insecurity and increase the bargaining power of many groups of employees. Other pressures for change are based on intergenerational attitude changes that are related to the emergence of an increasingly skilled labor force with a higher level of education, which has become more and more dissatisfied with the general quality of working life. The growth of bigger factories, vast impersonalized bureaucratic organizations, and work processes characterized by simple repetitive tasks needing deskilled workers have generated feelings of anomie and frustration among some segments of the work force and led to the proletarianization of other important groups. Worker readiness to express demands that include a call for more democratization at work have been aided and nurtured by influential consciousness-raising bodies, particularly the Institute for

Workers' Control, and by articulate union leaders who have propounded alternative ideologies with provision for a substantial measure of devolved industrial authority. Undoubtedly the momentum for change has also been greatly assisted by the continued growth in strength of workplace bargaining and attendant institutions. While accurate description of important facets of this process is impossible because of the absence of systematically collected data, most authorities agree that the number of shop stewards has continued to grow.* Accompanying these institutional developments there appears to have been a growing tendency for work groups to become increasingly aware of their latent power and for them to exercise this power in militant ways. Particularly important manifestations of direct shop-floor action are work-ins (beginning with Upper Clyde Side) and sit-ins, which have sometimes evolved into new worker cooperatives.†

Attitudinal change has not been confined to labor. British management is, on average, much less autocratic and more sympathetic to some participatory forms than previously. Economic and technological forces have probably helped to produce these changes: the superior efficiency of organization structures grounded on hierarchical relationships is no longer automatically accepted and often key management figures have lost their monopoly over basic knowledge and information that are essential for decision taking. The wider domestic and international climate is also less and less hostile toward changes in conventional industrial authority structures. The well-known fifth directive of the EEC and the proposed statute for European companies are of obvious import, as is the current widespread experimentation with diverse participatory forms throughout Europe, particularly in Yugoslavia. Important strides, both theoretical and empirical, have been taken in understanding the whole subject area and useful lessons can be drawn to assist the survival and success of existing participation forms and the formation of new viable types.

But not all socioeconomic forces point to increasing workers' participation in management. There is still considerable ideological resistance in some management circles to change, and it is worth repeating that thus far management-initiated participation schemes in Britain have predominantly been concerned with job enrichment and the like and have not involved any radical devolution of authority. It has also been forcefully argued by Brannen et al. (1976, Postscript)

---

*For a recent estimate of the number of shop stewards see Wilders and Parker (1975). Even less information is available on the numbers, industrial distribution, and so on, of joint shop-steward committees (in multiplant companies), institutions which appear to be increasingly prevalent.

†Again, reliable information on some of these phenomena is seldom available. Thus, with regard to sit-ins, Mills (1976) in his review of what appears to be the first overall evaluation by Keyer and Hemingway (1976), points out several sit-ins omitted from that study.

that if the British economic picture substantially improved, this would remove or at least drastically ameliorate many of the pressures that have led to demands for change. Yet on balance it seems as though the tide in Britain is flowing in the direction of increasing workers' participation in management. All political parties are intent on devising ways and means of introducing worker power into the control system so that it will play a more constructive and less reactive part than in the current conflict-resolving system. To this end it is clear that the substance of any proposed legislation is of vital significance to the forms that participation will increasingly tend to assume, and that the debate that will be engendered by forthcoming proposals will ensure that the subject will continue to burn brightly, at least during the rest of the 1970s.

REFERENCES

Alexander, K.J.W., and C.L. Jenkins, 1970. *Fairfields: A Study of Industrial Change*. London: Penguin.

Balfour, C., ed. 1973. *Participation in Industry*. London: Croom Helm.

Batstone, E., and P.L. Davies. 1976. *Industrial Democracy, European Experience* (Two Research Reports). London: HMSO.

Batstone, E., I. Boraston, and S. Frenkel. 1977. *Shop Stewards in Action: The Organisation of Workplace Conflict and Accommodation*. Oxford: Blackwell.

Bernstein, P. 1976. "Necessary Elements for Effective Worker Participation in Decision Making," *Journal of Economic Issues* 10, no. 2.

Best, R.D. 1964. "Management by Free Expression." *Industrial Newsletter*, no. 33, Second Quarter.

Best and Lloyd 1966. "Memorandum of Special Board Meetings ' Birmingham: Best and Lloyd.

Blum, F.H. 1968. *Work and Community*. London: Routledge & Kegan Paul.

Blumberg, P. 1968. *Industrial Democracy: The Sociology of Participation*. London: Constable.

Board of Trade. 1896. *Co-operative Contracts* London: HMSO, C-8233.

Brannen, P., et al. 1976. *The Worker Directors*. London: Hutchison.

Briston, R. 1976. "Scottish Daily News: Accountants View of Why it Went Wrong." *Accountants Weekly*, October 31.

British Broadcasting Corp. 1976. *Analysis: Industrial Democracy*. London: BBC, Radio 4, November 11.

Brown W. 1960. *Exploration in Management*. London: Heinemann.

Cadbury-Schweppes. 1976. *A Joint Working Party's Submission to the Committee of Inquiry on Industrial Democracy*. London: Cadbury-Schweppes.

Carnoy, M., and H.M. Levin. 1976. "Workers Triumph: the Meriden Experiment." *Working Papers*, Winter 1976.

City Company Law Committees. 1976. *Evidence Submitted to the Committee of Inquiry on Industrial Democracy*. London: Bank of England.

Clarke, O., D. Fatchett, and B.C. Roberts. 1972. *Workers' Participation in Management in Britain*. London: Heinemann.

Clegg, H.A. 1960. *A New Approach to Industrial Democracy*. London: Blackwell.

―――. 1976. *Trade Unionism under Collective Bargaining*. Oxford: Blackwell.

Coates, K., ed. 1968. *Can the Workers Run Industry?* London: Sphere Books.

―――, ed. 1976. *The New Worker Co-operatives* Nottingham: Spokesman.

―――, and A. Topham, eds. 1968. *Industrial Democracy in Great Britain*. London: Macgibbon & Kee.

Cole, G.D.H. 1919. *Self-government in Industry*. London: G. Bell & Sons.

Compen (Management Consultants). 1976. *Evidence Submitted to Bullock Committee on Industrial Democracy*. Belfast: Compen, March.

Constable, C.J. 1974. "Some Comparative Financial Ratios Comparing Scott Bader with Other Chemical Companies." Cranfield, Bedfordshire: Cranfield Institute of Technology, mimeographed.

Cooperative Productive Federation, 1897–1960. *Co-operators Yearbook*. Annual published in Leicester or London by Cooperative Productive Federation.

Dachler, H.P., and B. Wilpert. 1976. "On the Theoretical Dimensions and Boundaries of the Concept of Participation Within Organizations: Implications for Research and Practice." Berlin: International Institute of Management, mimeographed.

Daniel, W. W., and N. Mclintosh. *The Right to Manage*. London: Political and Economic Planning.

Derrick, P., and J.F. Phipps. 1969. *Co-ownership, Co-operation and Control*. London: Longmans.

Eccles, T. 1977a. "Sit-Ins, Woorker Co-operatives and Some Implications for Organization." *Personnel Review*.

Eccles, T. 1977b. "Industrial Democracy and Organisation Change." *Personnel Management*.

Edelstein, J.D. 1976. "The Origin, Structure and Problems of Four British Producers Co-operatives." Syracuse, N.Y.: Syracuse University, mimeographed.

Flanders, A., R. Pomeranz, and J. Woodward. 1968. *Experiment in Industrial Democracy*. London: Faber & Faber.

Goodrich, C.L. 1920. *The Frontier of Control*. London: G. Bell & Sons.

Gordon-Brown, I. 1972. *Participation in Industry: An Introductory Guide*. London: Industrial Copartnership Association.

Guest, D., and D. Fatchett. 1974. *Worker Participation: Individual Control and Performance*. London: Institute of Personnel Management.

Hewes, A. 1922. "Guild Socialism: A Two Years' Test." *American Economic Review* 12, no. 2, pp. 209–37.

Hobson, S.G. 1938. *Pilgrim to the Left*. London: E. Arnold.

Horvat, B., M. Markovic, and R. Supek. 1975. *Self-governing Socialism: A Reader*. 2 vols. New York: International Arts and Sciences Press.

Industrial Common Ownership Movement. 1975. *This is ICOM*. London: Bellers.

Industrial Participation Association. 1975. *Computer Management Group Ltd*. London: IPA Case Studies, no. 3.

Industrial Partnership Association. 1976. *Industrial Democracy 1976: The State of Play*, Study Paper no. 4. London: Industrial Partnership Association.

Industrial Relations Review and Report (IRRR). Published twice monthly by Unwin Brothers in London.

Jaques, E. 1951. *The Changing Culture of a Factory*. London: Tavistock.

Jarvie, M. 1968. "An Experiment in Industrial Democracy: The Rowen Engineering Company Ltd." Edinburgh: Edinburgh University, mimeographed.

Jay, P. 1976. "A General Hypothesis of Employment, Inflation and Politics." Sixth Wincott Memorial Lecture, Institute of Economic Affairs, Occasional paper no. 46.

Jones, B. 1894. *Co-operative Production*. Oxford: Oxford University Press.

Jones, D.C. 1974. "The Economics of British Producer Co-operatives." Ph.D. dissertation, Cornell University.

———. 1975a. "Workers' Management in Britain." *Economic Analysis and Workers' Management* 9, no. 3–4.

———. 1975b. "British Producers Co-operative and the Views of the Webbs on Participation and Ability to Survive." *Annals of Public and Collective Economy* 46 (January/March).

————. 1976. "British Orthodox Economic Thought on Associations of Labourers: 1848–1974." *Annals of Public and Co-operative Economy*, 47 (January/March).

————, and D.K. Backus. 1977. "British Producer Co-operatives in the Footwear Industry: An Empirical Examination of the Theory of Financing." *Economic Journal*.

Joslyn, C.S. 1922. "The British Building Guilds: A critical survey of Two Years' Work." *Quarterly Journal of Economics*, November, pp. 75–133.

————. 1923. "A Catastrophe in the British Building Guild." *Quarterly Journal of Economics*, pp. 523–37.

Keyer, W., and J. Hemingway. 1976. *Who's in Charge? Worker Sit-Ins in Britain Today*. Oxford: Metra Consulting Group.

Kirkham, M.J. 1973. "Industrial Procedure Co-operatives in Great Britain: Three Case Studies." M.A. thesis, Sheffield University.

Klein, L. 1976. *New Forms of Work Organisation*. Cambridge: Cambridge University Press.

London Borough of Wandsworth. 1976. *Prosperity or Slump? The Future of Wandsworth's Economy. A Report of the Policy Review Sub-Committee*.

Marshall, A. 1919. *Industry and Trade*. London: Macmillan.

Mathews, F. 1971. "The Building Guilds." In *Essays on Labour History*, vol. 2., ed. A. Briggs and J. Saville. London: Macmillan.

McCarthy, W.E.S. 1966. *The Role of Shop Stewards in British Industrial Relations*. Royal Commission on Trade Unions and Employers' Associations, Research Paper 1. London: HMSO.

Melman, S. 1958. *Decision Making and Productivity*. Oxford: Blackwell.

Mills, A.J. 1976. "Worker Sit-Ins." *Personnel Review* 5, no. 4.

National Federation of Building Trade Operatives. 1922. *Conference between Emergency Committee of the National Federation of Building Trade Operatives and the Representatives of the National Building Guild*. Manchester.

National Institute of Industrial Psychology. 1952. *Joint Consultation in British Industry*. London: Staples Press.

Ostergaard, G. 1957. "Membership Participation in Co-operative Co-Partnerships." In *Co-operators Yearbook for 1957*. Leicester: Leicester Printers.

Pateman, C. 1970. *Participation and Democratic Theory*. Cambridge: Cambridge University Press.

Poole, M. 1975. *Workers' Participation in Industry*. London: Routledge, Kegan & Paul.

Potter, B. 1891. *The Co-operative Movement in Britain*. London. Allen & Unwin.

Pribicevic, B. 1959. *The Shop Stewards Movement and Workers' Control*. Oxford: Blackwell.

Price, R., and G.S. Bain. 1976. "Union Growth Revisited: 1948–74 in Perspective." *British Journal of Industrial Relations* 14, no. 3, November.

Pritchard, R.L., ed. 1976. *Industrial Democracy in Australia*. Australia: C.C.H.

Radice, G., and R. Lewis. 1976. *Workers in the Boardroom*. Fabian Tract 441. London: Fabian Society.

Ramsay, H. 1976. "Participation: The Shop Floor View." *British Journal of Industrial Relations* 14, no. 2.

Rayton, D. 1972. *Shop Floor Democracy in Action: A Personal Account of the Coventry Gang System*. ICOM Pamphlet no. 1. Nottingham: Russell Press.

Renold, C.G. 1950. *Joint Consultation over Thirty Years*. London: Allen & Unwin.

Robertson, D.H. 1923. *The Control of Industry*. New York.

Royal Commission on Trade Unions and Employers Associations, 1965–68. *Report*. London: HMSO, Command 3623.

Sallis, H. 1959. "Joint Consultation in the Electricity Supply Industry, 1949–59." *Public Administration* 37, Summer.

Sawtell, R. 1968. *Sharing Our Industrial Future?* London: The Industrial Society.

Sorge, A. 1976. "The Evolution of Industrial Democracy in the Countries of the European Community." *British Journal of Industrial Relations* 14, no. 3, pp. 274–94.

Stock Exchange. 1976. *Submission of the Stock Exchange to Committee on Industrial Democracy*. London.

Vanek, J. 1970. *The General Theory of Labor-Managed Market Economies*. Ithaca: Cornell University Press.

———. 1971. "The Basic Theory of Financing of Participatory Firms." Working Paper no. 24. Ithaca: Cornell University, Department of Economics.

———, ed. 1975. *Self-Management: Economic Liberation of Man*. Harmondsworth: Penguin.

Vickers Northeast Combine Committee. 1975. "Worker Representation on Vickers' Boards—A Proposal." Newcastle: Tyneside *Free Press*.

Walker, K.F. 1974. "Workers' Participation in Management: Problems, Practice and Prospects." *Bulletin*, no. 12, International Institute for Labor Studies.

Webb, C. 1904. *The Story of a Peaceful Revolution*. Manchester.

Webb, S. and B. 1914. "Co-operative Production & Profit Sharing." *New Statesman*, Special Supplement.

Wilders, M.G., and S.R. Parker. 1975. "Changes in Workplace Industrial Relations 1966–1972." *British Journal of Industrial Relations* 13, no. 1, March.

Wright, R. 1961. "The Gang System in Coventry." *Anarchy*, no. 2, pp. 47–52.

CHAPTER

5

WORKER CONTROL IN FRANCE:
RECENT POLITICAL DEVELOPMENTS

Stephen Bornstein
Keitha S. Fine

During the 1960s self-management and workers' control became central issues in the programs of the major French unions and parties on the left. This ideological innovation must be seen against the background of a decade of unprecedentedly intense industrial conflict, featuring escalating demands by French workers for increased control over their jobs and participation in their unions, the political parties, and their state. The steadily growing militancy of workers throughout Western Europe since the mid-1960s helped to rekindle a search by the French left for theories and programs that would meet the demands of average French men and women for a transformation in the nature of everyday life. In addition, the spectacular events of May 1968 encouraged them to turn to a set of ideas that has traditionally been associated with workers' council movements throughout the continent. Popular response to the unions' platforms pushed first the government and then industrialists to seize upon these workers' participation issues, albeit retooling them to fit the economic and political needs of advanced industrial capitalism for a productive, well-integrated workforce.

There is no single generic term that can encompass either all the forms of workers' control currently debated on the French left or the limited allotment of workers' participation envisaged by government and industrialists. Each political actor has his own terminology corresponding to specific demands at one or another level of workers' struggles, and depending on who makes the demand

This chapter was originally prepared for delivery at the 1976 Annual Meeting of the American Political Science Association, at the Palmer House in Chicago, September 2-5, 1976.

and on whether the political thrust is working class or bourgeois, reformist, or revolutionary.[1]

Within this complicated lexicon, three terms are of particular interest to us: *participation, gestion democratique,* and *autogestion.* * *Participation*, a term used by the center and right, refers to worker or citizen or student involvement at some level of decision making. Involvement in decisions concerning such varied issues as working conditions, pensions and benefits, marketing policies, or profit sharing can all be subsumed under this category, as can de Gaulle's proposals, dating from 1946, for a "worker-management partnership" and the later government schemes that we discuss below. The term *gestion démocratique* refers specifically to a component of the political platforms of the French Communist party (PCF) and of the Communist-dominated *Conféderation général du travail* (CGT), the country's largest trade union.† It signifies both a strategy to topple the capitalist state and a program for the management of the state, society, and industry by the whole people under the leadership of a political party during the transitional period and under fully established socialism. Finally, *autogestion* or self-management, the expression most familiar to the English-speaking world since the celebrated strike at the LIP watch factory in 1973, is a complex term denoting the political platform of France's second largest union, the *Confédération française démocratique du travail* (CFDT) for

---

*Other specific terms include *cogestion*, or "joint management" in enterprises, as in German codetermination schemes or the English Scanlon arrangements. *Contrôle ouvrier*, or "workers' control," refers, in both France and Italy, to the power of workers to exercise (de jure or de facto) a negative control in the form of an effective veto over issues ranging from limited questions such as assembly-line speeds and working conditions to the most general aspects of national economic and social policy making. Another kind of *contrôle ouvrier* is exercised by collective worker-producers assembled in cooperatives based on their collective ownership of the means of production. *Gestion syndical* means, quite literally, "union management," and can refer to union ownership or management of industry in a network of cooperatives—as in the case of the *Histadrut* in Israel—or to the direction by the unions of the entire society, as envisioned in revolutionary syndicalist theory.

†The PCF was officially born in December 1920 out of a split at the Congress of Tours within the old Section française de l'International ouvrière (SFIO), the French section of the Second International. In the aftermath of World War I and the Russian Revolution, a left majority within the SFIO, pressured by Moscow to join the Third International, sought to redress the reformism into which the SFIO had slipped during the period of war socialism by creating a new revolutionary socialist party inspired by the success of the Bolshevik Revolution. The origins of the current CGT date from the same period of revolutionary/reformist conflicts when syndicalists sympathetic to the Bolshevik Revolution separated from the original CGT, founded in 1895, to form the Confédération général du travail unitaire (CGTU), whose ties to the PCF were made public in 1926. Reunification with the, by then, larger but open accommodationist CGT was concluded in 1936. Despite several periods of internal dissension between 1938 and the early post-World War II period, Communist hegemony within the reunified CGT has prevailed.

workers' control of all aspects of social and political life. Recently, it has also been adopted as a long-range objective by the Socialist party (PS).*

First introduced into France in the mid-1960s to describe the social and industrial organization of Yugoslavia and later that of Algeria, *autogestion* is now widely used by large sections of the left to invoke a vision of "another way," a decentralized classless society composed of equal associations of self-governing men and women. *Autogestion* has now become a catchall phrase that can mean almost anything and everything. It is not unusual to find reformist French owners and managers proclaiming their support for *autogestion* when all they really intend to grant is some sort of carefully delimited operational autonomy to experimentally constituted work teams. Even on the left, the term *autogestion* can have many meanings. Daniel Mothé has shown that the term can quite reasonably be applied to various forms of worker autonomy from the level of the relationship of the worker to his tools and materials and forms of labor, through teamwork; to collective management of enterprises or communities; to the level of an entire society managed by the whole people.[2] But only at the last two levels does *autogestion* take on a truly revolutionary character. It is in this global sense that we shall use the term. Specifically, we present *autogestion* as the principal plank of the CFDT and refer to *gestion démocratique* as the position of the PCF and CGT concerning the democratization of capitalism and the administration of a socialist society.

Since it was, however, only after 1968 that the idea of *autogestion* passed into general French political discourse and that decentralized, aggressive new forms of labor action became prevalent, we shall first review the challenge to the preexisting system of industrial relations posed by the events of 1968 before we examine the responses to it offered by the government, and by the two most important industrial unions, the CFDT and the CGT. Then we suggest four lines of analysis that we believe can help to account for the sudden massive popularity

---

*The PS is the product of the transformation of what remained of the old SFIO in the wake of the May-June events of 1968. The transformation involved both internal reorganization and fusion with a number of left clubs, and their merger with the *Convention des institutions republicaines* of François Mitterrand. He was elected first secretary of the PS at the Epinay Congress in June 1971. The CFDT, which claims a current membership of 800,000, is France's second largest union confederation. Its roots go back to the 1880s when the first Catholic workers' unions were formed. In 1919 under the leadership of the federation of Catholic white-collar employees, these various unions merged to form the *Confédération française des travailleur chrétiens* (CFTC), and the movement retained that name until 1964. At that date, efforts by militants finally succeeded in bringing about the movement's "deconfessionalization"; all references to Christianity and to the social teachings of the church were henceforth dropped from the union's name and statutes. A small fraction refused to accept the transformation and reconstituted itself as the CFTC. Since 1964 the CFDT has undergone a significant shift to the left.

of *autogestion* as the predominant expression of the demand for workers' control in France. We then consider the difficulties and possibilities of reorienting workers' struggles around decentralized socialist principles, and assess the relative cogency of the various available strategies on the left that aim at gaining popular control over the centers of economic and political life in contemporary France.

THE MAY-JUNE EVENTS OF 1968

The events of May-June 1968 were a culmination of social conflicts throughout the 1950s and 1960s embodying widespread discontent with the fabric of French life under de Gaulle's form of forced modernization.[3] Both student and labor actions reflected the crisis of the state and its institutions and were reactions against the centralization, bureaucracy, and the rigid structures of authority that permeated French life. But they also contained the possibility of important social change, perhaps best manifested in student and worker attempts to dissolve leader/follower dichotomies, and to replace quantitative demands by qualitative ones. Fired by this spirit, the "nation of shopkeepers" became, however briefly, demonstrators.

Throughout the postwar period, but especially during the 1960s, one model of industrial conflict crystallized at the national level among the government, public and private industry, and the unions. All parties shared a certain consensus about the desirability of steady economic growth based on technological progress and social peace. For its part, the government tried to institutionalize a new ideology around the concept of a "directed economy," secure in the knowledge that a relatively centralized, reformist syndicalism, responsible to the society because it was, on the whole, assured of continual satisfactory contracts, would help obscure the gaps in the system and restrain calls for excessive class conflict.[4] What 1968 revealed was that the weak link in the model lay at the enterprise level, where, prior to 1968, unions had no official recognition, and where all processes and any intermediary institutions had, in effect, been ignored or bypassed by all major participants in the national-level negotiation structure.

The students' strike was triggered by specific issues such as the archaic structure of the French university system, and the technological focus increasingly imposed on their disciplines. However, worker actions during the height of the conflicts were far from merely supportive or imitative of the student movement; they were notable on their own account for at least four reasons of interest to us. First, rank-and-file militancy clearly outran union leadership to become a direct challenge to the structures of postwar unionism. This fact was not mitigated by the early supportive role of the CFDT in some cases, by the election of union members to strike committees, or by the evidence that the trade unions began trying to impose their hegemony on the demonstrations at all levels as quickly as possible.[5] Second, during the height of the conflicts and during the period that has followed, many traditional trade union structures, long forgotten, were revived: strike committees, worker assemblies, citizen support committees, shop committees, all focused on strengthening workers' role at the enterprise level. This "radicalization" through structures has been as important and as lasting as the "radicalization" of the strike methods that tended to occur during the strikes themselves—for example, factory occupations, lock-ins of management personnel, or direct production by the workers. Third, both the explosive wave of strikes in the old anarcho-syndicalist tradition, and the seemingly planned, or at least more coordinated, series of smaller strike waves that have followed since 1968 have rejected the former rules of the game. In so doing, they have not only sought to impose new models of social relations in the factory, but also to institutionalize a renewed tradition of direct action, evidence to many of the growing autonomy of the base. Finally, worker militancy at the base, while pushing the government toward tough antistrike legislation, also, and more importantly, forced certain very real changes on relationships among the government, management, and unions.[6]

The institutionalization of some of these changes seems unavoidable; official recognition locks all parties into place, but especially the weaker ones.* What is of interest is whether, as in the 1960s, this new institutionalization will rechannel labor militancy. Considerable evidence points in that direction: the traditional bread-and-butter demands are less prominent; the level of strikes has remained very high; the actions have retained their explosive, spontaneous character; strikes have been called around such matters as layoffs, a break in the usual pattern; and the workers have attempted to perpetuate the new factory-level structures that emerged in the height of the strike waves. It is possible to argue that a massive reorientation of French labor struggles has taken place. At the very least, the politicization of strikes at all levels, and the inclusion in strikes of the "new working class," as well as various "marginal" groups such as unskilled workers, youth, women, peasant workers, and immigrants has forced the government, management, parties, and the unions into uncustomary defensive postures.

---

*For example, the Grenelle Agreements, signed at the end of May 1968, which "settled" the labor unrest, gave legal recognition to the unions at the enterprise level without the concomitant right of negotiation. As a sop, the purview of the *comités d'entreprise* was expanded to include input regarding the employment of women and youth, work conditions, and the like. In 1970 severe legislation against the right to strike was introduced, notably to limit radio-T.V. walkouts; however, enforcement of it was often lax.

LA PARTICIPATION: GOVERNMENT ATTEMPTS TO
INSTITUTIONALIZE WORKERS' PARTICIPATION

In the years since 1968, alarmed government and management circles have produced a raft of schemes aimed at pacifying industrial relations in the firms and at the national level and at restoring to the bourgeoisie its waning control over the course of French industrial development. Many of the schemes have involved some sort of proposal for the "democratization" of the French economy and the French workplace through the creation of mechanisms to increase the "participation" of workers in the management of production. These reform proposals did not need to be invented but could draw on a long tradition of French thought.

Serious proposals for the reform of the firm via some version of profit sharing were always a central element of social Catholic bourgeois thought. They can be found as early as 1879 when a Society for the Study of Participation was created and numerous socially minded industrialists introduced profit-sharing schemes into their factories.[7] In its other sense, of including workers in the decision-making process of the firm, *participation* was advocated as early as the 1930s by numerous reformers including the Catholic trade union, the *Confédération française des travailleurs chrétiens* (CFTC). It was also included as part of the program of the National Council of the Resistance and, in 1945 and 1946, it was embodied in the creation of a system of works councils, the *comités d'entreprise*. These councils, now obligatory in all companies employing more than 50 persons, were to be composed of representatives of management and of the workers, the latter elected from lists submitted by the unions. They were intended to give workers and their unions access to information concerning the operation of the firm and an effective voice in controlling its day-to-day operations and long-term policy making. Their creation was heralded as one of the most significant reforms of the Liberation period, but it rapidly became clear that the practical import of the legislation was extremely limited. Very few firms bothered to create the committees and even where they did come into being, management generally succeeded in presenting them from becoming anything more than powerless talk shops that added little—beyond some influence over minor social and recreational programs—to effective worker control over the activities of the firm.[8]

Between 1945 and 1968, numerous voices were raised in favor of a renewed attempt to reform the capitalist firm. Some of the advocates of such reform spoke from the center-left;[9] other reformist elements among owners and managers advocated reform of the firms as a means of reducing strikes and short-circuiting obstreperous unions, thereby facilitating economic expansion.[10] De

Gaulle, too, during his years out of power, made a restructuring of the capitalist enterprise an important plank of his platform. Beginning with his famous speech at Bayeux in 1946, he regularly presented a social platform for increased working-class participation in the firm as offering a "third road" between capitalism and communism. And in the early years of the Fifth Republic profit-sharing schemes variously labeled *la participation, l'intéressement,* or *l'association capital-travail* were established with considerable fanfare but significantly less concrete impact. Several attempts were even made by de Gaulle, with yet less success, to increase worker participation at the national level by transforming the Senate into a national economic parliament composed of representatives of unions and management.[11]

Proposals, ordinances, and proclamations notwithstanding, the French economy remained, as of 1968, one of the least democratic of Western capitalist economies. At the national level, the unions played only a token role in the formulation of economic and social policy through minimal representation in such essentially powerless, consultative bodies as the committees of the National Planning Commission and the Economic and Social Council. National "inter-professional" collective bargaining was a rare phenomenon whose absence was much lamented by liberal industrial relations specialists.[12] Inside the firm, the authority of the patron was absolute, untempered either by effective legal restrictions or by any legally sanctioned countervailing union power. Unions had no right to operate within factory walls, and union militants and members were offered no legal protection from arbitrary treatment by owners.[13]

The May strikes led management and government to make a number of important concessions to demands for increased economic democracy and for expanded workers' rights inside the factories. In the heat of the crisis, de Gaulle's old *participation* platform made a brief reappearance. In a nationally televised speech on May 24, he proposed *participation* as the remedy for all the nation's ills: it would, he promised, provide the basis of a genuine "revolution" that would "change the human condition in the midst of modern civilization."[14] The ultimate settlement of the strikes involved much more pedestrian but still quite significant alterations. The *comités d'entreprise* were given broader powers and the right of the unions to organize sections inside the factory was legally established.

Yet neither these gains nor the substantial salary increases granted at the famous Grenelle negotiations proved sufficient to restore tranquility to French industrial relations. Labor militancy in the years after May 1968 remained at an unprecedented level. The intensity of the strike waves, as well as the aggressive tactics and highly politicized character of the slogans used, induced conservative forces to seek new ways to pacify workers and unions in order to reassert control over French industrial development. Jacques Chaban-Delmas, for example, attempted to lure the unions into his "New Society" by expanding the powers of the *comités d'entreprise* in return for the unions' acceptance of long-term contracts (*contrats de progrès*), which linked salaries to productivity and included no-strike clauses. Innovative management circles have turned their attention to schemes imported from Sweden and the United States for job enrichment and the introduction of semiautonomous work teams who are allowed to make some decisions about their work speeds and methods.[15]

The attempts by the government of Valéry Giscard d'Estaing to introduce a "reform of the firm" constitute merely the latest incarnation of this conservative strategy. In June 1974, shortly after his narrow presidential election victory, Giscard set into motion another attempt to shore up, and improve the image of, the firm. Using language reminiscent of the Gaullist participation schemes, the new president created a special commission, headed by industrialist and centrist deputy Pierre Sudreau, to study the reform of the firm.[16] In the press conference called to announce the creation of the commission, Giscard expressed confidence that its proposals would venture "very far." Prime Minister Chirac boldly predicted that the commission's proposals would "bring democracy to the world of labor."[17] Such claims did little to mitigate the skepticism of the unions and parties of the left concerning the real intentions of the government. They saw as slim the likelihood of significant change under a president supported by a conservative majority and committed to a policy of "change without risk." The commission report, made public in January 1975, proved their skepticism justified.[18]

The commission report contained about 100 distinct proposals. Of these, some, such as proposals for aid to ailing firms and suggestions for increasing the power of individual shareholders, were of little direct relevance to workers. Others merely reiterated old themes such as establishing autonomous teams of workers or providing on-the-job training. Most of the proposals to give the *comités d'entreprise* greater access to bookkeeping information and planning goals of the firms were merely restatements of workers' rights established long ago by law or collective agreements, but which had never been enforced. However, in one area, the commission did recommend significant change: it suggested altering corporate structure in order to separate clearly the functions of *gestion* (management) from those of *surveillance* (supervision of the activities of management); workers in firms employing more than 1,000 or perhaps 2,000 people would then be given one-third representation on the body responsible for *surveillance* (hence the term *cosurveillance*). Although fairly audacious in the French context, this proposal fell far short of the systems already in operation in several other Western countries, such as the codetermination system in West Germany.

The major unions were, however, unimpressed with the Sudreau Commission's proposals. From the unions' point of view, *cosurveillance*, even if it were transformed from a proposal for widespread public debate on the issue to actual legislation, would really change very little in the power structure of the capitalist firm. The authority of the *chef d'entreprise* would remain unaltered without the unions' gaining any control over his designation. Restriction of *cosurveillance* to companies employing 1,000 or 2,000 people would leave the bulk of the French productive system unaffected. And the one-third representation would leave the workers in a minority even if they voted as a bloc. In sum, the unions felt that the commission had devoted far too much attention to an exotic scheme for corporate restructuring while completely ignoring some of the most glaring injustices about which unions had long complained. These included insufficient legal protection of workers and unionists from arbitrary discrimination, inadequate occupational training programs, legal restrictions on the right to strike, and inadequate administration of health and safety regulations. The extremely limited reformism of the Sudreau report seemed to justify almost completely the CGT's disdainful comment that "the supposed reform of the firms is simply a contemptible means of distracting attention from the very real austerity being imposed on the workers."[19]

Disappointing as it was, the Sudreau report now seems positively radical in comparison with the government declaration based on it and presented to parliament in mid-May 1976. The key proposal for *cosurveillance* has been weakened to the vanishing point. Whereas the commission wanted *cosurveillance* to be mandatory for all firms of 1,000 or perhaps 2,000 employees, the government declaration makes the reforms optional, to be applied at the discretion of management "where it will be opportune." Furthermore, it deliberately excludes all "small and medium-sized firms" not only from this part of the reform but from all the proposed changes.[20] Where the Sudreau Commission recommended that its proposals be enacted through legislation, the government now intended to avoid legislation (which is felt to be out of place in Giscard's "advanced liberal society") and to rely instead on the free contractual activity of the "social partners" who will be "urged" and "incited" to negotiate by governmental "proposals" and "recommendations."

The real conservatism of Giscardian politics and the function assigned to participation schemes in such a conservative project were strikingly illustrated in the declarations of the various government spokesmen at the parliamentary session. The government revealed, first of all, a clear awareness of the social composition of its electoral base. Prime Minister Chirac and Labor Minister Durafour concentrated, in their speeches, not on demonstrating how far the proposed reforms went, but rather on assering how cautiously the government had proceeded. Indeed, the whole section of measures to favor the development of small business was grafted onto the Sudreau proposals. Secondly, whereas in June 1974 Giscard had promised a "revolution" aimed at "restoring the value of manual labor," in May of 1976 Giscard's ministers spoke in very different tones, admitting much more openly that the primary role they hoped a reformed firm would play was a stabilizing one. Sudreau spoke of the reform as an "effort to transcend the bipolarization and the atmosphere of internal cold war" of contemporary industrial life. In presenting the government's plans, Chirac insisted that "economic efficiency comes, and will come increasingly, from social equilibrium."[21] Third, the parliamentary discussions made it clear that the government had no intention of tampering with any of the essentials of economic liberalism or with any of the structures—specifically the authority system—of the capitalist firm. Chirac assured the deputies that the government "has no intention of overthrowing social institutions," for the firm can only function properly if the "authority that directs it is full and entire." Finally, the government's conservatism was revealed in its attitude toward the unions. The Sudreau report recommended a series of changes aimed explicitly at "increasing the power of the unions." However unsatisfactory these were, the Chirac declaration reveals a very different approach. The workers' representatives to the supervisory boards are to be selected by methods to be determined in each firm by the general assembly of shareholders, bodies hardly likely to be sympathetic to unions. Any new rights of self-expression in the factory are to be granted not to the union sections, but only to the individual worker. In light of the declared intention of many leading Gaullists and Giscardians to "break the union monopoly" of workers' representation, and with organized business's insistence that any granting of new powers to the *comités d'entreprise* must be contingent on ending this "monopoly," it is not an exaggeration to see the government's project as explicitly antiunionist. It remains another attempt, in the words of one analyst, to "atomize the employees, to reduce them to a dustcloud of individuals."[22]

The latest government proposal for democratization of the workplace amounts, as we have seen, to little more than a public relations device. "The absurdity of the formula 'change without risk' could not be more clearly illustrated; by taking no risks, one introduces no change."[23] Even more clearly than in previous Gaullist endeavors, the Giscard government has illustrated the extent to which participation schemes function, for conservative governments, as means of pacifying workers, separating them from their unions, and integrating them into a rationalized neocapitalist institutional framework.

AUTOGESTION: THE CFDT AND THE PRINCIPLE OF SELF-MANAGEMENT

We have seen that the near revolution of May 1968 induced the French bourgeoisie to propose reforms purporting to democratize French industrial life. The strike wave was equally a challenge to the traditional strategies of the major unions and to their accustomed methods of controlling and channeling worker militancy. The most interesting response to the challenge came from the country's second largest union, the CFDT, which took advantage of the enthusiasm generated by the factory occupations to launch a new idea—*autogestion* (self-management). This term was first inserted into a CFDT official text on May 16, 1968 at the height of the street battles and factory occupations and it was adopted as the CFDT's primary objective at its next national congress in May of 1970.[24] From a hastily launched CFDT trial balloon, *autogestion* and the related notion of *socialisme autogestionaire* (loosely translatable as "self-managed socialism") have become the official platforms not only of the CFDT but of a large and steadily growing *courant autogestionnaire*,* including the United Socialist party (PSU), a number of Marxist splinter groups, several important left-Catholic political clubs, a few influential magazines, and, most importantly, the newly reorganized and increasingly dynamic PS.

Autogestion has clearly come to function not only as a stimulant for widespread debate on the issue of industrial democracy but above all as a crucial CFDT contribution to the renovation of the French non-Communist left. Unlike the bland democratic socialism of the old SFIO,† or of *Force Ouvrière* (FO),‡ *socialisme autogestionnaire* has rapidly proved to be both a rallying cry with enormous popular and intellectual appeal (especially to left-Catholics previously hesitant to declare themselves "socialists") and a powerful slogan around which tough, highly politicized strikes able to radicalize large numbers of previously apathetic workers could be organized. It is on this basis that the PS has pinned most of its hopes of dominating its difficult and competitive electoral alliance with the PCF, formalized in the Common Program signed in June 1972. The struggle for hegemony within the left alliance has frequently taken the form of acrimonious debates over the relative merits of *autogestion*—the approach of the PS and the CFDT to industrial and social reorganization—and *gestion démocratique*, which is the formula preferred by the Communists and their trade-union ally, the CGT.

The Aims of *Autogestion*

For the CFDT, the concept of *autogestion* represents the culmination of long years of reflection on the nature of capitalist society and on the potentials and pitfalls of socialism as a mode of social reorganization. It was the exhilarating experience of May 1968 that spurred the CFDT to abandon its hesitations

---

*The term *courant autogestionnaire* defies translation. The closest we have been able to come is "self-management wing" or "self-management tendency," with the phrase "of the French socialist movement" understood.

†The SFIO was the official name of the French Socialist party between April 1905 and July 1969, when it was renamed the *Parti Socialiste.*

‡FO is France's other major industrial union confederation in addition to the CGT and the CFDT. Created in 1947 by a secession of anti-Communists from the CGT, the FO currently claims a membership of 700,000 but is generally regarded by outside observers as somewhat smaller. During the Fourth Republic, FO was loosely allied with the Socialists but it has now shifted to the right.

and circumlocutions and to take at last a firm stand in favor of socialism.* The CFDT saw the events of May not merely as a movement for higher wages and increased benefits but rather as a genuine "revolution" containing a "global contestation of the society" and demanding its replacement with a socialist alternative.[25] Furthermore, the CFDT saw in the *gauchiste* criticisms of the bureaucratic centralism of the PCF and the CGT a confirmation of its own refusal to identify socialism exclusively with the centralized Soviet model.[26] For the CFDT, as the the students, socialism—if it were to constitute a real alternative—would have to be capable of realizing the aspirations of the May movement for freedom of expression and personal autonomy. Combining this reading of the May events with research previously carried out by some of its component federations on workers' control systems in Yugoslavia and Algeria, the CFDT produced over the course of the next few years a set of reports and resolutions proposing a system of *socialisme autogestionnaire* for France. This was to be a decentralized socialist society based on a dense network of small, autonomous, self-managed units, that is, units managed directly by all those immediately involved in their operations. Simultaneously, the CFDT attempted to sketch out a union strategy for bringing such a society into existence.

Autogestion is not, therefore, intended as a program for piecemeal reforms within the capitalist system. Nor is it merely a slightly more radical version of German codetermination dressed up in fancy leftist terminology. When the CFDT rejects out of hand government reform schemes such as de Gaulle's *participation* or Giscard's "reform of the firm" as having nothing at all to do with *autogestion*, it does so not because of verbal purism or because of minor specific objections to the details of such programs, but because of a rejection in principle of all piecemeal, incremental reformism inside the capitalist system. For the CFDT, *autogestion* is inconceivable without socialism because capitalism, even in its most attenuated social democratic forms, is an utterly unacceptable social system. Capitalism is, by its very nature, a system that exploits some men for the benefit of others, alienates human beings from their work and their fellows, and dominates them within an interlocking series of hierarchical institutions based on authoritarian, elitist, and fundamentally anti-human cultural models. It is not to be tinkered with but scrapped. Only when the

---

*Since its "deconfessionalization" in 1964, the CFDT had moved slowly toward a mild form of democratic socialism but its leaders were squeamish about using socialist terminology. Instead, the union's documents referred to "a different society," "social and economic democracy," or "democratic planning." A left-wing minority within the leadership group was quite aware of the dangers of employing such ambiguous language but did not, before the May events, feel that the mood of the French working class under Gaullist neocapitalism justified any attempts at ideological experimentation.

primary means of production and exchange have been socialized can people begin to live truly human lives.

But the CFDT's vision of socialism is a peculiar one. It is informed almost equally by a powerful anticapitalism and by a severe condemnation of Soviet and East European communism. In the CFDT's eyes, the Soviet experiment has failed because it has not accomplished anything beyond transferring ownership of the means of production from private capitalists to state bureaucrats. The status of ordinary men and women as wage workers has remained unaltered, as have their alienation from their work and their domination by pyramidal authority structures in factory, family, school, and state. The CFDT's project attempts to imagine institutions and strategies that will free France from the multiple oppressions of capitalism without plunging it into a "stifling order of a centralized and authoritarian socialism."[27]

The Structures of Self-Managed Socialism

How does the CFDT hope to organize such a truly democratic socialism in which the hitherto impossible task of reconciling equality and freedom will be fulfilled? The central principles of the CFDT's attempt to square this political circle are extreme decentralization and radical egalitarianism. The essential precondition is the socialization of the productive apparatus, to begin immediately upon the accession of socialist forces to political power and to continue gradually until almost no significant activity or firm remains privately owned.[28] Institutions of credit, the dominant groups of each economic branch, the strategic industrial firms, the major means of culture, information, and education, are to be socialized at once. It is important to note that the CFDT insists on a distinction between "nationalization"—which, it argues, produces "public" or "state" ownership with the attendant risks of a centralized, bureaucratic state capitalism—and "socialization," which will create a decentralized pattern of "social" ownership by an assortment of collectivities going from workers' collectives to municipalities, regions, and, in some cases, the national community.[29]

The socialized part of the national economic apparatus as well as the preexisting public sector will be divided into the smallest possible autonomous units consistent with reasonable efficiency.[30] In principle, each unit will then be self-managed, that is, managed directly and entirely by workers themselves, subject only to accountability before the public collectivity at the appropriate level. Except in the smallest shops (where workers' control will operate directly) most ordinary decision making will occur within a new type of democratically elected body to be called an enterprise council, which will combine the tasks presently divided between the enterprise committee and the administrative council.[31] This new council will possess enormous powers including the election and supervision of the top managers of the firm and negotiations with the unions. In those firms still under private ownership the prerogatives of management will be drastically reduced; all major decisions concerning investment, hiring, firing, and work conditions will be subject to public scrutiny, to a strict veto power by the unions, and to a review by a *comité d'entreprise* invested with greatly expanded powers.[32]

Within the individual socialized firm, decision making will take the form of pluralistic confrontation among the workers, elected representatives of the workers, elected representatives of the various parts of the firm, and the unions. A decentralized network of democratically elected planning boards topped by a national planning commission will harmonize the long-range decisions of the individual economic units into a coherent pattern of economic development.[33] All these decisions, which balance the desires, requirements, and capabilities of the various units at different levels, will be subject to open debate in a new network of national and regional social and economic councils.*

The principle of self-management—"the direct intervention of individuals and groups in every domain where their own destiny is played out"—will be applied not only in productive units but in all the basic institutions of society.[34] Schools, hospitals, stores, residential units, neighborhoods, communications networks, will be run directly by the people involved in their day-to-day operation, rather than by managerial elites. In the words of one CFDT leader: "It would be an error to limit it [self-management] to production units; it aims higher. Its principle involves the whole society. It is the globalization of workers' democracy, from the firms all the way to the highest level of decisions and including the political parties, public bodies, social service institutions, etc."[35]

Additionally, as this quotation suggests, the principle of *autogestion* also applies to the mechanisms of the state, which are to be drastically decentralized and then run directly by the citizens. In the political as in the economic world, decisions are always to be taken at the "most centralized level consistent with the public good."[36] Thus the bulk of the decisions now made at the national level will be transferred downward to small territorial councils at the level of region, department, city, ward, neighborhood, and even individual housing projects. The national parliament will decide only those issues that cannot be resolved at lower levels. The goal is not, as Marx foresaw, to "transcend" the state but rather to "socialize" it, to turn it into a "voluntary institution."[37] The CFDT hopes that this "parcellization" of the state will serve as a major bulwark against the emergence of the centralized totalitarian bureaucracy that it believes has poisoned the Soviet version of socialism.

---

*The National Economic and Social Council, which is currently an appointed body, would become a democratically elected one, and a similar set of regional councils would be established.

In self-managed socialist society, power and initiative are to flow as much as possible from the bottom up. Radical decentralization is seen as a prerequisite for such a redirection of the flow of power in society. It aims at a form of socialist pluralism in which a multitude of small independent power centers will "balance one another, confront one another, exercise mutual control, thus guaranteeing the reality and viability of the process of democratization of economic and social life."[38] But decentralization and pluralism are not sufficient. It is also necessary to ensure that within each of the many power units individuals will be able to participate in a meaningful way in the making of decisions. The object is not merely, then, to give each institution direct control over its own affairs but to ensure that within each unit decisions are made collectively rather than emanating from the manipulations of a few leaders. The aim is not to replace illegitimate authority by legitimate, but rather to replace all relations of authority by a radical egalitarianism.

According to the CFDT this will require a profound cultural revolution. Since capitalism consists not only of a system of property relations but also of a complex of cultural models and ideological structures, man cannot be truly liberated merely by socializing the ownership of property.[39] Capitalist culture with its hierarchical conception of human relations, its rigid distinctions between leaders and followers, thinkers and doers, men and women, teachers and students, city and country, rational and irrational, must also be cast off. In the words of one CFDT document, "It is the very concept of the boss, of the leader, which must be revised. It is the very organization of power, its structure, which must be recast, rethought."[40] Socialist substructures without a truly egalitarian socialist culture will lead only to new forms of enslavement. The CFDT envisions a massive restructuring of education and information systems, a radical reduction of salary differentials, a regular rotation of tasks, and a reorientation of the way knowledge and competence are acquired and socially rewarded as among the means necessary for creating a culture compatible with *autogestion.*

The Role of the Unions

The CFDT maintains that self-managed socialism is distinguished from both capitalism and centralized socialism by the role of the ordinary citizens, the masses. *Autogestion* involves keeping the real power, the real initiative at the bottom of the society rather than at the top. In the CFDT's conception, one of the principal guarantors of the predominance of the masses in socialist society will be the unions. Self-managed socialism requires a novel form of union structure and practice, which the CFDT sees itself as in the process of inventing. This new unionism has four major dimensions.

First, in the period of the struggle to abolish capitalism, unions must insist on their right to have their own independent socialist project and autonomous strategy. The CFDT sees grave risks of "totalitarian deviation" in any union-party partnership based on a functional division of labor that confines the union to short-range bread-and-butter struggles and entrusts to the party exclusive responsibility for long-range strategy and ideological reflection. This, the CFDT believes, has been the decisive error of Soviet unionism, an error which it accuses its rival, the CGT, of duplicating in its present relationship with the PCF. It is interesting to note that the CFDT's insistence on the universal competence of the union resembles the antiparty "pansyndicalism" of the old revolutionary syndicalists of the CGT in the period before the First World War. The recent resurgence of the PS and the establishment of the Common Program have induced the CFDT to temper somewhat its earlier tendency to see the union as sufficient in itself for the liberation of the working class. The CFDT now looks to a "union of popular forces" based on the "convergence" of parties and unions of the left but it still persists in minimizing the importance of political action as compared to "mass struggles," and in zealously defending its right to total ideological and strategic autonomy. Thus, for example, it refuses to commit itself to the terms of the Common Program, which it regards as a party matter in which unions should not become involved.[41]

The union, then, must have its own strategy linked in an effective way with that of a political formation capable of assuming political power. Secondly, connected to this strategy, the union needs a tactical approach to day-to-day union struggles so conceived as to achieve immediate concrete improvements in the material conditions of the workers, while at the same time contributing to the defeat of capitalism. The immediate demands of the workers must not be neglected but the traditional tendency toward a drastic separation between short-term demands and long-range socialist objectives must at all costs be avoided. The CFDT sees two ways to resolve this classic dilemma of socialist unionism. One is to emphasize what the CFDT calls "qualitative" demands, that is, the kinds of immediate demands that point to the limits of reform within capitalism and thus foster among workers a growing consciousness of the necessity of socialism. These "qualitative" demands—such as for the reduction of salary differentials, or for increased civil and political liberties inside the factory—are not intended to displace "quantitative," that is, bread-and-butter demands, but rather to supplement them.[42] The advantage of such "qualitative" demands is that their very nature enables the union to link daily action with long-term objectives. Through them, the union can politicize even the most banal bread-and-butter conflicts by placing them within the context of a global "challenge to capitalist power taken as a totality."[43] The CFDT's other answer to the reform-or-revolution dilemma consists of the attempt to orient daily struggles whenever possible to the issue of control over the process of production. The CFDT conceives of union action as the sort of "revolutionary reformism" advocated by André Gorz: as the workers, by means of their struggles, gain progressive control over the workplace, they not only undermine the powers of management but they acquire confidence in their own competence to run the factories themselves.[44]

This vision of union action as a progressive conquest of power through the gradual augmentation of workers' consciousness, power, competence, and self-confidence has exposed the CFDT to charges of reformism both from within its own ranks and from outside. The CFDT defends itself indignantly against such charges of gradualist optimism. "We have never recommended," they insist, "trying to set us islands of self-management within capitalist society."[45] The gradual augmentation of workers' hegemony does not obviate the necessity for a "global rupture" with capitalism, but rather provides "indispensable steps in gaining [socialist] consciousness and preparing the necessary conditions of victory."[46]

The third dimension of the CDFT's vision of the role of the unions in the struggle for *autogestion* is the obvious connection between this vision and the events of May 1968. It is clear that the CFDT's approach to union structure and tactics represents a deliberate attempt to accept as valid the criticisms of union methods presented by young workers and students during the May 1968 strikes. In the months following May, the CFDT deliberately accommodated itself to the new militancy of the workers, trying to become the organizational embodiment of the May revolt, partially in order to improve its competitive position vis-a-vis its larger rival, the CGT. It eagerly adopted many of the organizational innovations of the May strikes, such as regular general assemblies of unionized and non-unionized workers, the formation of strike committees independent of the unions, the use of illegal and often violent tactics—such as the barricading of management personnel inside their offices; and it displayed a tolerant attitude to the activities of "support committees" organized by extreme-left political groups from outside the factory during strike actions.[47] However, CFDT has since retreated somewhat from these audacious positions. Its return to a more conventional approach to organizational questions reflects a twofold concern: first, its recognition of the difficulties of blending spontaneity with effective organization; and second, a desire to improve its deteriorating relations with the CGT, which found many of the CFDT's practices intolerable.[48]

The fourth aspect of the union's role in the movement for self-managed socialism concerns the later phases of the anticapitalist struggle. At no point, even after socialism has been fully established, must the unions abandon their role as "contestatory forces" in society to become part of the administrative machinery of the state and the economy. Within the self-managed firm, then, the unions must not accept managerial roles but must remain the direct voice of the masses, "the organization expressing, in opposition to the elected delegates, the preoccupations, the unsatisfied aspirations, of the workers."[49] This oppositional role is seen by the CFDT as a crucial guarantee of the pluralism and openness of the future socialist society.

The idea of *socialisme autogestionnaire* has brought the CFDT to the center of the French political stage. It has also brought the union a great deal of criticism not only from the right, as might have been expected, but also from the left. Among the most vociferous of the CFDT's critics have been the PCF and its trade-union ally, the CGT.

GESTION DEMOCRATIQUE: THE CGT PROGRAM OF ECO- NOMIC AND POLITICAL DEMOCRACY FOR FRANCE

CGT Positions Prior to 1968

The CGT's contribution to the debate on the content, meaning, and viability of *autogestion* must be seen in the context of the political struggles on the French parliamentary left.[50] Before the events of 1968, and the CFDT's subsequent decision to develop *autogestion* as a way of embodying and furthering the social movements that had been unleashed in France, it is fair to say that the CGT envisioned its philosophy and actions as part of a broader movement of anticapitalist working-class struggles, spearheaded by the PCF, to bring about, in its language, a "fundamental change in the political life" of France. To this end, party and union activities were directed both against the government, as in demands for the introduction or revision of legislation or the extension of social security programs, and against big business regarding concrete work-related demands, such as for salary increments and for the recognition of union rights in the factory. Since 1926, when the ties between the PCF and the old CGTU were first made public and the CGT acquiesced in calling the PCF the "*avant-garde dirigeant du mouvement ouvrier*," the CGT has largely abided by the terms of the PCF's economic and political analysis of what is now called state monopoly capitalism.[51] Three of their assumptions remain pertinent to this discussion.

First, the PCF and CGT argue that the political and economic power of the state, together with that of the major capitalists and financiers, cannot be analyzed apart from its penetration into all areas of social life. At the same time, the capitalist state, a necessary stage on the road to socialism, will maintain itself until a major crisis of capitalism, along with the revolutionary activity of workers, ushers in socialism. This means that all political and union activities under capitalism have a twofold function: to democratize daily socioeconomic esistence for all as one way to provide the preconditions for the transition to socialism; and, simultaneously, to force capitalism to its point of highest development, meanwhile exacerbating the smaller crises of capitalism that appear along the way.

Second, only very belatedly has the PCF recognized the changing nature of class structure under advanced monopoly capitalism, as evidenced by its dropping of the shibboleth "dictatorship of the proletariat."* Previously, the PCF and CGT had clung tenaciously to the orthodox line that it is the traditional working class, in alliance with other categories of workers, that must play the leading role in the revolutionary struggle for democracy, both before and after the socialist revolution. In other words, the CGT believed, as did the PCF, that the role of unions and parties under state monopoly capitalism was to facilitate the *"organization de masse et de classe,"* incorporating new strata as they emerged from the social relations of production of advanced capitalism, and to build alliances with other unions and parties around concrete goals. After about 1956, both as an effect of cold-war anticommunism, which spurred it to adopt a "responsible" image, and as a parallel to the PCF's parliamentary road to socialism, the CGT often consciously depoliticized strike actions. It chose shorter, precise strikes over long, drawn-out ones, and generally attempted to enter strikes only where quick settlement of bread-and-butter issues was assured.

Third, the PCF and CGT continue to point out that the management crisis in the country and enterprises is fundamentally a crisis of the entire capitalist system, and insist that this be kept sharply in mind when structural changes are introduced at the enterprise level. The implication of this position is that real self-management at the level of firm and community is completely impossible under the capitalist mode of production. This argument is not unlike that of the CFDT, except that the PCF and CGT place more emphasis on bread-and-butter demands and want to put a foot in the door of management through the as yet largely ineffectual *comités d'entreprise.* [52]

Criticisms of the CGT during the 1960s

The implications of these assumptions for political action drew several trenchant criticisms from the rest of the French left during the 1960s. First, the PCF, and by association the CGT, were accused of simply reproducing the bureaucratic centralist model of state socialism characteristic of the Soviet Union and Eastern Europe. Not only the CFDT, but almost the entire non-Communist left, considered the Communist analysis and political strategy a sophisticated but unacceptable rationalization for democratic centralism, that is,

---

*At its twenty-second congress in February 1976, the PCF finally abandoned the orthodox Marxist idea that a "dictatorship of the proletariat" would be the necessary form of government in the period immediately following the revolution. This phrase, clung to so tenaciously over the years, had provided fuel for the non-Communist left's fears that the party had not de-Stalinized after all. One can speculate that the change was accomplished so easily in 1976 partly because of an increasingly youthful membership not wedded to old ideas.

for "Stalinist" organizational structures. A second and more serious criticism of the CGT was that it accepted a framework of labor struggles that was in effect imposed on it by a combination of Gaullist ideology, national legislation, and the tripartite form that French negotiations took. Both the PCF and CGT were then unable to make salient criticisms of the authority structure in which they participated at the national level, and this in turn left them unable to perceive or contest the authoritarian character of decision making and daily life at the factory level. Third, their rigid version of Marxist class analysis retarded their recognition of the changing nature of class structures; consequently, they were slow to accept different forms of workers' struggles over new demands. As a result, the CGT never sought to capitalize on the militant struggles and factory occupations of the early and mid-1960s, actions generally outside the unions and often against them. Additionally, they were especially insensitive to the rising discontent among French youth, particularly students (of whom relatively few were the children of workers) but also among young workers who were not affiliated with the unions.

The Impact of 1968

Even after it was clear that the student uprisings had detonated massive revolts of both unionized and nonunionized workers—because both they and the students were responding to the same cracks in French society—the CGT could only respond along traditional lines. It moved, often with success, to impose a union focus on the outbreaks in 1968; it tried to split the student-worker contacts that had been made; it accused students and renegade workers of being "extreme leftists," "Trotskyists," "Maoists," "anarchists," and "pseudorevolutionaries"; and it acted to quell all acts of provocation in the demonstrations— despite the far more outrageous behavior of the state security police.* The spirit reminiscent of anarcho-syndicalism that was manifested in the many unconnected spontaneous actions, the myriad *groupuscules*, and the workers' committees that emerged to lead strikes and organize essential services were anathema to both the PCF and CGT.[53] Because of its opposition to these kinds of activity, the CGT was contemptuous of the CFDT's support of both student protests and spontaneous worker actions, and afterward ridiculed the concept of *autogestion*. Indeed, at the height of the events both Georges Marchais, secretary general of the PCF, and Georges Séguy, secretary general of the CGT, referred to it as a "hollow idea." Yet, in the aftermath of 1968, the development and successful popularization of *autogestion* by the CFDT and the PS forced the

---

*Of the student leader, Daniel Cohn-Bendit, Georges Séguy, secretary general of the CGT, said derisively, *"Cohn-Bendit, qui c'est?" (Cohn-Bendit? Who is he?)*

CGT and PCF first to develop a cogent critique of it, and then to elaborate their own project, *gestion démocratique*, as a way to democratize capitalism and move toward socialism simultaneously.

CGT and PCF Criticisms of Autogestion

The CGT and PCF critique of *autogestion* pivots on the level of generalization at which they feel the CFDT has kept the discussion.[54] *Autogestion*, they argue, is too global a term. It is more a sensibility than a strategy, covering a range of ideologies including anarchism. In the lingering revolutionary-syndicalist promise of *autogestion* to negate the role of the state, the CGT and PCF see a utopianism that cannot be materialized either by democratizing the factory or by dismembering the state prior to the revolution. From the CGT and PCF points of view, the *autogestionnaires* avoid analyzing the nature of contemporary capitalism: its giant enterprises; the complex international systems of finance, technology, resources and marketing; the internationalization of production and of the labor market; and the interlocking of state and industry. Above all, the CFDT lacks an analysis of the crisis of advanced capitalism that recognizes the pivotal place of the state. Rather, it presents an abstract version of political economy, avoids contemporary realities, and misses completely the need to build a political organization of all workers and democratic forces capable of opposing the state and of assuming political power. Its singular misunderstanding of the role of the state in perpetuating monopoly capitalism leads it to mistake the appropriate arena for political struggle. Thus, the CFDT takes refuge in a vision of decentralized small and middle-sized industries compatible only with the economic structure of a former era.

By keeping the focus at the enterprise level, and by supporting spontaneous actions, the CGT maintains, the CFDT betrays the long-range needs of factory workers to organize themselves to control the entire spectrum of activities that comprise political and social life.* In fact, the very spontaneity of the actions will ensure their vulnerability to monopoly and state repression; neither workers' self-management nor absolute pay-scale equalization nor workers' assemblies will alone or in combination democratize an industry. For example, the CGT and PCF argue that the notion that all categories of work in the factory are equal will lead to resentments among the various segments of the workforce, obscuring their common interests and thereby delaying the struggle against the

---

*In the midst of 1968, the now ousted PCF philosopher, Roger Garaudy, said, "You can't have a socialist university in a capitalist state."

true source of despotism in the enterprise.* Furthermore, they suggest, the *auto-gestionnaire* emphasis on the problems of the enterprise encourages the class collaboration that provides the foundation for the comanagement and participation schemes that management, hand in hand with the state, then imposes as a palliative for profound discontent. Finally, the CGT and PCF think that all these weaknesses undermine the Common Program. They also argue that the CFDT's obsession with the ideology of *autogestion* compromises its commitment to the union agreements made during the same period.

CGT Assimilation of the Spirit of Autogestion

The CGT and PCF criticisms clearly suffer from their attempt to limit the interpretation of the CFDT conception of *autogestion* only to the enterprise. Additionally, they use the term as a catchall to include the many cooptive forms of participation introduced by government officials and industrialists. Yet these criticisms must be taken seriously because they are part of the ongoing ideological warfare on the French left. But while the CGT and PCF reject *autogestion* as a political theory helpful for understanding state monopoly capitalism, and characterize it as deficient in method and as a blend of "just aspirations and dangerous illusions,"[55] they have also accepted in general the need for a new interpretation of work conditions and social life. This is evident both in the PCF reliance on alienation theory to explain worker discontent, and in their compromise over the inclusion of the term *autogestion* in the Common Program. Georges Marchais said before the Central Committee of the PCF:

> If what certain persons call *autogestion* is not separated from the collective ownership of the major means of production and exchange, nor from democratic planning at the national level, nor from the political power of workers; if it more generally represents democratic socialism in perpetual progress, trying to perfect itself towards higher and higher forms of development in order to achieve the management of all the affairs of society by all, then we have already said that we do not have a fetishism about words. It's the content that counts.[56]

For its part, the CGT is slightly less conciliatory than the PCF. Its major criticisms of the Common Program are specifically of those aspects that address *autogestion*. In the words of Georges Séguy:

---

*Wage stabilization from the bottom up has been a constant CFDT plank, which the CGT has been forced to incorporate into its own program. The CGT's reluctance to do so can be traced to its analysis of the capitalist state, according to which, wage hierarchies under capitalism help, in theory, to exacerbate class conflict.

> We have an opinion a little different—not so much an opinion, but
> an attitude . . . [and] we, too, at the CGT could formulate a certain
> number of reservations about some chapters of the Common
> Program that do not go as far as we could have wished, not as far as
> the program of the CGT; but we are well aware of the fact that what
> is involved is an agreement concluded between the three principal
> parties of the Left. . . .[57]

In this statement, Séguy is reflecting two political dictates: first, the CGT's
political need to criticize the CFDT, but second, the CGT's accurate perception
that its own stance must be differentiated somehow from that of the PCF in
order to increase its appeal among all sectors of French workers.*

Séguy continued:

> We do not claim that we have nothing to learn from the CFDT's
> ideas. On the contrary, the exchange of opinions, the dialogue are
> mutually beneficial, so long as they avoid preconceived ideas . . .
> institutional chauvinism . . . competition. The discussion . . . can
> lead toward surmounting the divergences which exist with a view
> toward a long-term goal of trade-union unification. I am not going to
> claim that there is nothing left to accomplish in this regard. . . . I
> believe, to the contrary, like all my CGT comrades, that there is a
> lot to do; but I am convinced that we are making realistic progress.[58]

Gestion Démocratique

The CGT conception of "realistic progress" is embedded in *gestion démocratique*, in some ways a summary term for its position that essential bread-and-
butter demands, the extension of liberties, economic viability, and democratic
management cannot be separated.[59] But not surprisingly, the CGT's immediate
goals revolve around satisfying many of the same worker demands and needs at
the enterprise level as those pinpointed by the CFDT. *Gestion démocratique*
rests on three pillars: a "democratic plan," which will, after being elaborated by
the masses, define the new antimonopolistic political economy at the national
and regional levels, reorient collective national interests, and define new modes
of enterprise management; the nationalization of crucial sectors of the economy,
which will result in their management autonomy within the parameters of the
plan; and the kind of mass organization at the base that can democratize the

---

*In 1974 the CGT prepared its own document on participation in unions and among
workers, which it circulated to all parties of the left and to the CFDT. The document was
based on the statement of the 37th Congress of the CGT, in 1969, entitled, "Thèmes de
réflexion sur les perspectives du socialisme pour la France et le rôle des syndicats."

state and public life in order to replace capitalism. The plan and the nationalization program stand in a reciprocal relationship to each other. Under socialism, the plan would emerge from public discussions by representatives of the new, democratic enterprises, other collectivities, and workers' organizations. It would then be approved by an elected National Assembly. During the period of the transition from capitalism to socialism, the plan is the outcome of the gradual nationalization of crucial sectors of the economy. However, in contrast to the CFDT's intentions, in both periods the CGT plan also provides for the continuation of a smaller private sector whose production objectives are set to fulfill needs not met by public industries, and for a sector of smaller public firms at the regional or local level whose internal structures would parallel those of the nationalized firms.

In the nationalized sector each firm would be directed by an administrative council composed of elected representatives of workers, appropriate consumers, and a lesser number of other persons designated by the new government. They would, in turn, elect a president. The council's policy tasks are to contribute to elaborating the plan, design the overall direction of each firm, and set immediate goals concerning budgets, markets, interfirm agreements, and the like. In addition, the council will choose a technical management staff responsible to it and thereby, in effect, directly oversee the various sectors of the firm.

Because of their central place in production, the workers are the linchpin of this essentially pyramidal structure. Their first priority, both during the transitional stage and under socialism, is to insure that the needs of all workers are met through the socialization of production. What workers want to do (*vouloir faire*) should take priority even over technical "know-how" (*savoir faire*). They must play a role in all questions that touch, for example, on production and the means of production, research, investments, finances, the conception and materialization of the products of work, working conditions, and all relevant social questions. In the period of transition this role must be raised to the level of a general political struggle—that struggle that will, in fact, lead immediately to nationalizing the major part of the economy. To accomplish this, organized workers must actively participate at all levels of the enterprise. The CGT and PCF also believe that they must reinforce the functions of the already existent *comités d'entreprise*.[60] Another tactic is to press for fuller disclosure of information relevant to ever wider areas of decision making. A third is to agitate continuously for expanded rights of representation and expression in the factory at all levels. But perhaps the most important thing is to expand the sphere of influence of the unions, which, even under socialism, will form the counterweight necessary for harmonious and balanced development of the firm and society. Under *gestion démocratique* unions would elect representatives to the administrative councils and to the *comités d'entreprise*, which would receive orders from, and be accountable to, the unions. Union activity, then, provides the essential means through which workers become the core of the firm.

The CGT and PCF believe that *gestion démocratique*, with its heavy emphasis on unionism and political organization, stands in direct opposition to *gestion bureaucratique* (bureaucratic management) and to the further centralization of the capitalist state. They maintain that what differentiates them from the CFDT is the realism and specificity of their blueprint for the structural reorganization of France, built up from the level of the firms, where the fundamental class struggle continues to occur. And they believe that *gestion démocratique* satisfies all the fundamental human needs for self-determination without incurring the risks of chaos and confusion that *autogestion* would generate.

IN PLACE OF A CONCLUSION

It is evident by now that the theoretical and practical success of *autogestion* has been enough both to force government and industrialists to make gestures in the direction of workers' participation, and to push the CGT to make some political concessions to the idea. Two tasks confront us. First we must attempt to account for the success of *autogestion*. Then we must assess its political effects on the United Left Alliance both during the current struggle for power and during the critical early years of the left coalition government that now seems likely to emerge during the late 1970s. There are at least four explanatory hypotheses that can help us understand the development and popularity of *autogestion* in the current French political climate.

The first hypothesis rests on an analysis of French cultural patterns and suggests that the idea of *autogestion* derives much of its appeal from its ability to touch certain aspects of French national character.[61] The French, this theory reads, are notoriously individualistic, difficult to organize, and impulsive—all characteristics they share with other Latin and Catholic peoples. To this, they add a history of resistance to authority that is peculiarly French and that makes the antiauthoritarian and anticentralist tone of *autogestionnaire* schemes appeal to them. The French like to think of themselves as beleaguered individuals, struggling valiantly, along with a small coterie of allies, against the oppressive, invasive encroachment of various nefarious large-scale institutions, organizations, and social forces. This antiauthoritarian individualism pervades all social strata in France. Moreover, that kind of individualism fits with the all too frequent characterization of French political life as suffering from a dearth of intermediate institutions and an absence of group life. In the context of this hypothesis this is not a criticism of the French, but a cultural variable important to understanding the reemergence of a *courant autogestionnaire* in French life; in other words, the "current" was there all the time. The French worker's vision of himself as an autonomous worker-producer finds its parallel in the self-image of French businessmen for whom—no matter how large the enterprise they actually direct—

the ideal model remains the small, familial firm. The French, then, are seen in this hypothesis as naturally anarchistic and this national character trait finds its natural expression in what would otherwise appear to be irreconcilable political projects, ranging all the way from the revolutionary spontaneity manifested in 1968 to the wildcat strikes of the 1970s, to Giscard's attempt to reform the firm, and to the proposals of the French regional planning commissions during the past several years to revive a small and medium-sized industrial sector.[62]

The cultural approach is superficially appealing: it is only in France that *autogestion* has had such widespread popularity. But, as presented above, the hypothesis has two obvious flaws. It minimizes the distinctiveness of *autogestion* as a workers' control ideology by reducing it to one manifestation of national culture whose appeal thereby transcends all class lines to apply as much to the assembly-line worker as to the managing director of Renault. And, like all cultural explanations, it lacks historical specificity, ignoring the conditions under which cultural traits come into existence and the circumstances that permit their perpetuation.

One step can be taken toward correcting these failings by focusing our examination exclusively on the French working class in an historical perspective. The historical hypothesis points to the fact that at the turn of the century the idea of the autonomous worker-producer was not a cultural abstraction for the skilled craftsmen who formed the nucleus of the Revolutionary Syndicalist movement but was, rather, firmly grounded in the actual conditions of production that they sought to defend against the onslaught of mechanization and industrial rationalization. The Revolutionary Syndicalists, this hypothesis continues, established a powerful tradition within the French working-class movement of which *autogestion* is the latest avatar.

It is undeniable that *autogestion* resembles in both the goals it proposes and the means of action it espouses the strategy and tactics of the Revolutionary Syndicalists who dominated the French union movement in the late nineteenth and early twentieth centuries. The objectives of the Revolutionary Syndicalists— the overthrow of the capitalist system and its replacement with a system of decentralized socialism in which workers would reassume control of the means of production and in which the unions would serve as the fundamental social unit, "the structure of production and distribution, the basis of social reorganization"[63] —are very much akin to the societal vision of *autogestion*. Similarly, the methods advocated by the Revolutionary Syndicalists—the rejection of political parties and parliamentary action in favor of direct action in the form of strikes, boycotts, sabotage, and agitation culminating in the revolutionary general strike—bear striking resemblance to the tactical and strategic preferences of unions that today advocate *autogestion*. Moreover, the current debates between the CFDT and the CGT—over the importance of parliamentary and political action, over the relative merits of *autogestion* and *gestion démocratique*, over the ability of unions alone, without the leadership of political parties, to bring about fundamental political change—all correspond in astonishing detail to the debates within the pre-World War I labor movement in France.[64] This historical approach sees the revival of workers' control debates not as a phenomenon emerging exclusively as the consequence of new social and economic developments, but rather as a recurrent historical issue deeply embedded in the history of the French labor movement.

The historical hypothesis has much to recommend it. The parallels between CFDT unionism and Revolutionary Syndicalism are indeed remarkable, even though they are at least in part deliberately cultivated by the CFDT. French revolutionaries in general and the French working-class movement in particular continue to be very tradition oriented and it seems reasonable that such traditionalism could account for some of the strength of the response to *autogestion*. But the hypothesis does not explain why or how unskilled workers under monopoly capitalism can think of themselves as autonomous producers, given the structure of their work, their lack of autonomy in the job hierarchy, the fragmentation of their lives, and the alienation that follows. Moreover, even if the historical hypothesis is correct in labeling *autogestion* as a revival of the Revolutionary Syndicalist tradition, it offers no explanation for the occurrence and success of such a revival in the present period. For such an explanation we must turn to disciplines other than history.

The third hypothesis—basically a sociological one—may help provide some clues as to the timing of this revival. This hypothesis—drawn from the writings of Serge Mallet, André Gorz, and Alain Touraine[65]—suggests that advanced industrial capitalism (characterized by the internationalization and concentration of finance capital, the need for a carefully planned market and for wide-scale state intervention in economic life, a heavy reliance on automation and a growing institutionalization of industrial conflict, and expansion into a newly developed service sector) has given rise to a situation in which the old distinctions between productive and unproductive labor as a means of distinguishing classes are no longer of use. Under these conditions, a new working class has emerged. It is composed of white-collar workers including engineers, researchers, bureaucrats, high-level technicians, even salaried doctors and lawyers—all persons who may live bourgeois lifestyles as consumers, but whose relationship to both the consumer society and their work is one of alienation and one that reproduces in a new way the powerlessness of the factory workers in their relationship to the forces of production. More specifically, the conditions of work of the new working class resemble in important ways those of the Revolutionary Syndicalist craftsmen of the turn of the century; therefore, the idea of *autogestion* makes considerable sense to them.

In this situation the unions have, to be sure, managed to incorporate a relatively high percentage of the expanded workforce, but unionism itself, instead of becoming increasingly radical, has been coopted by a long history of tripartite bargaining. Under these conditions, the workers' response to the neocapitalist system into which their unions have become integrated, has been, in Serge Mallet's words, "new forms of anarcho-syndicalism": thus we see the resurgence of the wildcat strikes, of short but critical work stoppages, high rates of absenteeism, consumer boycotts, and the like by all sectors of the new working class demanding qualitative control of their own lives as workers and consumers. This then becomes the basis upon which unions and political parties must organize the "revolutionary reforms," to borrow André Gorz's language, that will herald the new socialist society. It is these spontaneous actions—flying in the face of the legality and logic of advanced capitalism and the sterile demands of the unions and left-wing practices—that culminate in the demands for self-management in the workplace and the society which *autogestion* embodies.

The limitations of this sociological hypothesis are fairly evident. First are the criticisms that can be leveled at the peculiar determinism of new working-class theories and at their tendency to oversimplify the highly complex and differentiated impact of advanced capitalist development of the conditions of work, skills, and internal differentiations of this fraction of the working class. Furthermore, the theory assumes an identity of interests and consciousness among all sectors of the old proletariat and new working class, a phenomenon we know to be variable from the numerous occurrences where skilled workers simultaneously embraced socialist ideas and opposed the authority of an employer, while defending their own position against the demands of less-skilled workers in a firm.[66] Moreover, increasing levels of technology under capitalism almost inevitably create more highly differentiated hierarchies based on skills or functions while at the same time increasing competition for jobs—a situation that tends to make the workplace rather than the union the object of the worker's primary identification. In this situation alone it is not immediately clear why unions should ever be the agents of "revolutionary reforms" for either the "old" or "new" working class. Again, new working-class theory presents a plausible, if debatable, argument for the popularity of *autogestion* and industrial militancy by analogy to the craftsmen of revolutionary syndicalism. Yet it also points to the ironic fact that it is the bourgeois and petit bourgeois social orientation of the new working class that may contribute to demands for more autonomy in and control over their work lives. But the theory makes no attempt to account for the obvious success of *autogestion* among the "old" working class.

What is needed is an analysis of the working class as a whole such as that provided in the writings of Ernest Mandel, the Belgian Marxist economist. From his work, as well as from that of Pierre Dubois of the *Groupe de Sociologie du travail* in Paris, we have drawn a fourth hypothesis, which we have labeled "economic/structural."[67] This explanation suggests that the economic structures and the resulting class configuration of the "third industrial revolution" help explain the emergence of militancy in all sectors of the working class; *autogestion* then becomes the appropriate expression of that militancy. First, in the absence of strong wage controls, a situation of nearly full employment coupled with inflation leads unions to assume that bread-and-butter demands will usually be granted, freeing them to concentrate on other grievances centering on the structure and control of the workplace. Second, large-scale capitalism, state and private, requires both careful planning and predictive mechanisms and a stable, integrated workforce. The government, and public and private industry, therefore seek to integrate the unions into the system and to institutionalize labor conflicts as much as possible. Their strategy often includes one variety or another of plans for *participation*. The institutionalization of conflict contains the seeds of its own negation because it drives radical demands outside the unions into wildcats, factory takeovers, lockins, and the like. Spontaneous, extralegal labor activity, then, takes place whether or not unions are in favor of it. It will be recalled that in 1968, both the CFDT and the CGT dragged their feet behind their memberships long after major worker unrest had begun. Finally, it is argued that while highly technological capital-intensive industry has its own forms of job parcellization and repression through the monopoly of knowledge, its requirements for a more highly developed workforce also produce people who at all skill levels and in all sectors of the economy perceive needs that transcend old boundaries. Such workers become increasingly receptive to the analyses and political ideologies of the radical left. Thus while strict laws against the right to strike may be passed (as in France after 1968), raised consciousness leads to increased flouting of the law and a return to explicitly political—and illegal—labor actions, containing escalating demands from the base for control of both the actions and their results.

This hypothesis obviously has large areas of overlap with new working-class theory, and to that extent we maintain our objections to the assumption that different class sectors will inherently perceive their interests similarly. And just as new-working class theory errs in its suggestion that unions and parties should and can be agents of "revolutionary reforms," this hypothesis errs in its argument that radical demands must occur outside the unions, a situation manifestly contradicted by the leadership of the CFDT militants in many of the smaller local strikes during the 1970s, and its national role in propelling demands for *autogestion* to the forefront of the French labor scene. The hypothesis, however, does contribute the important suggestion that changes in both economic and class structures will produce new forms of class actions.

Taken together, these four hypotheses, which we have somewhat arbitrarily labeled the cultural, the historical, the sociological and the economic/structural, help provide some perspective on the dramatic reception of *autogestion* at all levels in France since the mid-1960s. In addition, we must take into account the impact of the May-June 1968 events—in particular their influence on the decentralized forms of labor action that have been a feature of French labor struggles since then—and the effects of the decisions of two of France's largest mass organizations, the CFDT and the PS, to push *autogestion* as their ticket to power and influence within the French left. Taken together, all these factors can provide the beginnings of an explanatory configuration. They also suggest that *autogestion*, with its bases in French culture, history, and economic development, is likely to remain an important aspect of French socialist ideology and politics for the foreseeable future.

Ramifications for the United Left Alliance

We must thus examine some ramifications of *autogestion* for the United Left Alliance both now and under any future socialist government. Its possible significance, we believe, is twofold: first, its contribution to the selection of effective union strategies for mobilizing broad support for a left government before it comes to power; second, its contributions to defining the contours of the future socialist society in light of its effects on the balance of power within the United Left.

The first important aspect of the relevance of *autogestion* is the question of its efficacy as a mobilizing strategy for organizing workers against capitalist domination at the factory level and for creating broad social support for left political battles. Debate on this question crystallized sharply during the spectacular and protracted strike at the LIP watch factory in Besançon from June 1973 to February 1974.[68] The precipitating event was the sale of this old, family-owned French factory to a Swiss concern, and the universal belief among workers that it would shortly afterward be closed. In a move they presented as a fight to protect their jobs, the LIP workers, many of whom were CFDT and CGT members, broke with traditional union strategy and seized control of the firm. Although many maintained they did not have an explicitly socialist ideology, they organized the plant into a work cooperative, sequestered the existing supply of watches, continued to assemble new ones from available parts (while organizing work in new, nonhierarchical ways), and established an effective black market for their sales. Thanks to the active publicity cmapaign mounted by the workers and various other left groups, the romantic strike immediately aroused enthusiastic support throughout France and attracted the attention of leftists in many other countries. These practices also helped put the two major unions on a collision course with each other.

The CGT was less than enthusiastic about the strike from the outset. It seemed to agree with the Swiss owners' analysis that regarded as foolhardy the decision of the strikers to demand that none of the present LIP employees lose their jobs in any reorganization of the company. In fact, the CGT was largely unsympathetic to those actions that constituted the novelty of the LIP strike: occupying the factory, barricading the managers, seizing watches and parts, resuming autonomous production, and selling illegally made watches on the black market. It was even less sympathetic to the way in which the occupation strike was administered. It did not approve of the frequent convocation of general assemblies of strikers to make all the crucial decisions concerning production, sales, and strike tactics. Nor did it agree with the formation of an independent steering committee that included nonunionized workers and was entrusted by the general assembly with the role of negotiating with prospective owners and with the government, a function normally reserved for union delegations. Moreover, it was opposed to the role played in the strike by a support committee composed not only of interested political and religious figures from the Besançon area, but also of young political militants of the far left who flocked to LIP offering money, assistance, and advice of all sorts. Finally, the CGT was very critical of the extent of the autonomy that the local CFDT leaders enjoyed in their relations with the CFDT's national leadership. Besides questions of methods and tactics, the CGT was also annoyed by the ideological halo surrounding the strike. In the press of the extreme left, in the minds of a public fascinated by the LIP affair, and even in the mouths of some of the more idealistic of the strikers, the LIP strike had become "the first strike for *autogestion.*" The CGT insisted that it was ridiculous to collapse self-management into proto-socialism within the boundaries of capitalist society, and that a union ideology that gave rise to such utopianism was irresponsible and dangerous.

For its part, the CFDT, despite constant difficulties between national and local leaderships, enjoyed the ideological gains that the strike was bringing it. It accused the CGT of "defeatism," of "excessive timidity," and of gullibility in accepting the company's analysis of LIP's economic situation when a CFDT-PSU-sponsored study of the books found that the firm had been mismanaged and was still economically viable. Furthermore, the CFDT insisted that none of its official spokesmen had ever encouraged thinking of LIP as the "setting up of an island of self-management within a sea of capitalism." The strike had always been presented quite lucidly as the defense of the right of workers to keep their jobs. If, while it was run by the workers, the LIP factory had come to acquire some of the characteristics of the self-managed firm, such as the creation of autonomous work teams, or the regular rotation of menial tasks among all the personnel including supervisors, or the establishment of production quotas and work methods by collective decision, this was so much the better. As for the use of illegal tactics, nonunion steering committees, and outside support committees, what really counted, the CFDT proclaimed, was results.

For a while the results of the strike appeared excellent: after ten months of strike, agreements were signed in February 1974 that reopened the factory under new ownership and with three-quarters of the original employees retaining their jobs. But by the spring of 1976, bankruptcy had again been declared and LIP seemed in its final death throes, bearing out the CGT's most pessimistic prognostications. At last word, LIP workers were once again on strike in the summer of 1976. However, in the meantime, the idea of *autogestion* had made enormously popular gains, in part riding the wave of the more than "200 children of LIP," worker actions centered on local control issues, that followed the LIP strike between 1973 and 1975.

But more important than the propaganda effects of the strike, or even its domino effect, is the answer to the following question: What does the "LIP affair"—its evident capacity to generate enthusiasm, its ultimate failure to protect the workers of Besançon from losing their jobs, the vicious interunion warfare it fomented—tell us about *autogestion* as an organizational strategy in the struggle against capitalism in the period of transition toward socialism?

The lessons of LIP are, we believe, the following. In the present phase, separate strikes demanding self-management are doomed to failure, and workers who engage idealistically in such strikes will be discouraged rather than having their political consciousness raised, perfecting new forms of action, or restructuring their work. In hindsight, the CFDT agrees with this, and has acknowledged the need to avoid such misunderstanding of its intentions and such discouragement of its followers by altering its terminology somewhat. In recent documents, it refers not simply to *autogestion* but to the much less ambiguous, if more ambitious, *socialisme autogestionnaire*. As a mobilizing slogan, as a critical yardstick against which to measure existing capitalist institutions, as a term capable of exciting people about the possibility of a different way of organizing everyday life, self-management is clearly an idea with great power. And in the final phase of a capitalist crisis, strikes for self-management occurring simultaneously in many of the major plants of France could indeed provide a decisive fillip to the defeat of capitalism.

As to whether, in such a strike wave, the CGT and the CFDT could cooperate more effectively than LIP, or at any of the similar strikes that have copied the LIP approach, the answer is uncertain.[69] Since 1973, the CFDT has moderated its position on the issues of illegal strike tactics, extraunion steering committees, outside support committees, and so on. These changes could make future interactions with the CGT somewhat easier. But the persistence of major disagreements between the two unions on such crucial issues as the autonomy of local unions to strike as they choose and the role of strikes, especially wildcats, under the left government makes it clear that they still conceive the process of the transition to socialism in very different terms.

The second issue to consider is the suitability of *autogestion* for defining the contours of French socialism both in the long run and more immediately in light of the very real possibility of the election of a government of the United Left in the next parliamentary elections. To begin with, it is clear that *autogestion* has been at least partly responsible for the revival of interest in socialism in France and, more specifically, for the dramatic renaissance of the PS. This contribution of *autogestion* should initially be treated from an historical perspective. Previous coalitions of Socialists and Communists in France, and elsewhere in Europe, have proven extremely unstable. During the 1930s and again in the 1940s, even when the French Socialists gained an electoral advantage over their Communist allies, they always felt dwarfed by the solid mass base of the Communists in the factories and municipalities. Moreover, the Socialists' vague, loosely constructed brand of reformist socialism was no match for the analytical power and intellectual cogency of communist social and economic theory. In such circumstances, the most effective drawing card of the Socialists usually was an appeal to the visceral anticommunism that was almost as pervasive on the left as it was on the right. In sum, the ideological insecurity and organizational fragmentation of the non-Communist forces combined with their anti-Stalinism to undermine left coalitions.

Unlike earlier social democratic ideology, *socialisme autogestionnaire* seems attractive enough to give the non-Communist left an alternative to communism that is both intellectually cogent and popular beyond the minimal requirements of electoral victories. In conjunction with the organizing activities of the CFDT, the concept has so far been surprisingly successful in creating a mass base and a broad network of effectively placed militants throughout firms, the bureaucracy, and the society. *Autogestionnaires* have already started to develop a non-Communist subculture around political clubs, journals, colloquia, law collectives, and child-care institutions on the grounds that *autogestion* is a positive, autonomous social theory with an organizational logic of its own.

The idea of *autogestion* has not only given the PS a badly needed intellectual transfusion, but it has also made an important contribution to the debate between Socialists and Communists, between CFDT and CGT, on the contours of future socialist society. Despite its utopian aspects, *autogestion* has brought a new focus to all left critiques of bureaucratic socialism and has provoked serious reflection on the French left concerning ways to organize socialist society in a democratic fashion. Moreover, the growth of the *courant autogestionnaire* has had a definite effect on the CGT and the PCF. It has pushed the CGT and PCF to face the strengths of the new qualitative demands emanating from all segments of the French working class, especially youth, women, and the "new working class." It has encouraged the Communists to produce a vision of future society acceptable enough to the Socialists so that the Common Program could be established. It has also pushed the CGT and PCF to talk about decentralized workers' participation and management autonomy at the level of the firm.

However, the extent of ideological and strategic change engendered as a response to *autogestion* by the CGT and PCF should certainly not be exaggerated. A conceptual and programmatic examination of *gestion démocratique* does not reveal extensive modification of fundamental PCF analysis of French socioeconomic conditions. The CFDT and others still see, with some justification, a contradiction between the PCF's nationalizations policy and *la dynamique autogestionnaire*, not to mention the implicit contradiction between a policy that advocates widespread decentralization and one that assigns a central place to a political party as the primary workers' organization.

In turn, the Communists feel that although *autogestion* is less likely than earlier forms of social democratic socialism to serve merely as a cover for opportunism and anticommunism, the danger is still very much alive that the PS will become, as in Portugal, a heterogeneous haven for many people who lack a real commitment to fundamental social change. Further, they argue that yet another risk attached to *autogestion*'s popularity is the possibility of the direct repression it could provoke from the state. The recent political history of Chile has alerted the entire European left to this danger, and some fear that direct state repression could also occur in Western Europe to quell the wildcat labor struggles that the *autogestionnaires* support. They also anticipate indirect repression against advocates of *autogestion* through the subtle cooptive strategies frequently employed by the modern state.

This debate on the merits of *autogestion* has gained in urgency and concreteness with the approach of the 1978 legislative elections. The Communists fear that *autogestion* is more likely to undermine the chances of the United Left than to advance them. The CGT and PCF also fear that *autogestion* may undermine the unity of the United Left coalition during the crucial period preceding the 1978 elections and especially after a left victory. The Communists see in *autogestion* a subtle new form of anticommunism that can be used by their Socialist colleagues to undermine the United Left from within, by invoking *autogestion* to criticize the Common Program. This threat from within would be reinforced by attacks on left unity from the center/right also centering on *autogestion*. The residual ambiguities of the term—particularly those revolving around where the revolution begins and where it ends—as well as its patina of revolutionary syndicalism and its potential as a fuel for anticommunism all make it obvious to them that the center and right will also try to use *autogestion* to drive a wedge between the Socialists and the Communists within the Common Program. These fears rest on the increasing references to *autogestion* being made in centrist and rightist circles and also on the CFDT's continuing refusal to endorse the Common Program, which, the Communists feel, makes the CFDT a potential Trojan horse on the labor front quite apart from any designs of the center or the right.

Thus another question in the current debate concerns union activities in the wake of a potential left electoral victory. The PCF and the CGT—firmly dedicated to the parliamentary road to socialism and pointing to the narrow margin by which Mitterrand lost to Giscard in 1974—feel that the 1978 elections are a crucial turning point for France and for the left. Reflecting on the events of 1936, they feat that the CFDT's approach to strikes, as manifested in its continued support for wildcats, could bring disaster to a left government, and is counterproductive in terms of a winning electoral strategy. Because the CGT and

PCF realistically expect that the left will come to power in the midst of an economic crisis, they also fear the impact of spontaneous 1936-style strike waves in the period of enthusiasm and raised expectations that would follow a left electoral victory. In this situation it is not inconceivable that the CGT would lay down a no-strike pledge (despite advance statements to the contrary) and act to hold back wage demands. In such a case the way would be clear for radical elements in the CFDT openly to oppose the Common Program by riding their *autogestionnaire* ideology into a series of wildcat strikes. Even if the CFDT's national leadership opposed such action, the union's commitment to the autonomy of its base-level organizations could force the national union into supporting strikes against the left government. It is clear that at this point the political trouble inevitable between the unions would be reflected in the parties and then in the government, with obviously deleterious consequences.

The leadership of the CFDT is not unaware of these potential dangers. It has attempted to strengthen its influence over local sections by weeding out extreme-left militants from positions of power and by initiating internal discussion of the responsibilities of the unions during the early period of a left government.[70] But it has, thus far, refused to make any concessions on the issue of internal organizational autonomy and refused to condemn in advance any possible postelection strike wave. In the report on its latest concgress, the CFDT makes it clear that such 1936-style strikes ought to be viewed by a newly elected left government not as a challenge to its authority, as Léon Blum viewed it, but as an indispensable contribution to the setting in motion of a broadly based revolutionary process.[71] It follows from these disagreements that it is likely that the PCF and CGT will each continue its own interpretation of a proper strike strategy for unions to follow where a Socialist government is in power.

The contribution of *autogestion* to the French left is thus complex and debatable. It is certain that the ideology of *socialisme autogestionnaire* and CGT compromises on previously rigid positions have provided a way for large numbers of people to begin to see themselves as socialists here and now without being immobilized by the specter of Stalinism. This breakthrough in consciousness has enabled many to engage in the kind of ongoing political and cultural reconstruction that can contribute to creating the forms of a new society. *Autogestion* has also helped workers to understand more clearly the necessary articulation among abstract models of society, daily demands, and the organizational means needed to link the two. And most concretely, it has indeed contributed to the rapid buildup of votes on the left since the electoral disasters of 1968 and 1969. However, it should not be thought that the future contributions of *socialisme autogestionnaire* to the solidarity of the United Left and to the capacity of a potential left government to govern effectively remain anything but problematic.

NOTES

1. See Alain Guillerm and Yvon Bourdet, *Clefs pour l'autogestion* (Paris: Editions Seghers, 1975), pp. 5-50; Yvon Bourdet, "L'Autogestion no. 5," *Autogestion et Socialisme*, no. 30-31 (March-June 1975): 91-94; Ernest Mandel, ed., *Contrôle ouvrier, conseils ouvriers, autogestion: Anthologie* (Paris: Maspéro, 1970), pp. 7-45.

2. Daniel Mothé, "Où en est le courant autogestionnaire?" *Esprit*, no. 442 (January 1975): 16-33. For another theoretical model see Roberto Massari, "From Workers' Control to Self-Management: Elements for the Construction of a Theoretical Model," mimeographed (Rome: Institute of Sociology, n.d..).

3. George Ross's felicitous phrase in "The May Revolt in France," *New Politics* 7, no. 1 (Winter 1968): 42. In 1968 after two years of recession, 600,000 people were jobless (this was double the 1966 figure); nine million workers at virtually every level of French society went out on strike.

4. Pierre Dubois, *Les nouvelles formes des conflits du travail: 1960-1974* (CNRS monograph, November 1974), pp. 62-63.

5. The following table of strike waves illustrates the increasing militancy in the labor movement between 1958 and 1973. Ibid., p. 2.

France	No. of Strikes (yearly average)	No. of workers Involved (yearly average in millions)	Work Days Lost (yearly average in millions)
a. 1958-67	1,753	1,979	2,484
b. 1968-73	?	3,483 (est.)	26,000 (est.)
c. 1969-73	3,467	2,180	3,204
progression b/a	?	+76%	+946%
progression c/a	+97%	+10%	+29%

6. The literature on May-June 1968 is too numerous to mention. On this specific point see ibid., and, in English, Andrée Hoyles, *Imagination in Power: the Occupation of Factories in France in 1968* (Nottingham: Spokesman Books, 1973).

7. For early proposals of *participation* and for the history of attempts to implement profit sharing and share distribution in the late nineteenth and early twentieth centuries see Maurice Vanlaer, *La Participation aux bénéfices* (Paris: Rousseau, 1898); Roger Beynet, *De l'influence de la participation sur la production, la situation de l'ouvrier et les grèves* (Paris: 1908), and Maurice Duhamel, *Participation aux bénéfices et participation au capital* (Lille: 1912).

8. For an ambivalent CGT view of the *comités d'entreprise* see "Le Rôle des comités d'entreprise," *La Nouvelle Critique*, no. 35 (June 1970): 10-15.

9. The most important of such reform proposals came from François Bloch-Lainé, a very high-ranking career civil servant and president of one of the nation's largest national-ized banks. See his *Pour une Réforme de l'entreprise* (Paris: Seuil, 1963).

10. In 1964 both the Confédération française des patrons chrétiens and the Centre national des jeunes patrons (CNJP) devoted sessions of their annual conventions to discus-sions of participation. See *L'année politique 1964* (Paris: Presses universitaires de France, 1965), pp. 174-78. On the CNJP, see Philippe Bernoux, *Les Nouveaux patrons* (Paris: Editions ouvrières, 1974), especially chap. 2.

11. For Gaullist domestic policies the reader can refer to Jean Charlot, *Le Gaullisme* (Paris: Colin, 1970), and Pierre Viansson-Ponté, *Histoire de la république gaullienne*, 2 vols. (Paris: Fayard, 1970 and 1971).

12. See, for example, Jean-Daniel Reynaud, Jean-Maurice Verdier, and Gérard Adam,

La Négociation collective en France (Paris: Edition ouvrières, 1972).

13. Hubert Lesire-Ogrel, *Le Syndicat dans l'entreprise* (Paris: Seuil, 1967). In 1965, the president of the CNPF (the central organization of French industrialists) declared: "We willingly accept the *comités d'entreprise*, but we will never accept the entry of union action into the firm. That would have to be imposed on us by force, which is fortunately not yet the case."

14. Excerpts of the speech appear in *L'année politique 1968* (Paris: Presses universitaires de France, 1969), p. 384.

15. Very few large-scale experiments have actually been undertaken in France. See Jean Dubois, "Les bonnes intentions patronales," *Projet*, no. 95 (May 1975): 546–54.

16. For the contents of the Sudreau report see *Le Monde* January 29, February 8, 13, 14, 15, and 16–17, 1975.

17. Cited in Jean Dubois, "Requiem pour une réforme défunte," *Projet*, no. 106 (June 1976): 629.

18. Henri Krasucki, quoted in *Le Monde*, February 15, 1975.

19. See *Le Monde*, May 13, 1976.

20. Ibid.

21. Ibid.

22. Dubois, "Requiem pour une réforme défunte," op. cit., p. 631.

23. Ibid., p. 630.

24. The communique was issued by the CFDT's Confederal Bureau and is cited in Albert Detraz, *Positions et action de la CFDT au cours des événements de mai-juin 1968* (a special issue of the CFDT weekly newspaper *Syndicalisme*, no. 1266A), p. 54. For the texts adopted at the 1970 Congress see *CFDT: Textes de base* (Paris: CFDT/Réflexion, 1974), pp. 31–50.

25. The quotations are taken from Detraz, op. cit. p. 168.

26. For the CFDT's evaluation of Soviet socialism, see Edmond Maire, *Pour un Socialisme démocratique: Contribution de la CFDT* (Paris: Epi, 1971), pp. 45–46, and Edmond Maire and Jacques Julliard, *La CFDT d'aujourd'hui* (Paris: Seuil, 1975), pp. 164–66.

27. Albert Detraz, Edmond Maire, and Fredo Krumnow, *La CFDT et l'autogestion* (Paris: Cerf, 1973), p. 34.

28. See CFDT, Conseil National, "Des Objectifs de transformation conduisant au socialisme autogestionnaire," April 19, 1974, in *Syndicalisme*, April 25, 1974, p. 8 (hereafter cited as "Objectifs de transformation").

29. See Detraz, Maire, and Krumnow, op. cit., pp. 42–43. For the CFDT's insistence on the difference between nationalization and socialization, see Maire, *Pour un Socialisme démocratique: Contribution de la CFDT*, op. cit., p. 48.

30. "Objectifs de transformation," p. 7.

31. Ibid., p. 7. The *conseil d'administration* corresponds more or less to the board of directors of an American corporation.

32. Ibid., p. 8.

33. For the interaction between self-management and planning see Detraz, Maire, and Krumnow, op. cit., pp. 46–50.

34. Maire and Julliard, op. cit., p. 174.

35. Albert Detraz, "Réflexions sur l'origine, les expériences et la théorie de l'autogestion," *Formation* (the CFDT's magazine for its militants), no. 82 (March-April, 1969): 19.

36. Detraz, Maire, and Krumnow, op. cit., p. 43.

37. Maire and Julliard, op. cit., p. 185.

38. Detraz, Maire, and Krumnow, op. cit., p. 49.

39. For the CFDT's analysis of capitalism and for the importance assigned to non-economic aspects, see the General Resolution of the 1976 congress, section 203, in *Syndicalisme*, no. 1603, p. 23. This analysis dates back to the 1970 congress's "Document d'orientation," which can be found in *CFDT: Textes de base*, op. cit., pp. 31–50, specifically pp. 36–37.

40. Detraz, Maire, and Krumnow, op. cit., p. 5.

41. For the CFDT's post-May pansyndicalism, see Detraz, "Réflexions sur l'origine, les expériences et la théorie de l'autogestion," op. cit. For the "Union des forces populaires," see *CFDT: Textes de base*, op. cit., pp. 107–22, especially p. 119. For the CFDT's refusal to sign, or to pledge itself to abide by, the Common Program, see, for example, the General Resolution of the 1976 congress, section 230, in *Syndicalisme*, no. 1603, p. 24.

42. See Maire, *Pour un Socialisme démocratique*, op. cit., pp. 53–54, and Maire, "Rapport Général," (Report presented to the CFDT's 37th Congress, Annecy, May 1976), chap. 2.

43. The CFDT's latest expression of its longstanding preoccupation with what it calls "linking 'today' with 'tomorrow,'" can be found in section 230 of the General Resolution of the 1976 congress, in *Syndicalisme*, no. 1603, p. 23. Similarly, for the "politicization" of demands, see Maire, "Rapport général" to the same congress, op. cit., p. 57.

44. Gorz's positions can be found, in English, in *Strategy for Labor: a Radical Proposal* (Boston: Beacon Press, 1969) and in *Socialism and Revolution* (Garden City, N.Y.: Anchor Books, 1973).

45. Maire and Julliard, op. cit., p. 186.

46. Edmond Maire et al., "Pour une Démocratisation de l'entreprise dans une perspective de transformation sociale et d'autogestion" (Report presented to the CFDT's 35th Congress, May 1970), p. 13.

47. For the CFDT's attitude toward radical strike methods, see Edmund Maire, "A propos des formes d'action," *Syndicalisme*, no. 1328, and Pierre Dubois and Claude Durand, *La grève: Enquête sociologie* (Paris: Armand Colin, 1975), pp. 237–42.

48. The CFDT began to moderate its positions in early 1972 apparently in response to disappointing results in factory elections held in plants where the CFDT had led radical strikes. The documents of the 1973 congress reflect the new moderation concerning tactics. See Edmond Maire, "Rapport général" (Report presented to the CFDT's 36th Congress, Nantes, May 30-June 3), 1973, pp. 64-67.

49. Maire, *Pour un Socialisme démocratique: Contribution de la CFDT*, op. cit., p. 70.

50. CGT membership is approximately 1.6 to 1.7 million workers, approximately four times that of the PCF and two to two-and-one-half times that of the CFDT. The PCF has many adherents who are not members of the CGT, and the same is true in reverse. A fairly reliable estimate of Communist party members in the CGT is found in André Barjonet, *La CGT* (Paris: Editions du Seuil, 1971), p. 124. It would be a simplistic error to identify the CGT today as a "transmission belt" for the PCF. The CGT's membership includes many diverse Socialists, Communists, Christians, and even a vestigial anarchist contingent. Yet, it is true that the leadership and the militants of the union tend to be Communists. Barjonet offers four explanations for this: the more professional commitment and discipline of Communists at the base; a certain inhibition that non-Communists in the CGT feel vis-a-vis the PCF; the majority of Communists in several of the more powerful federations and departments; and the leading role of Communists in the Bureau Confédéral. For a fuller discussion see Barjonet, chap. 5, "La CGT et le parti communiste," pp. 124-36. Specifically, four members of the Political Bureau of the PCF are now members of the Executive Commission of the CGT: Benôit Frachon, Georges Frishchmann, Henri Krasucki,

and Georges Séguy. Often the most promising young CGT members are proposed for membership in the PCF.

51. Jean Montreuil, *Histoire du mouvement ouvrier en France: les origines à nos jours* (Paris, 1948), p. 382, cited in Robert Wohl, *French Communism in the Making* (Stanford: Stanford University Press, 1966), p. 347, fn. 148.

52. The CGT's views of the *comités d'entreprise* are, however, ambivalent. See the aforementioned colloquium "Le Rôle des comités d'entreprise," loc. cit.

53. For CGT hindsight on May-June 1968 see Georges Séguy, *le Mai de la CGT* (Paris: Juillard, 1972).

54. The CGT and PCF literature on *autogestion* and *gestion démocratique* is ballooning rapidly. The following sources are immediately helpful: Barjonet, op. cit.; Henri Krasucki, *Syndicats et socialisme* (Paris: Editions Sociales, 1972); Georges Séguy, *Lutter* (Paris: Stock, 1975); "La Gestion démocratique et l'intervention des travailleurs dans l'entreprise," *Economie et Politique*, no. 229-30 (August-September, 1973); see especially the articles by Georges Marchais, Jean Fabre, Paul Boccara, Jacques Brière, and Daniel Adam. See also Jacques Brière, "Autogestion, autonomie de gestion et démocratie avancée," *La Nouvelle Critique*, no. 37 (October 1970): 6-13; "Le Rôle des comités d'entreprise," loc. cit.; George Marchais, *Le Défi démocratique* (Paris: Grasset, 1973); and the *Programme Commun de gouvernement du parti communiste et du parti socialiste* (Paris: Editions Sociales, 1972).

55. Boccara, in *Economie et Politique*, op. cit., p. 49.

56. "Démocratie politique et démocratie économique sont indissociables," *Economie et Politique*, op. cit., pp. 19-20.

57. Séguy, op. cit., p. 312.

58. Séguy, op. cit., p. 315.

59. More extensive theoretical elaboration can be found in Krasucki, op. cit., and in the Marchais and Fabre articles in *Economie et Politique*, op. cit.

60. "Le Rôle des comités d'entreprise," op. cit.

61. For two well-known elaborations of this point of view see Stanley Hoffmann, "Paradoxes of the French Political Community," in *In Search of France*, ed. Stanley Hoffmann (New York: Harper Torchbook, 1965), pp. 1-17; and Michel Crozier, *The Bureaucratic Phenomenon* (Chicago: University of Chicago Press, 1964).

62. This is particularly interesting in light of the evidence that the most radical strikes since 1968, that is, those controlled from the base, have occurred in the smaller factories located in the countryside where the unions are less firmly ensconced. See Dubois, op. cit., p. 50.

63. Cited from the Amiens Charter of 1906. This was the declaration of principles of the CGT at the apogee of revolutionary-syndicalist influence. See Jean-Daniel Reynaud, *Les Syndicats en France*, vol. 2, *Textes et Documents* (Paris: Seuil, 1975), pp. 26-27.

64. Conflicts in the pre-World War I labor movement among Socialists, anarcho-syndicalists, "pure" syndicalists, and First International Communists are far too complicated to relate here. Suffice it to say that the lines were drawn early within each group as well as among them in regard to questions of both ideology and tactics. At the same time, the strange bedfellows in the old CGT and the Socialists in the SFIO wove a complicated, fragile pattern of alliances in both the union and the party. For background on this period see Val Lorwin, *The French Labor Movement* (Cambridge: Harvard University Press, 1968); F.F. Ridley, *Revolutionary Syndicalism in France* (Cambridge: Cambridge University Press, 1970); Robert Wohl, *French Communism in the Making* (Stanford: Stanford University Press, 1966); Reynaud, op. cit., vol. 1; and Jean Montreuil, op. cit.

65. See, for example, the still untranslated seminal work by Serge Mallet, *La nouvelle Classe ouvrière* (Paris: Editions du Seuil, 1969); André Gorz, op. cit.; Alain Touraine, *The Post-Industrial Society* (New York: Random House, 1971); and André Gorz, ed., *Critique de la Division du travail* (Paris: Seuil, 1973), part 2.

66. For a discussion of this point see Charles F. Sabel, "Industrial Conflict and the Sociology of the Labor Market," mimeographed (Cambridge: Center for European Studies, Harvard University, 1976).

67. Mandel, op. cit.; Dubois, op. cit.

68. At this point the literature on the LIP strike is almost overwhelming. Some convenient sources in English are Peter Herman, "Workers, Watches, and Self-Management," *Working Papers*, Winter 1974, pp. 18–25; "The Lip Watch Strike," *Cahiers de Mai* translated in *Radical America* 7, no. 6 (November-December 1973): 1–18; and *Lip and the Self-Managed Counter-Revolution*, pamphlet translated from *Negation*, no. 5 (Detroit: Black and Red Press, 1975). For French sources see, among others, *Le Monde*; articles in *Autogestion et Socialisme*, no. 28–29 (October 1974–January 1975); "Lip: qui a tue?," *Le Nouvel Observateur* (April 12, 1976); Charles Piaget, *Lip: Charles Piaget et les Lip recontent* (Paris: Stock, 1973).

69. For a list of these occupation strikes and an analysis of the parallels to LIP, see "Les Enfants de LIP," *CFDT Aujourd'hui*, no. 15 (September-October 1975): 17–26, expecially the tables on pp. 21 and 23–24.

70. For this discussion see the following CFDT texts: "La CFDT et la gauche," special issue of *Syndicalisme*, no. 1493 (May 1974), and "Les Rapports syndicals-partis," special issue of *Syndicalisms*, no. 1550 (May 29, 1975). The elimination of left-wing militants is obviously not a matter for open discussion within the union. It can be gleaned from reading the left-wing press, and is occasionally reported in *Le Monde*.

71. See Maire, "Rapport général" (Report presented to the CFDT's 37th Congress), op. cit.

6

WORKER COUNCILS IN ITALY: PAST DEVELOPMENTS AND FUTURE PROSPECTS

Martin Slater

INTRODUCTION

In September 1969, the Fiat management, responding to a strike by 800 workers in a single department, closed the gates to their factories in Turin. This lockout, which resulted in the temporary unemployment of 30,000 workers, sparked sympathy strikes in other northern factories, and led the metalworkers' unions to begin immediate strike action for the renewal of their national contract, which expired at the end of the year. In the next several week, which became known as the "hot autumn," the worst fears of Italian capital were realized. The strike actions of one and a half million metalworkers were soon followed by workers in other sectors of the economy whose contracts were due for renewal. Over four million workers, a major portion of the industrial workforce, participated in strike activity. Their settlement was such that, following the intervention of the Ministry of Labor in the disputes, 80 percent of their grievances were satisfied. The increase in costs to Italian industry of this settlement was estimated to be 28 percent over the next three years.[1]

The 1969 strikes were remarkable for the vigor with which they were fought. More remarkable still, the high level of strike activity did not collapse immediately in subsequent years as it had tended to do in other West European countries. Sustaining this level of activity were new structures of workers' participation. These structures, consisting of shop-floor and factory assemblies, elected workplace delegates, and factory councils, allowed much stronger expression of working-class interests. They also permitted a considerable broadening of the scope of topics raised in negotiations with public and private employers. Workers on the shop floor not only controlled the content of their grievances, but also, through their elected delegates, they fully controlled the negotiating process. The delegates, despite their name, were not representatives of the workers in any Burkeian sense; there was no delegation of authority. They were, and in most cases remain, an organic part of the working class, and the expression of each homogeneous group of workers in the workplace.

The new structures of workers' participation came to maturity in 1969, and it was then also that they were embraced by important elements within the three major unions—the *Confederazione Generale Italiana del Lavoro* (CGIL), *Confederazione Italiana Sindicati Lavorati* (CISI), and *Unione Italiana del Lavoro* (UIL). The delegates and councils, however, had hade their first appearance somewhat earlier, in late 1968 and the spring of 1969. They had arisen spontaneously on the shop floors of a number of large northern factories, principally in the industrial cities of Milan and Turin. The workers of Pirelli (Bicocca) are generally credited with having formed the first shop-floor committees.[2] The forms of organization and demands that were developed in a series of wildcat strikes in a few major firms laid the groundwork for the movements of 1969 and later years. In integrating the new democratic structures into their own organization, the unions succeeded in generalizing workers' councils and the delegate system for large numbers of firms throughout Italy.

The new system of industrial relations has now become firmly established in the workplace, replacing in most cases the preexisting union and representative structures. The democratization of the workplace appears to have had far-reaching social and political effects throughout the nation. The united front presented by the workers' councils has encouraged the movement for the unification of the main union confederations.[3] This confederal unity, while still not fully achieved, allowed the unions to assume a new role in Italian society as immediate guardians of working-class interests. They thus ceased to be mere representatives of their own members. The unions, as indicated by their program and action on social reforms, have directly expressed working-class interests at the national level. Their actions have, in fact, destroyed the hegemony of the Communist and other left-wing parties in the expression of these interests. The traditional dominance of politics in Italy has ended.[4] Within the workplace, employers' prerogatives have been challenged and upset by workers, who have found themselves with sufficient contractual and political power to negotiate on such issues as the organization of work and even the investment programs of firms.

In view of the important political changes that have taken place as a result of the development of new forms of workplace organization, it is opportune at this time to review the experiences of the postwar period. This chapter addresses three sets of questions. First, we will examine the principal ways in which workers' councils have changed the system of industrial relations and workers' representation in Italy. Second, we will suggest an explanation for the development of the councils. Finally, we will consider the experiences of the councils since their formation, assessing both how successfully they have represented working-class interests and what their likely prospects are in the future.

WORKERS' COUNCILS: NEW FORMS OF
DEMOCRATIC PARTICIPATION

The workers' councils constituted a major turning point with regard to previous forms of organization for the decentralization and democratization of bargaining, the extension of workers' control in the form of contestation of a wide range of decisions previously the prerogative of management, and the growth of a unified, class-based movement.

The workers' councils were the first instance in which workers directly controlled both the expression and the settlement of their grievances at the plant level. The grievances expressed in strike platforms, whether at national, local, or plant level are discussed and approved by popular assemblies on each shop floor and in each plant. Each homogeneous group of workers within the plant—that is, each group of workers doing similar work in a particular department—chooses a delegate to represent it in the factory council. This council then negotiates with management, reporting back to the assemblies to gain approval for any proposed settlement. Each delegate will normally represent between 20 and 50 workers. Thus in a large factory, with more than 20,000 employees, there may be as many as 350 delegates in the council* In these cases, it is common to elect an executive council with perhaps ten or 12 workers who devote themselves full time to running the day-to-day business of the council. The assemblies, however, remain the highest authority, and time during working hours is made available for their convocation.† An example of the authority of the assemblies is provided by the 1969 metalworkers' contract where between 2,000 and 3,000 meetings were held to determine the content of the national platform.[5] The system, therefore, is democratic insofar as workers on the shop floor directly control demands and their settlement. This decentralization of decision making is complemented by decentralization of the levels of collective bargaining. Plant and shop-floor agreements have become the norm.

If, prior to the late 1960s, there had been little progress with regard to the democratization of the workplace, this was not so for decentralization. Since the Second World War, there had been a constant trend toward the progressive decentralization of the bargaining process. Until 1954, the confederations alone had held responsibility for salary negotiations. Agreements were applicable only at the most general level. Their effects, incidentally, were hardly noticeable because of the effective blockage of salary gains during the early 1950s. After

---

*The Alfa Romeo (Portello and Arese) council has 350 members; the firm employs approximately 20,000 workers in its two Milanese plants.

†Under national and plant agreements, unions have obtained work release with full pay for delegates and union representatives. In addition, 10 hours per year are made available to every employee for attendance at factory or departmental assemblies.

1954, two changes took place that led to considerable decentralization of the bargaining process. First, the industrial federations of the unions took responsibility for the negotiation of national contracts in the industries that they represented. The role of the confederations was thus diminished. Second, plant-level accords began to take place on an increasing scale. The latter were as yet confined to agreements on work conditions, while salaries continued to be negotiated at the national level. Nevertheless, with 670 plant-level accords in the four years from 1953 to 1957 and a full 562 in a single year in 1960,[6] the trend toward decentralization was unmistakable. In 1962, the notion of plant-level bargaining was officially acknowledged in an agreement between the metalworkers' unions and the state enterprise boards (*Instituto per la Ricostuzione Industriale* [IRI] and *Ente Nazionale Idrocarburi* [ENI]). In the following year, the private employers' association, *Confindustria*, also acknowledged the need for collective bargaining at the plant level. Both agreements provided for complementary bargaining at four separate levels: national, industrial, branch, and plant.

For some contemporary observers the developments of the early 1960s marked a momentous change in the Italian system of industrial relations.[7] But decentralization of the levels of bargaining had involved neither decentralization in decision making nor democratization of representative structures. The main negotiating bodies continued to be the union structures outside the firm. For plant-level contracts, the provincial union offices held primary responsibility. Officials in these offices were career unionists, appointed by the unions. For agreements at other levels, the industrial federations and confederations continued to be the chief negotiators.

The two principal organizations within the workplace, the internal commissions and the union sections, had no contractual power. The union sections acted as no more than communication channels for the provincial unions. In addition, the union representatives were not democratically elected, but appointed by the unions. The only elected representative organization in the factory was the internal commission. It was not a union organization. The unions, however, could present their lists of candidates for election to the commission, and it was common for all elected officials to be active in the union. All workers, whether members of unions or otherwise, had the right to vote in professional elections and to stand for election themselves. The commission, however, by the 1960s, was an organization in decline. During the 1950s, commissions had exerted considerable influence in plant-level agreements. But, with the institutionalization of plant-level bargaining in the early 1960s, they had been obliged to relinquish much of their influence to the provincial unions.[8] The internal commission might have been able to ride the crest of the popular movements in the late 1960s but for two additional factors. First, it had too few members to be a truly representative body. In the very largest firms, the commission had a maximum membership of 21 workers. Many parts of a large factory could not be adequately represented. Second, and making matters still worse, the commission was elected by plantwide elections. Thus there was no guarantee of adequate representation for many departments.[9] Other minor organizations within the workplace were the technical committees, which were involved mainly in negotiations over work conditions. These committees were relatively ineffective. Their joint composition of management and union representatives meant that they could never become the expression of working-class interests. Formed in 1962 in the textile industry and in 1966 in the metal and mechanical engineering industry, they had only a short existence in the large northern factories.*

Against this background, the arrival of the workers' councils in 1968 constituted a radical departure. As noted earlier, the councils developed spontaneously on the shop floors of the large northern factories. Popular assemblies, through their elected delegates, controlled all aspects of the factory struggles. For several months, the councils and the preexisting structures of workers' representation lived alongside one another. The old internal commissions hoped initially to increase their own influence by harnessing the force of the popular movement. But the commissions often found themselves in conflict with the councils.[10] This conflict centered not only on the substantive demands to be proposed in negotiations with employers, but also on which organizations should be responsible for such negotiation. Since the councils continued to command popular support on the shop floor, it was clear which organization held the contractual power necessary for successful negotiating. The internal commissions soon became somewhat anomalous. Long since deprived of any negotiating power, they were now no longer regarded as representative of the vast mass of workers. In this condition, they had no further reason for existence. By the early 1970s, they had disappeared from view in most factories.

The unions were much more successful than the commissions in adjusting to the presence of the councils. Major adjustments were required. The provincial unions gave up much of their negotiating powers. Today, their major role is that of coordinating strike activity within the province. In integrating the councils into the union movement, the unions avoided a fight with the councils. But conflicts still remain over the question of loyalties in the workplace. Is loyalty owed to the union or to the immediate group of workers that each delegate represents? In the factories where the councils developed spontaneously, it seems that the first loyalty was to the workers. Union representatives, however, as opposed to workers' delegates, are still active in the factory. Under the terms of the Workers' Charter,† passed in 1970, the unions gained the right to appoint their

---

*Joint committees have, in fact, continued in a number of more traditional industries where the contractual power of workers is considerably less than those in more advanced sectors of the economy. In the construction industry, for instance, joint committees still negotiate on work conditions.

†The Workers' Charter (*Lo Statuto dei Lavoratori*), passed into law on May 20, 1970, guarantees the presence of unions in firms with more than 15 employees.

own representatives within the factory. These representatives were afforded wide negotiating powers by the new law. The intention was clearly to shift power away from the provincial unions. In practice, it is not the formal power of union representatives that determines their effectiveness, but their level of support on the shop floor. It is unthinkable for unions to appoint representatives who are not also delegates to the workers' council. The council, therefore, remains the source of workers' power within the factory. This point is further illustrated by the number of nonunionists (usually members of small leftist groups) who continue to be active in the council, and who have authority to negotiate with management.[11]

The Extension of Workers' Control and the Development of Permanent Confrontation

Closely linked to the democratization of the workplace and the decentralization of bargaining is the extension of workers' control over areas of decision making that were once the prerogative of management. In the early postwar years, under the confederal agreements, salaries were virtually the only topic of negotiations. During the 1950s and 1960s, however, the increasing number of plant-level agreements meant that work conditions became a common area of collective bargaining. With the development of articulated bargaining in 1962, which included provisions for plant-level agreements, there was official recognition of the right of unions to negotiate piece rates, job evaluation systems, and productivity bonuses. Unions' negotiating power in this regard could not always be realized. The main problem for the unions was their lack of technical competence in negotiating issues such as piece rates and other aspects of work organization. Only consultation with workers on the shop floor could have provided the unions with the requisite technical knowledge.[12] But the structures that might have made possible such consultation did not yet exist. Thus the technical committees present in the workplace since 1966, although they included workers appointed by the union, were ineffective because they lacked a democratic structure for shop-floor consultation or participation. The committees, with their joint membership of management and union representatives, were also indicative of a trend in collective bargaining that ran counter to workers' control. This trend was toward the acceptance of binding contracts. The metal workers' unions were practically alone among the industrial union federations in rejecting the notion of binding contracts. The extension of collective bargaining, however, had tended to lessen confrontation and facilitated the growth of stable contractual relationships.

The workers' councils were unusual in extending the area of bargaining while bringing permanent confrontation into the workplace. The councils accepted no limitation on which topics could be brought up in negotiations.

However, labor tribunals have increasingly concerned themselves with the question of dismissals. The control of the courts has not been widely contested by the workers' movement, at least in the northern cities, where many court decisions have been favorable to dismissed workers.

The significance of the councils has not been just in the fact that they now confront the employer on an unlimited range of issues, but in that they now define the issues. An example is provided by bargaining on job classifications. Under the system of job evaluation, a different rate of pay was determined for every job. Minute differences in tasks would result in hundreds of different pay scales throughout the factory. Instead of bargaining with employers about how the various jobs should be evaluated, the councils demanded an end to this divisive system. In calling for flat-rate pay increases, the councils contested the system of merit payments. In the early 1970s, traditional concepts of skill were also brought into question; delegates demanded a system of automatic promotion within the factory, based on length of service, not skill. Linked to these platforms were the statements by workers that their health was not for sale. Workers insisted on improvements in work conditions, and the provision of job enrichment programs, refusing to accept mere monetary increases for the same conditions.

The above demands challenged the power of employers with regard to the work organization of the factory. At the same time, the movement also challenged the power of employers in the sphere of planned investments. In 1970, Fiat workers consented to spread an agreed reduction in working hours over a longer period in return for a commitment on the part of management to invest in southern Italy.[13] The agreements of later years laid out specific plans for this investment and also specified provisions for social infrastructure in the areas where the new plants were to be built.[14] In 1972 and 1973 Alfa Romeo workers also called for southern investments, contesting plans of management to expand production in the north. The 1972 struggle at Alfa Romeo was extremely bitter. The government saw an opportunity in a state-run concern to inflict a serious defeat on the workers' movement.[15] Luraghi, the president of Alfa Romeo, explained his tough stance by claiming that workers "want to take the instruments of production out of our hands; it is a problem which concerns not only our firm."[16] In this situation, the government's and Alfa Romeo's strategy was defeated. Changes took place in both the investment programs of the firm and the organization of work (promotion became automatic for most categories of workers). In other advanced sectors of the economy, similar demands contesting management prerogatives were being made. Thus in 1973, chemical workers called for tighter pollution control measures.[17]

From the challenge to management prerogatives in the workplace, it was a short step for the union confederations to launch a platform for social reforms at the national level. The union program, initiated in 1970, called for increased government investment in the south, in schools, transport, and other social infrastructure.[18] The program for social reforms may not have had the success for which unions hoped.[19] But it is clear that the program was strongly supported by the new democratic structures within the workplace. This support came in the form of strike action, and was most successfully carried out in the factories where the councils had their greatest strength.

The platforms that they advanced and their unitary structure in the workplace indicated that the councils were unified, class-based organizations. Elected by all workers within the factory, they were fully representative of all employees. This is not to say that ideological divisions did not exist within the councils. Indeed they did and still do. But, in most cases, the councils have been concerned about preserving a united front in negotiations with management. This unity has been easier to maintain as a result of the elimination of political office-holders from union positions. Such officials were given the choice of union or political loyalties.* They may still maintain their membership in both organizations, but they can only hold office in one.

Formal unity of the workers' movement has been achieved in the past. The 1944 Pact of Rome unified the entire labor movement under the banner of the CGIL. This unity, however, could not be maintained beyond the end of the decade. In the 1940s, arguments over the Marshall Plan and the political role of the union movement led first to the breaking away of Christian unionists and later of the Republicans, Social Democrats, and some Socialists. The cold-war atmosphere of the 1950s did not further the cause of union unity; the Christians formed their own confederation, the CISL; and the Republicans and Social Democrats formed the UIL; meanwhile the majority of unionists, mainly Communists but also some Socialists, remained in the CGIL.[20] The latter organization regularly defended the notion of unity, but it was not until the 1960s that some unified actions began to take place.[21] Effective unity, however, only came with the arrival of the workers' councils. That there have been some limits to this unity is because of the uneven strength of the councils throughout Italian industry.

Besides being unified, the councils also constituted a class-based movement. The councils, in fact, are an embryonic form of workers' power that is inimical to participation in management of the type that has taken place in Northern European nations. In the most militant councils in the Italian metalworking industry, workers have rejected, as noted earlier, the joint committees on technical conditions that included management as well as workers' representatives. The CGIL, of the major union confederations, because of its close

---

*On March 23, 1970, for instance, Novella, the former general secretary of the CGIL, resigned his union office in order to maintain his position as a Communist party deputy in parliament.

links to the Communist party, has generally opposed participationist ideologies. This was not always true of the other union confederations, and particularly the CISL with its strong Christian ethic. The trend of collective bargaining during the 1960s supported this ethic, but the strength of the CGIL ensured that participationist doctrines were never strong in Italy. A similar state of affairs existed in the French labor movement, where the principal confederation, the *Confédération générale du travail* (CGT), was also Communist dominated.

The councils expressed class interests in representing all workers within the factory, regardless of their particular ideological confictions. In taking control of the delegates' movement, the unions were obliged to abandon policies of representing only their members. This transition was no problem for the CGIL, which had always regarded itself as a voice of the working class. The metalworkers' federations of all three major unions had also developed into class-based unions in the 1960s. But for some union federations, the transition was more difficult.*

The assemblies, delegates, and councils that arrived in 1968 substantially altered the Italian system of industrial relations. Why did these changes take place? How, also, can their timing be explained?

AN EXPLANATION OF THE DEVELOPMENT OF WORKERS' COUNCILS

Among the major social changes that have taken place in Italy since the Second World War, four can be singled out as having an important effect on the workers' movement: the high rate of economic growth and the virtual elimination of unemployment; technical development in the firm, which resulted in a massive disqualification of the labor force in the major industries; the migration of millions of southern Italians to the northern factories; and finally, a considerable rejuvenation of union cadres making the unions more receptive to new ideas.

There is little doubt that workers' militancy in Italy during the postwar years was closely linked to cyclical trends in the economy. This is especially clear when examining the movements of the 1960s. Economic growth, therefore, was a permissive factor in the development of the councils, and helps explain the timing of their arrival. The years of the Italian economic miracle were from 1958 to 1962. Until this time, unemployment had remained at relatively high levels. By 1963, however, unemployment had fallen to a mere 2.6

---

*For those federations not representing workers in the advanced sectors of the economy, the transition to class action remains difficult at the time of this writing.

percent. The northern industrial regions felt the effects of a tight labor market most severely. The majority of new employment opportunities had been created in the north. With low unemployment in 1963, the unions were able to exert considerable contractual power in the firms.[22] This was the year in which major concessions were won on the level and scope of collective bargaining. Major salary increases were also achieved. The economic depression and rise in unemployment over the next two years tied the hands of the unions. Thus the 1966 national contracts were regarded by many as a step backward for the workers' movement.[23] Despite some hard-fought strikes in certain factories, the gains, particularly with regard to salary, were modest. By 1966, the economy, in the north, though not in the south, was on the move again. It was, therefore, in the context of an increasingly tight labor market that wildcat strikes broke out in 1968, and continued into the major movements of 1969 and the early 1970s. The employment figures of Alfa Romeo, one of the major arenas for the conflicts of the 1960s, provides an illustration of how much the large factories were affected by cyclical trends in the economy; between 1960 and 1963 employment increased by 42 percent from 7,578 to 10,772. Over the next three years, there was actually a decline in employment. These were years of ineffective union activity. Then from 1967 to 1971, employment increased by 80 per cent from 10,167 to 18,158.[24] The size of the plant, grouping together large numbers of workers, and the enormous expansion in employment served to sustain the conflicts of the late 1960s in which the workers' councils emerged.

While the cycles of economic growth determined the timing of strike activity, it was the manner in which growth was achieved that largely determined the organizational form of the struggles. Of particular importance in the expansion of employment in the major firms had been the change in work organization, which caused an enormous increase in the numbers of low-skilled production workers. The round of wage increases in 1963 highlighted some of the weaknesses of Italian capitalism. Wage increases in the more capital-intensive economies of Northern Europe had a much less severe effect than in the labor-intensive Italian economy. Italian industry suddenly found itself uncompetitive with others.[25] The solution for the most advanced sectors of the Italian economy was the rationalization of production and intensification of exploitation.

The example of Alfa Romeo is again instructive of what was taking place in the major firms. Until the early 1960s, the firm concentrated mainly on the production of luxury sports cars, and a high proportion of skilled craftsmen were employed in production. In 1962, the firm changed its model range to include family cars, built a new factory outside Milan, and considerably extended its assembly-line production. The introduction of more specialized and automatic machines reduced the requirement for skilled labor.[26] By 1971, only 16.1 percent of the work force was skilled. The skilled workers who remained were not employed in the production departments, but in the service and maintenance departments. Alternatively, a few were employed in specialist production departments. The main production departments, however, are today noticeable for their total absence of traditionally skilled workers. In other major firms, the transition to mass production may not have been so sudden. What was clear, however, was that the great expansion of production was being achieved with organizational methods that required massive increases in the numbers and proportions of low-skilled workers.

To understand the effect of the employment of low-skilled workers, it is first necessary to understand how their work conditions differed from those of other workers. The difference is in some respects one of degree. The low-skilled production worker, more than any other worker in the factory, lacks control over the tasks he carries out, the manner in which they might be accomplished, and the speed with which they are to be done. Surveillance and control by others in authority is constant. This control is achieved by strict discipline, the enforcement of production quotas, or the mechanical pacing of the production line. If the intellectual effort is low, the mental and physical effort is considerable. The work is strenuous and constant attention is required of the worker. Environmental conditions, including excessive noise, heat, dirt, fumes, and greasy floors, also contribute to the arduousness of the work. What is most important is that there is no mobility out of these positions. Since the job can be performed proficiently within a few hours, no skills are learned on the job. Besides, the skilled positions in the factory are of a technical nature. Most skilled workers, especially the younger ones, will have undergone at least two years of intensive course work, learning how to repair and set up the machines within a particular factory.[27] The low-skilled workers, effectively barred from apprenticeship schemes by their lack of formal education, faced the frustrating and daunting prospect of a lifetime on the line.

It was in large measure the frustrations of the low-skilled workers that led to the formation of the first factory councils and that gave the movement its particular character. The influx of low-skilled workers revealed how inadequate were the existing forms of representation within the factory. The provincial union officials who had responsibility for workplace negotiations were unable to understand the particular needs of low-skilled workers.* The union officials within the factory and the members of the internal commission, besides having no negotiating power, failed to express the exigencies of the low-skilled workers. The officials and internal commission members appeared to be drawn overwhelmingly from the ranks of skilled workers, and they tended to express the interests of this latter group. With no likelihood of promotion to the skilled

---

*Many union cadres have never worked in a factory. Their career is made within the territorial structures of the union.

positions, the low-skilled workers were hardly interested in programs from which they could not even benefit in the long term. There thus grew a crisis of faith between workers and unionists in the major factories.

In spontaneously forming workers' councils to express their interests, workers challenged not so much the union but the existing skill hierarchy of the factory, the system of job evaluation, and the methods of retribution. They also demanded job enrichment programs and improved working conditions. Many of the wildcat strikes in 1969 were over promotion to higher skill categories. In 1970, elimination of the lowest skill categories and automatic promotion for all workers were two principal elements in the strike platform. In 1969, in contrast to 1966, workers won flat-rate pay increases rather than percentage increases. These had the effect of lowering differentials between categories of workers, countering the previous trends produced by percentage increases.[28] These and other challenges to the organization of work by the councils were the means by which low-skilled workers (and others too as it turned out) liberated themselves from what could be aptly described as a prison factory.

While not overtly antiunion, except in isolated instances, it was clear that the unions had not encouraged the development of the movement. One worker at Alfa Romeo claimed that in 1969 "the only thing that the union was prepared to do was to prevent the struggle from developing any further."[29] This reserve of the unions allowed a number of left-wing political groups to play an active role in the leadership of the movement.* These groups were not concerned about observing traditional procedures of collective bargaining. They were active in encouraging the development of spontaneous and contestatory movements. The leftist groups had their greatest success in those large factories where management repression had been most severe and where the unions were, in consequence, weak. Such was the case at Fiat where, until 1969, the largest union in the factory was one of class collaboration (SIDA).† The CGIL, the principal class-based union, was virtually absent. Spontaneity in the movements at Fiat was more apparent than in other firms.[30] In Alfa Romeo, where the CGIL had remained dominant, the leftist groups exerted somewhat less influence. This eventually meant that the workers' councils that emerged were composed of many active unionists.

It should not be forgotten that the workers in the northern factories who spontaneously formed shop-floors councils were for the most part southern migrants. The period of economic expansion from 1958 to 1962 saw the first

---

*The principal radical groups active in the factory have been *Lotta Continua, Avanguardia Operaia, Il Manifesto,* and *Assemblea Autonoma.*

†SIDA (*Sindacato dell'Industria dell'Automobile*) was formed in 1958 as a breakaway group from the Turin CISL.

massive migration of southern Italians to northern industry. The latter also became increasingly reliant on southern labor for its expansion. In previous years, southerners had been attracted abroad rather than to the north.[31] The north, for its part, relied on migrant labor supplies from local provinces within the northern regions or from the northeastern part of the country, around the Veneto region. By 1962, however, over half of all migrants to Milan came from the south. By 1969, the figure was over 90 percent. Natural increase and older migration flows continued to meet certain labor needs during the 1960s, but these labor needs were increasingly in the tertiary sector of the economy. The needs of industry, on the other hand, were met almost exclusively by southerners. They were young, resilient, and willing, and their lack of skill was unimportant to industry. They came to dominate in the industrial sectors of the economy, and particularly in the least pleasant low-skilled jobs that had been vacated by indigenous workers and earlier migrants from the north and northeast. Southern migrants were most heavily employed in the metalworking industries and construction sites. By the late 1960s, it is fair to say that most of the low-skilled workers on the assembly lines of the major northern factories were southern immigrants.[32] A survey at Alfa Romeo in 1971 revealed, in fact, that southern migrants filled 76 percent of the low- and semi-skilled jobs.[33]

What effect did migrants have? For some observers, such as G. Bianchi, R. Aglieta, and P. Merli-Brandini,[34] southern immigrants had an important effect on the struggles, particularly in such cities as Turin. The southern migrants' traditions of independence supposedly set them apart from other workers. Dissatisfactions with both the workplace and living conditions in the urban community became the frustrations of a social group. The conditions of migrants politicized the struggles, and turned them into antisystem movements.

The above view of the role of migrants risks ignoring the fact that, for the migrants who did participate in forming the councils, there were many more who played no active role. In the construction industry, for instance, a major employer of souther migrant labor, there was no spontaneous development of shop-floor councils. The migrants in the construction industry were no better off in terms of their integration into the urban environment than were migrants in the metalworking industries. The differences lay in the types of firms in which they were employed, and could be observed for nonmigrants as well as migrants from the south.[35]

The point about the independence of southern migrants can also be misunderstood. During the 1960s, there were certainly a number of southern migrants arriving in the north who had been active in land occupations and farm-laborer struggles in the south. But despite the pride with which the migrants view the radical traditions of the southern peasants, few had personal experience of such struggles. One southerner, a delegate in Alfa Romeo's foundry and active in the 1969 movements in the factory, noted that "most of the workers who came here had not been involved in the struggles of southern Italy, and certainly did not know how to express themselves politically when they first arrived."[36] The evidence points, therefore, to the political inexperience of the southern migrants during the early part of the 1960s.

The conversion of a politically illiterate group into a leading element of a united class movement testifies to the harsh realities of the modern factories in which the southern migrants came to the fore. The experience of other countries in Europe, however, suggests that migrants might delay the development of conflicts even in the large factories. In France and Germany, for instance, migrants come from abroad, from several different ethnic groups, and many are only temporary settlers. These factors hinder the development of class or even ethnic solidarity. In contrast, the migration in Italy is distinct. Migrants come from internal regions. They thus have full political rights. They have also tended to become permanent settlers. Dreams of a return to the land distract few migrants from the reality of the workplace. Finally, migrants are from a single geographical area. Under these circumstances, and with migrants constituting the majority of employees in the large factories, ethnic solidarity could build up and serve as a strong basis for the 1969 movements. As a social group feeling discriminated against both in the factory and the urban environment, the migrants could also be expected to turn away from traditional organizations, developing their own structures of representation.

In many countries, during periods of intense strike activity, embryonic structures have arisen reflecting shop-floor democracy. Seldom, however, have the structures survived beyond an initial period of enthusiasm. Thus in France in May 1968 and later in the early 1970s, a series of strikes took place in which shop-floor committees in the form of strike committees directed all aspects of the conflicts.* These committees did not survive. The Italian experience is unusual in that the workers' councils not only survived, but were also extended throughout Italian industry. Bruno Trentin is surely correct when he writes:

> The main reason for the affirmation, the diffusion, and above all the survival of the workers' councils can lie only in the capacity that the union movement, despite its great limitations and delays, had for internalizing the crisis of the old structures, the criticisms and protests of younger generations of workers, the stimuli of the students' movement, and the arguments over old canons of grievances and old relations of faith between workers and union leaders.[37]

The metamorphosis of the unions was remarkable. Skeptics can argue that in a system of competitive voluntary unionism, the unions had no choice but to keep

---

*The strikes in the early 1970s included those at Renault-Le Mans in 1971 and Renault-Billancourt in 1973. Both these strikes involved the formation of autonomous strike committees by low-skilled workers.

pace with the fastest runners. There is, however, strong evidence to suggest that major elements in the union movement, though not the entire movement, were favorable to the developments that took place. The stability of the new structures was aided by their smooth integration into the union movement.

In the 1950s, the union confederations acknowledged the need for further decentralization of the bargaining process. As early as 1953, the CISL had broken with the notion of confederal agreements and called for salaries to be negotiated at the plant level. This change in policy on the part of the CISL did not signify subversion by radicals. Quite the contrary. The CISL saw itself as an American-style union. With its Christian, participationist ideals, it believed that salary increases should be tied to productivity.[38] This type of policy could only be successful if salaries were negotiated at plant level. In calling for plant-level accords, the CISL also hoped to reinforce its position in the workplace at the expense of the CGIL, which was already dominant. The very success of this strategy soon led the CGIL to accept plant-level bargaining as part of its overall strategy. The CGIL did poorly in the internal commission elections of 1954–55, and the change in policy was officially announced at its Fourth Congress in Rome in 1956.

During the 1960s, after the institutionalization of plant-level bargaining in 1963, the main impetus for change came not from the union confederations, which saw any further decentralization as removing control still further from their hands, but from the industrial union federations, and particularly the metalworkers' unions, the *Federazione Italiana Operai Metalmeccanici* (FIOM [CCIL]), the *Federazione Italiana Metalmeccanici* (FIM [CISL]), and the *Unione Italiana Lavoratori Metalmeccanici* (UILM [UIL]). In 1966, open conflict of views was shown between the three federations and their confederations over the question of decentralization of bargaining.[39] That the metalworkers' federations had been able to move toward a more democratic and decentralized view of bargaining was because of a considerable rejuvenation of their cadres, which had taken place during the 1960s.[40] The change within the CGIL was especially remarkable, for centralized organization of the workers' movement had long been regarded as the best guardian of working-class solidarity. Nevertheless, when the councils arrived, the major elements in all three unions, led by the metalworkers' federations, were quickly able to see the possibilities that existed for the development of a powerful and unified workers' movement. Regaining control of the movement was not always easy for the unions, especially in firms such as Fiat where the councils had been antiunionist in character. Overall, though, a large proportion of the new delegates were unionists, and this made the transition somewhat easier. In extending the councils to other firms where they had not developed spontaneously, the unions were aided by the new 1970 Workers' Charter; this Charter, passed with the backing of the Socialist Party and left-wing elements among the Christian Democrats, both members of the governing coalition, gave the unions (as we noted) a legal right of existence in all firms with more than 15 employees.

WORKERS' COUNCILS AND THE ITALIAN LABOR MOVEMENT: SUCCESS OR FAILURE?

How does one judge the success or failure of the workers' councils? In terms of their staying power, and also of the momentous changes in Italian industrial relations, they must be regarded as a success. But to what extent have the ideals of democratic participation and a unified class movement been maintained? The experience of the councils is somewhat uneven. Councils have played a vastly different role according to the type of firm in which they are situated. At the national level, union leaders can be pleased with the renewed strength and vigor of the union movement. The unions have never had so many members and have never been so well organized in terms of the numbers of full-time union officials. But organic unity at the national level is not being achieved (and may never be achieved) as quickly as many had hoped. Open divisions within two of the confederations are apparent. Preoccupations with running the day-to-day business of the union and coordinating its policies with political parties has led the union leadership to drift away from close consultation with the shop floor. For example, the union leadership's tacit support of the 1976 Andreotti government's austerity plan was called into question by a series of October strikes in northern factories, protesting the government's measures. That the union leadership hastily changed its policy as a consequence of the strikes augurs well for the democratic ideals of the movement. But it does show the tendency for the union leadership to become increasingly divorced from the shop floor.

What accounts for the continuing weaknesses in the workers' movement as it has evolved since 1969? Two factors, stemming from deep divisions within Italian society, appear to be important. First, there are the divisions between different types of firms and workers, those who are in the modern sector, those in the traditional sector, and those in government agencies. Not all workers perceive themselves as having similar interests. These perceptions are often deeply rooted in their industrial experience. Second, and related to the first issue, there is the stark division between north and south in Italy. The success of the neo-fascists in the southern cities during the early 1970s points to a failure of the workers' movement to develop unified and solid support among the working class.

The workers' councils developed, as we saw, in the large modern factories where the rationalization of production had involved the employment of significant numbers of low-skilled workers. In all other firms, the workers' councils were imposed by the unions. In these other firms, the levels of unionization or strike activity were often low or nonexistent. It is to the credit of the unions that in many of these small and medium-sized firms a successful union movement was able to develop. But there have been limitations to this development. In many small firms, for instance, the workers have little contractual power. High mobility of labor and fragmentation of the productive structure into large numbers of small firms hinders the development of a militant workers' movement.

Workers in the large northern firms are also distinct in the type of interests they express. They constitute a modern industrial proletariat—low-skilled labor, alienated in the world of machinery, and concentrated in large units of production. It was the very fact that they saw no possibility of advancement in the factory that prompted them to express a series of egalitarian demands and challenge the existing work organization. Such contestation has not been apparent in, for instance, the construction industry. In the latter industry, workers raise grievances about the work conditions, but because of the possibility of on-the-job training, even low-skilled workers can appreciate the possibilities of career advancement. There is, therefore, little direct challenge to work organization, the system of qualifications, and the pay hierarchy.

While workers in a large number of traditional firms have been integrated into the union movement, or at least are sympathetic toward its goals, this is not the case with some public service employees. They have been antagonized by a union movement that is egalitarian in its aims. Their chief concern, in fact, is to retain their hard-earned status and pay differentials. These groups, who number among them airline pilots and magistrates, have pursued strike action for their own goals within autonomous unions. The strength of autonomous unions appears to have increased, and they have also become far more militant in their actions.

The corporatism of autonomous groups within and outside the labor movement has been one of the chief preoccupations of the union leadership, and particularly the CGIL. For the latter, it is proof of the dangers of too much decentralization, and means have been sought to correct these corporatist trends. One means is to develop the strength of workers' councils in all firms, thus ensuring that no particular group of workers has a disproportionately strong voice. The unions have attempted to follow such a policy.[41] In conjunction with this move, they have also initiated zonal councils to strengthen the movement at the territorial level. The zonal councils are, in fact, the key to the unions' anticorporatism drive. Luciano Lama, the general secretary of the CGIL, noted in 1973:

> Today we need to generalize these structures (the councils) . . . and bring them outside the factory so that they become the unitary base at the territorial level of the various industries and of the horizontal

structures of the union. . . . There are branches of the economy and work-place where there are no councils and where perhaps there never will be. . . . but even these groups of workers should have their representatives, and in the zonal councils their participation can be assured.[42]

As well as combating corporatism, the zonal councils might also have served the confederations in moving the class struggle outside the factory to a point where the union leadership could better maintain its overall direction of the movement. It is, however, too soon to say how successfully the zonal councils have combated corporatism. At this juncture, it seems that the mainstay of the zonal councils are the very groups of workers who built up powerful workers' councils in the workplace. The zonal councils, therefore, have not as yet been an effective means of integrating backward sectors of the working class into the workers' movement.

Even in modern large-scale factories, examples of corporatism exist, so it is not surprising to see how powerful the divisions and differences can be among separate firms. In Alfa Romeo, for instance, corporatist struggles were in evidence in 1973 among the foundry workers, who, unlike all other workers in the factory, were prepared to accept pay increases rather than improvements in working conditions. With the vast majority of delegates in the factory council opposing their actions, the foundry workers could not be convinced to change their views. The problems of unity at plant level have been magnified at the national level. In 1972, important factions within the CISL and the UIL opposed organic unity of the confederations. These factions consisted of union federations in some of the more traditional industries. The metalworkers' union, on the other hand, achieved its own organic unity among its three federations before the formal unity of the confederations, and despite the reserves of the latter.[43] Thus the readiness of workers to organize in a unified class-based movement depended very much on the types of industries in which they were employed.

If the workers' councils developed first in the major factories, they were also a phenomenon of northern Italy. In southern Italy, there are few plants of the type in which workers' councils might have developed. The councils had, therefore, to be imposed throughout the south by the unions. The results have not been unfavorable. Between 1968 and 1972, there was a 50 percent increase in union membership in the south. This increase in membership, however, occurred mainly in industry, where union membership increased by over 90 percent. In other sectors of the economy, notably agriculture and public employment, there was relative stagnation. Further, the horizontal organization of the unions remained weak. In 1972, there were local offices in only about 20 percent of southern communes, and there was a heavy reliance on individual unionists prepared to take on organizational work.[44] The lack of success of the unions' programs for social reforms no doubt also disenchanted many southern workers. In any event, in 1972 it appeared to be Fascist groups, among whom was the Fascist workers' union, *Confederacione Italiana dei Sindacati Nazionali dei Lavoratori* (CISNAL), who held the initiative in the south, gaining large percentages of the popular vote in elections in southern cities. In 1975 and 1976, the boot appears to be on the other foot. Support for Fascist groups has declined, owing probably to the latter's own excesses. At the same time, the Communist party made its largest electoral gains of those years in southern cities. This suggests that the solutions proposed by the left have finally struck a chord among the working population in the south.*

That the formation of the workers' councils has marked a major change in the political role of the Italian working class is undoubted. What is less certain is the permanency of the changes that have taken place. In this last section, the focus has been less on how effectively the councils operate at the level of the firm, but more on how they have evolved as a national expression of working-class interest. It is their performance at this level that will eventually determine the strength of the movement. We have noted that the workers' councils do suffer serious weaknesses owing to the basic structure of Italian society. The unions and political parties of the left, however, are also aware of these weaknesses, and considerable efforts have been mounted to maintain a unified movement. That the movement is still relatively unified despite the divisions and despite a major economic recession is a major achievement. The next few years will show if any further progress can be made.

NOTES

1. For estimate of costs, see Gino Giugni, "Recent trends in collective bargaining in Italy," *International Labour Review* 104, no. 4, October 1971, p. 320; for the previous figure of percentage of grievances satisfied, see Gino Giugni, "L'automne chaud syndical," *Sociologie du Travail* 13 (April-June 1971): 163.

2. For specific accounts and documentation of the 1968 movement at Pirelli, see Ellida Pietropaolo, "Pirelli '68; contro l'organizzazione capitalistica del lavoro e per la democrazia diretta," in *Classe, Due, Le Lotte Operaie del 1968-69* Dedalo Libri, 1970), pp. 67-90; "Le lotte alla Pirelli: Documenti," in ibid., pp. 93-132, is a reproduction of union and shop-floor tracts from the strike; see also Fabrizio d'Agostini, *La Condizione Operaia e i Consigli di Fabbrica* (Rome: Editori Riuniti, 1974), passim., for a series of interviews with participants in the Pirelli conflicts.

3. On July 3, 1972, a federative pact was signed by the three major union confederations (CGIL, CSIL, and UIL). A series of articles and reports on union unity is contained in *Quaderni di Rassegna Sindacale* 9, no. 29 (March-April 1971).

---

*Certainly, the Communist party is now proclaiming the success of its southern strategy.

4. On the changing role of unions in Italian politics, see Alessandro Pizzorno, "Les syndicats et l'action politique," *Sociologie du Travail* 13 (April-June 1971): 115–40; see also Peter R. Weitz, "Labor and politics in a divided movement: the Italian case," *Industrial and Labor Relations Review* 28, no. 2 (January 1975): 226–42.

5. Giugni, "Recent trends in collective bargaining in Italy," op. cit., p. 317.

6. See F. Drago et al., *Movimento sindacale e contrattazione collettiva* (Milan: Franco Angeli, 1971), pp. 207–85.

7. Gino Giugni, "Recent developments in collective bargaining in Italy," *International Labour Review* 91, no. 4 (April 1965): 273–91; writing in the middle 1960s, Giugni considered the introduction of articulated bargaining to be a revolutionary change in the Italian system of industrial relations. He certainly did not anticipate the far more radical changes of the late 1960s.

8. The proportion of plant-level accords signed by internal commissions diminished from 51 percent in 1953–57, to 36.7 percent in 1960, to 13 percent in 1968, and to 7 percent in 1970; see Bernadette Mauerhofer-Mourize, *Les Syndicats Italiens*, Notes et Etudes Documentaires, nos. 4068–4069, La Documentation Francaise (March 15, 1974), p. 40, ff. 149.

9. An internal commission could only be elected in firms with more than 40 employees. It was composed of three members in firms with 41 to 175 employees, five members in those with 176 to 500 employees. The maximum number of members was 21 for firms with more than 40,000 employees. The larger the plant, therefore, the less adequate was the representation. Under these circumstances, many departments within the factory had no one to speak for them in meetings of the internal commission; see ibid., p. 41.

10. Such was the case, for instance, at Alfa Romeo (Portello and Arese); see Armando Sandretti, *Lotte all'Alfa Romeo 1970–1972* (Milan: Tesi di Laurea, Universita degli Studi Sociali di Milano, Facolta di Scienze Politiche, 1971-72).

11. The number of nonunionists in the workers' councils appears to have diminished. Even in the most radical factory environments, they rarely made up more than 10 or 20 percent of the delegates; see G. Bianchi, R. Aglieta, and P. Merli-Brandini, *I Delegati Operai: Ricerca su Nuove Forme di Rappresentanze Operaie*, Quaderni ISRIL, (Rome: Coines, December 1970). The presence, however small, of nonunionists in a negotiating capacity confirms that contractual power rested with the shop floor, not the unions.

12. It was for this reason that the joint committees were initially formed. The current union position, however, goes further than calling for joint committees. It is argued that only workers directly experiencing work conditions in the factory can fully understand how their health and general well-being (for example, degree of anxiety) is affected by work conditions. See Gastone Marri, "La riforma sanitaria come partecipazione," *Rassegna Sindacale* 18, no. 232 (March 26–April 9, 1972): 15–18.

13. Giugni, "Recent trends in collective bargaining in Italy," op. cit., p. 323.

14. "Il detonatore Fiat per lo sviluppo del Sud," *Rinascita* 30, no. 44 (November 9, 1973).

15. Leonardo Banfi, "Dove vuole arrivare il padrone pubblico," *Rassegna Sindacale* 18, no. 230 (February 20–March 5, 1972): 15–16; Bruno Ugolini, "L'operazione centro-destra vista dalle fabbriche," *Rinascita* 29, no. 3 (January 21, 1972): 10.

16. Banfi, op. cit., p. 15.

17. Fernando di Giulio, "Per l'unita sindacale," *Rinascita* 30, no. 46 (November 23, 1973): 1.

18. On reforms and strike action in support of reforms, see *Quaderni di Rassegna Sindacale* 10, no. 36 (May-June 1972), "Sindacate e Riforme"; see also various issues of *Rassegna Sindacale*, Quindicinale della CGIL, 1970–74.

19. This was noted by Luciano Lama, general secretary of the CGIL; see Fabrizio D'Agostini, "Colloquio con Luciano Lama: lo stato del movimento," *Rinascita* 29, no. 7 (February 18, 1972): 8. Lama says that greater coordination is needed between factory and territorial struggles. He also notes the greater combativity of workers in the large northern factories such as Fiat, Alfa Romeo, and Pirelli.

20. For a history of the Italian labor movement, see Daniel Horowitz, *The Italian Labor Movement* (Cambridge: Harvard University Press, 1962).

21. See Mauerhofer-Mourize, op. cit., pp. 46–50.

22. On the effects of the labor market on workers' militancy, see Massimo Paci, *Mercato del Lavoro e Classi Sociali in Italia* (Bologna: Il Mulino, 1974), especially chap. 6.

23. See Giugni, "Recent trends in collective bargaining in Italy," op. cit., p. 312.

24. Figures from Sandretti, op. cit., app. 2a.

25. Paci, op. cit., especially chap. 3.

26. For an account of the technical innovations at Alfa Romeo, see Istituto Gramsci, Scienze e Organizazzione del Lavoro, "Alfa Romeo: Comunicazione al Convegno," mimeographed (Turin, June 8–10, 1973).

27. On the mobility of different categories of workers in Italy, see Paci, op. cit., chap. 6.

28. For the specific forms of struggle in the major northern factories, comparing their experience with those of more traditional industries, see Martin Slater, "Migration and Workers' Conflicts in Western Europe" (Ph.D. diss., Massachusetts Institute of Technology, 1976), chap. 6.

29. Interview with CGIL foundry delegate, Alfa Romeo (Arese), May 7, 1975.

30. See Bianchi et al., op. cit.; see also a shorter article in French by the same authors, "Les delegues ouvriers: nouvelles formes de representation ouvriere," *Sociologie du Travail* 8 (April-June 1971): 178–90.

31. On the development of southern migration flows to the north and abroad, see Giovanni Mottura and Enrico Pugliese, "Mercato del lavoro e caratteristiche della emigrazione italiana nell'ultimo quindicennio," in *Sviluppo economico italiano e forza-lavoro*, ed. P. Leon and M. Marocchi (Padua: Marsilio Editori, 1973); Claudio Francia, *Il Fenomeno Migratorio in Italia* (Rome: Ente Italiano di Servizio Sociale. 1967).

32. For an account in English of southern migration to northern Italy, see Slater, op. cit., chap. 3.

33. Scuola di Formazione in Sociologia, "Gli operai comuni all'Alfa Romeo" (Milan, *Classe, Otto*), pp. 31–191.

34. Bianchi et al., op. cit.

35. See Slater, op. cit., chap. 5.

36. Interview with CGIL foundry delegate, Alfa Romeo (Arese), May 7, 1975.

37. Trentin, "Introduzione," in D'Agostini, op. cit., p. xii.

38. See Mauerhofer-Mourize, op. cit., pp. 25–29.

39. Giugni, "L'automne chaud syndical," op. cit., p. 169; Francois Sellier, "Les transformations de la negociation collective et de l'organisation syndicale en Italie," *Sociologie du Travail* 8 (April-June 1971): 150.

40. Giugni, "L'automne chaud syndical," op. cit.

41. Agostino Marianetti, "Le stutture di base e il sindacato unitario," *Rassegna Sindacale* 18, no. 227 (January 9–23, 1972): 5.

42. Luciano Lama, speech to Eighth Congress of the CGIL, Bari, July 2–7, 1973, reported in *Rassegna Sindacale* 19, no. 267–68 (July 15, 1973): 11.

43. At a meeting in January 1972 at Ariccia, the general councils of the FIOM, FIM, and UILM determined to proceed with their own planned unification for October 1972, despite the delays at the confederal level; see Sesa Tato, "Metallurgici: l'unita della

categoria sotto il segno dei delegati," *Rassegna Sindacale* 18, no. 227 (January 9–23, 1972): 14.

44. See Aldo Giunti, "Quanti siamo: inchiesta dibattito sul sindacato nel Mezzogiorno." *Rassegna Sindacale* 18, no. 248 (November 12–16, 1972): 8-9.

CHAPTER

7

PARADOXES OF
WORKER PARTICIPATION
G. David Garson

Worker participation in West European management is neither socialism nor simply one more human relations device adopted by management to manipulate workers. It is at once a subject of deep-felt idealism and cynicism. It is apt to be discussed by administrative technocrats as well as by philosophers. Perhaps no single development in the 1960 and 1970s has been publicized among West European businessmen as such an imminent danger to the capitalist order. Yet throughout Western Europe the strongest opponents of worker participation have been the Communist parties. Seeming paradoxes like these abound.

In this chapter we shall examine five of these paradoxes. First, why is it that the movement for workers' control, which sounds so revolutionary to North American ears, has found the poorest reception in countries with the most radical labor movements? Second, why is it that the rise of the workers' control movement has corresponded to the rise of European prosperity after the war, when radicals have asserted that prosperity makes capitalism better able to resist working-class radicalism? Third, why, when national traditions have so clearly favored voluntaristic collective bargaining, has it been possible for the workers' control movement to have such success, given its heavy emphasis on legal institutionalization of workers' rights? Fourth, why is it that the current period of economic problems has not caused industrial democracy to wither away in favor of bread-and-butter issues? Finally, why is it, given the similarities of all capitalist democracies, that North American workers have not followed the example of West European unions in demanding an increased, direct say in management?

The answers to these questions help to explain why worker participation has a potential to become something that is neither socialism nor simply capitalism with human relations management. The debate over capitalism versus socialism has long accustomed us to think in falsely dichotomous terms.

Worker participation, an old idea but in terms of practice still an infant, contains the seed ideas of self-management as a world order alternative to capitalism or socialism.[1] But it also contains the potential to collapse back into being a minor variant of either of these two world orders. What limited insight exists as to the future of workers' control may be gained by a closer examination of the paradoxes surrounding this movement.

WHY HAS THE MOVEMENT FOR WORKERS' PARTICIPATION FARED LEAST WELL IN COUNTRIES WITH RADICAL UNIONISM?

Indicative of Communist antipathy toward the movement for workers' control was the reaction of the *Confédération général du travail* (CGT) toward the 1973–74 strike at the LIP watch factory in Besançon, France. As Bornstein and Fine note in Chapter 5 of this volume, the Communist unions were unsympathetic to the strike from the outset. Though it was hailed internationally as a major labor uprising for workers' control, with workers taking over and running the factory without management, the Communist union (the CGT) was angered by the view that worker self-management might advance under capitalism. Better, they argued, to understand clearly that workers' control can be achieved only under socialism. At present worker militance must be channeled into confrontation with management, not collaboration with management or acceptance of managerial responsibilities. Accordingly the CGT did not support occupying the factory, resuming production, or holding general worker assemblies to decide on matters of production, sales, and strike strategy. And the CGT would have nothing to do at all with the many intellectuals, journalists, and activists who rallied to support the ideal of worker self-management at LIP.

Speaking of the prospects for workers' participation in France, David Jenkins noted, "Recently, employers have been changing with the times, while the unions have not."[2] For example, in 1974, prodding by the government led the major employers' confederation (CNPF) to propose a quite progressive set of reforms. These included decentralization of supervision, changes in work organization, job redesign to reduce monotony, more flexible hours, and other changes often associated with a participatory approach to management. In 1975 the unions rejected this and the government has temporarily dropped the proposals. When the Sudreau Commission then brought forth a report containing an even more comprehensive package of participatory reforms (for example, redesigning assembly lines, voting seats for worker representatives on company boards) it was rejected out of hand by the CGT as a "reform gimmick." In this the CGT was simply paralleling the Europeanwide opposition of Communist unions to the codetermination model of workers' participation.

Communist opposition to workers' control under capitalism is based on Leninism. Lenin insisted that the introduction of workers' control was possible only when five conditions had been met: nationalization of the banks, nationalization of monopolies, abolition of commercial secrecy, amalgamation of industrialists, merchants, and employers generally, and compulsory organization of citizens into consumers' societies.[3] In this context workers' control of production could be subject to people's control of the economy.

A very different reality lies beneath the rhetoric, however, In fact, the Communist countries have adopted industrial reforms analogous in general intent to Western participatory management techniques. And even in capitalist countries with strong Communist labor movements, industry is evolving in the direction of greater workers' participation.

Contrary to the rhetorical assertion that workers' participation will necessarily be profoundly different under socialism, industrial reforms in Communist countries have had a similar general scope and nature. The Soviet model of industrial relations is characterized by a complex network of worker committees and productivity meetings, and capped by a union council.[4] In Bulgaria enterprises are headed by economic committees supervised by the unions. These committees endorse principles of remuneration, veto illegal management activities, and pass on changes affecting working conditions. In Rumania enterprises are directed by comanagement committees composed of management, union, and worker representatives. In addition, a general meeting of workers has the power to supervise management. Since 1945 Poland has had a system of worker production councils very similar to the works councils established in various West European nations at the same time. Similarly in Czechoslovakia, a system of factory councils was established at the war's end. These councils, formed from a plan of the Central Council of Trade Unions, participate in hiring, firing, introduction of new technology, and similar policies; they offer suggestions for improvement of production; and they attempt to hold management responsible to general laws and government regulations pertaining to work. In Hungary worker control commissions have rights to management information, similar to their West European counterparts, and, also like them, consult with management in certain decisions affecting the enterprise. While one may argue that the Communist workers' participation organs are simply manipulated by the party, the evidence for this charge is quite analogous to similar contentions that in Western Europe the works councils are manipulated by management or by the unions. Overall, the intent and limited scope of worker participation is quite similar.*

---

*The Chinese model is somewhat different. Since the West European Communist parties take the Soviet bloc system as a model, however, the Chinese example is not discussed here.

Even in capitalist nations, with strong Communist labor movements, limited forms of workers' participation in management have been making headway. Though they are not as extensive as the West German codetermination system, it is quite invalid to assume that West European-style industrial participation is making no headway in such countries. In both Italy and France, the major countries with strong Communist unions, the opposite is true.

Superficially Italy might seem to be an unfavorable milieu for the development of a workers' control movement. The dominant force in working-class politics, the Communist party of Italy, has traditionally rejected workers' direct control in favor of channeling workers' struggles through union and party demands. Codetermination is rejected in the strongest possible terms. At the other end of the spectrum, Italian management has been paternalistic at best and dogmatically hierarchical at worst. Until the 1970s Italian managers showed virtually no interest in job humanization experiments, for example. And workers themselves were confronted with the negative example of meaningless pseudo-participation in the works councils (*commissioni interne d'azienda*), established in 1963 and extended in 1966. These councils served only as transmission belts for management and union information. They were devoid of power and their existence tended to discredit proposals for direct worker participation. Furthermore, the workers' movement as a whole lacked a strong tradition of shop-floor democracy. Italian collective bargaining had been among the most centralized in Europe. Regional bodies played little role, let alone local workers' organizations.

Today, Italy displays a dense network of shop-floor-level labor organizations whose struggles for workers' interests rival in scope those of any labor movement in the world. How did this happen so rapidly, and does it provide a clear alternative to codetermination?

In 1960 the center-right cabinet of Tambroni was ousted from power. This opened a period of raised expectations and new political strategies. For its part, the Communist party began moving toward a new popular front.[5] A revolutionary fringe became more active. This periphery was expressed in the journal *Quaderni Rossi* and in various local labor activist groups that were to unite as *Potere Operaio* in 1967 or as *Lotta Continua* in 1969. These in turn drew upon the influx of more radical workers from the south. These men and women came from agricultural communities with traditions of rural radicalism.[6]

At the same time the pattern of rigidly centralized collective bargaining began to break down in the 1960s, starting with the move of the engineering unions toward a contract providing for plant-level negotiations on details of collective agreements. Though supposedly limited by a no-strike provision, this constraint was ignored in practice. As a result grassroots union militancy grew in importance. This tendency was accelerated by a shift in policy of the Communist labor confederation (CGIL), whose new strategy emphasized decentalization. This new grassroots strategy served to build factory delegate councils that were the organizational basis for union mergers and a rapprochement between the CGIL and its Christian Democratic counterpart (CISL).

The rebirth of a decentralized labor movement, moribund since World War II, was aided greatly by the social crisis of 1969. This crisis was marked by intense social movement activity including mass strikes, occupations of factories and schools, rent strikes, widespread absenteeism, and sabotage, followed by waves of arrests and political repression.

Although revolutionary groups viewed the crisis as a prelude to revolution, the Communists sought to harmonize institutionalized relationships with the newly emerged delegate councils and other grassroots organs. By one estimate, by 1974 some 60,000 worker delegates were organized into 6,000 delegate councils.[7] These new organs have already largely displaced the internal commissions of the 1960s. In addition, union leaders have created zone councils as higher-level organs for coordinating labor struggles. In essence, the zone committees have functioned to support reform efforts of the union centrals without much possibility of rank-and-file intervention.

Critics of the Communist party have charged that the new delegate councils and zone committees are being undermined by reformist union and party groups. On the other hand, while in principle confined to a shop-steward role, worker delegates at Fiat and elsewhere have in practice used their positions as a cover for activities in direct labor struggles. This covert function has been critical to the spread of the council movement in Italy.

Employers have been forced to accept delegate council committees composed in many cases of activists as well as union and party leaders. On this basis higher levels of union organization have been able to assert unprecedented influence in collective bargaining. In spring, 1974, for example, Fiat negotiations resulted in a contract that contained provisions on location of investment (more to go to the south) and changes in the basic plan of production (increasing public transport). These achievements indicate a scope of workers' influence well beyond that of the West German codetermination model.

The Italian strategy of union militancy has not, however, led to a clear alternative to participation of the codetermination sort. It has, to be sure, precluded worker representatives on corporate boards. But it has also promoted profound changes in Italian labor relations, which draw Italy closer to the German example when one looks below the level of rhetoric.

Italian management opinion is shedding its traditional paternalism in favor of a more participative managerial style, as in other countries more directly influenced by codetermination. Italian opinion surveys show, for example, that employers increasingly see improving working conditions, encouraging employee participation, and granting more decision-making responsibility as critical to attracting and keeping an efficient labor force.[8] A June 1976 interview with Agnelli, managing director of Fiat, for instance, elicited views along these lines. Agnelli stated that Italian management must encourage full involvement and participation of all segments of society; only a pattern of consultation and co-operative decision making could enable a return to more productive management in Italy, he stated.[9]

Similarly, unions such as the Italian metalworkers' union have begun demanding management consult with unions on major decisions. The Fiat contracts have been a national example in this direction. Though labor-management relations are still acrimonious in Italy and bear the burden of class-struggle rhetoric, a different reality is emerging beneath this surface. With the increasing control exerted by the Communist unions over the factory delegate councils, the shift toward participative management among employers, the increasing willingness of the government to intervene in labor-management relations, and the expanding scope of national collective bargaining, differences between the Italian system and codetermination have become obscure. As Jenkins has noted, the effect of Italian labor relations in similar to that of codetermination even if unions condemn board representation and other symbols of the West German model.[10]

A similar pattern exists in France. There the Communist CGT has rejected the codetermination model of workers' participation with equal vehemence. But in spite of the aftermath of the social crisis of May 1968, here too a different reality lies just below the surface. Ironically the events of May 1968 augmented the role of the moribund works councils, which had been created at the end of World War II. The unions were given official recognition within enterprise representative bodies in December 1968. By 1972 unionists held over 50 percent of the seats on such groups.[11] A 1969 national collective agreement required employers to consult with the works councils in advance of proposed layoffs. Legislation in 1971 extended the councils' functions to worker training. And on top of this expansion of the works councils has come board representation of workers. Legislation in 1972 has allowed four nonvoting workers to sit on corporate boards. And in February 1975, the Sudreau Commission recommended workers hold one-third of seats on supervisory boards. Along with this has come a striking shift in management opinion in the direction of support for workers' participation in management.[12] Though union resistance to the codedetermination model continues, the movement toward codetermination-like practices has been the major development of French labor relations since 1968.

That workers' control (in the sense of codetermination) is weakest in the countries with the greatest degree of radical (Communist) unionism is thus not a paradox at all. In actual labor relations practices Italy as well as West Germany, France as well as Scandinavia, are moving in the direction of greater workers' participation in management within the context of limited overall power. The greatest difference comes in the symbols of the codetermination model, especially board representation, but the actual substance of workers' influence is not as much at variance. If anything, the scope of decisions affected may indeed be great in a country marked by radical unionism (as in Italy). This reconciliation of the seeming paradox requires an understanding that workers' actual control cannot be equated with any given institutional form, whether works councils, board representation, or collective bargaining. Actual workers' control has to do not with the existence of a given form but rather with the degree and type of use of any of these forms. And at the other end of the argument, radical cannot be equated with Communist. If what is radical is greater actual workers' control, the countries with the most radical labor movements would include West Germany (which otherwide would be termed moderate due to its ideological distance from communism). The Communist-dominated labor movement of Italy would also rank high, but so would the social democratic labor movement of Sweden, while the Communist labor movement of Frrance would be considered less radical in terms of workers' actual control. This foreshadows a point to be made later, that worker self-management is a concept transcending traditional capitalist-versus-Communist stereotyped analyses of work relations.

WHY HAS THE WORKERS' CONTROL MOVEMENT ARISEN IN A PERIOD OF PROSPERITY WHEN AFFLUENCE IS THOUGHT TO STIFLE RADICALISM?

It is commonly believed in the United States that American workers, bathed in relative affluence, have rejected radicalism in favor of bourgeois pleasures. More generally, affluence is seen as the great legitimator of any economic system that enjoys its mark. Where workers prosper, the system is supported and radicalism languishes on the sidelines of politics. It seems paradoxical, then, that the workers' control movement—which seems radical to even European businessmen—has arisen at the very time the European economy enjoys relative affluence. How is this to be explained?

First, the most significant early steps toward workers' participation, the German system of codetermination, were taken immediately after the war, before recovery had really begun. These reforms, moreover, were introduced for reasons of denazification and political control and were not dependent on considerations of affluence or deprivation. After their establishment the codetermination reforms came to be seen as a major cause of prosperity. Chancellor Schmidt has referred to codetermination, for example, as "that which has accounted for the competitive economic advantage we have enjoyed internationally thus far."[13] This in turn has provided the motivation for the spread of the codetermination model and related ideas to other European capitals. When Britain's Bullock Committee on Industrial Democracy (set up in 1975) developed its legislative proposals for industrial democracy, for instance, it prepared itself by making a pilgrimage to West Germany. There Schmidt told them that the key to his country's "post-war economic miracle was its sophisticated system of worker participation."[14]

Some social scientists have attempted to conceive of affluence as the parent of demands for workers' control. Notable is the work of Abraham Maslow, whose concept of a "need hierarchy" suggests that once basic economic needs and needs for security are met, the worker is freed to "advance" toward fulfilling needs for self-actualization—with which worker participation is thought to be associated.[15] While one may question whether human beings ever "move beyond" economic demands, there is evidence that affluence encourages participatory political goals.[16] This may be in part a function of the higher educational levels that successful industrialization brings to the workforce along with relative prosperity. As Gerald Susman has noted, "When the educated worker compares the routinization and submissiveness required of the work place with the values he has embraced and the experiences he has had at school, he is likely to react with anger and frustration."[17]

Not only are participatory management techniques needed, given the changed workforce associated with postwar affluence, but such methods emerge from other administrative needs of contemporary enterprises. Complex technology in a rapidly evolving environment makes more valuable organizational controls that are flexible, task- rather than structure-oriented, and that delegate task management to direct producers, leaving top management free to concentrate on policy and strategy.[18]

From a managerial point of view relative affluence has made both necessary and possible reforms leading toward opening the decision process. It is not so much that worker radicalism is advancing in spite of affluence. Rather affluence has brought a process of deradicalization and institutionalization of goals that had once seemed the epitomy of labor militancy, leading possibly to syndicalism and worse. In retrospect this change has built on a long tradition of respect for the rights of the workplace, common on the continent. Just as Republicans in the United States reluctantly came to accept Social Security and the Wagner Act, and as British doctors learned to live with socialized medicine, now European managers are in the process of learning that limited worker participation may not be so radical after all. It may even prove helpful. If it seems paradoxical that workers' control is advancing in spite of relative affluence, it is partly because, contrary to common opinion, affluence can be radicalizing, and it is partly because workers' control as practiced in West Europe is not yet very radical.

HOW HAS IT BEEN POSSIBLE FOR THE WORKERS' CONTROL MOVEMENT TO ADVANCE IN COUNTRIES WITH STRONG TRADITIONS OF VOLUNTARISM?

Sweden, long a stronghold of the purely voluntaristic approach to labor relations, has now started moving toward making various industrial democracy reforms compulsory by law. This dramatic shift has already begun to spread to other Scandinavian countries. And in Great Britain, the Trades Union Congress (TUC) has reversed its longstanding opposition to labor representation on corporate boards and has specified details of the legislation it advocates. Since the voluntaristic tradition is also strong in the United States, it is particularly interesting to investigate why those nations whose labor relations systems have an affinity with our own are now shifting toward the continental, government-intervention model.

In Sweden, which has often been cited as a participatory labor relations model for the United States,[19] the voluntaristic approach was best known for national labor-management agreements that sponsored a series of experiments in work democratization. These experiments, as at Volvo, seemed to illustrate the success of the Swedish system and its ability to forge worker-management unity. This appraisal was superficial. The much-vaunted Volvo experiments were not idealistic; rather they were a response to high absenteeism and labor shortages, and were explicitly contingent on no drop in worker productivity. The democratization involved in such experiments entailed little more than control over work relations on the shop-floor level and more open communications with higher levels. It did not alter the basic (capitalist) nature of the enterprise or substantially change power relations.

Over time Swedish unions became increasingly critical of the democratization experiments in spite of their yielding generally increased levels of job satisfaction and productivity.[20] The central problem arose not from the effects of participation per se, but from the failure of such experiments to spread outside a small experimental sector of the economy. A review of such experiments by Lars Ødegaard showed they tended to become encapsulated and stagnate. "This seems to take place," he noted, "in the phase of development where it becomes ncessary to consider fundamental conditions or features of the superimposed organizational authority structure in order to establish necessary conditions for the continued growth and development on the factory floor level of the organization."[21] That is, stagnation occurred because of the unwillingness to democratize higher levels of the power structure of the enterprise.

The limits of the voluntaristic approach became glaringly evident to Swedish unionists by the early 1970s. Unionists began to abandon the voluntaristic model in favor of legislated workers' rights. The image of labor-management harmony was deeply disrupted by a wave of strikes in 1970. Innis Macbeath has noted how, after these strikes, the "spirit of cooperation has lately changed" and how, starting in 1971, the Swedish unions began to reverse their former positions.[22] Later Norway joined the trend, passing legislation in 1973 requiring company assemblies with one-third worker representation and conferring on these assemblies final jurisdiction over major investments, reorganizations, and other important decisions.

Plans for the implementation of the Norwegian legislation provide an indication of the degree to which the old voluntaristic approach may be being abandoned. Bjørn Gustavsen anticipates three stages of enforcement: issuance of a 30-to-40-point guideline setting forth issues and criteria for organization, but not constituting strict standards; a later set of specific directives demanding changes in particular companies, enforced by legal sanctions; and much later, sanctions for negative (antiparticipative) practices even when work inspectorate authorities have issued no prior directive.[23] If implemented in this way, particularly in its intended aspect of prohibiting authoritarian power structures within enterprises, this legislation would represent the most comprehensive attempt to date to institutionalize participative work relations in the compulsory bonds of law.

The shift away from voluntarism has occurred for somewhat different reasons in Great Britain. While a movement for new forms of worker participation in management had been growing among unionists, the catalyst was the necessity for the TUC to take a position on the new Common Market company law. Under the proposed law, European companies would have a system of worker representation at the board level, works councils with moderate but significant powers, and some participation in other areas. The TUC, seeing the writing on the wall, reversed its traditional opposition to this form of workers' participation and instead began to concentrate on what it might do to influence implementation of such reforms in the United Kingdom. By endorsing parity labor representation on corporate boards and strengthening of shop-floor democracy, the TUC sought to affect the Labour government proposals for industrial democracy to be put before parliament in the 1976-1977 session. This reversal of attitude, from voluntarism to legislated requirements for participation, has had far-reaching implications. The Labour government, for example, has now announced draft legislation for greater worker participation in the Post Office Corporation, and has put a participation amendment in the Aircraft and Shipbuilding Industries Nationalization bill.[24]

The prospect is for further extension of the legislative approach to worker participation in management. While accepting the TUC's insistence on central emphasis on collective bargaining, the Labour government is now in the process of adopting a far more interventionist policy in these matters, designed to augment industrial democracy. Ronald Hayward, general secretary of the Labour party, articulated this new orientation:

> We believe that the scope of collective bargaining must be increased to cover all aspects of working life, including production planning, factory layout, investment decisions and the rest. . . . Industrial democracy to us means joint control and joint regulation of industry. We want a positive form of control. Workers must not be placed in a position in which all they can say is "no." They do not want to be asked for their views after the decisions have been made.[25]

This is not to say that the turn away from pure voluntarism represents the same social process in Great Britain as in Sweden. Swedes, for example, tend to see worker participation as a step toward a more classless society, whereas the British tend to discuss it as an aspect of class struggle.[26] But in both countries the tradition of voluntarism has failed to meet changing industrial needs and, in reaction to this failure, a compulsory or legislative approach has arisen. This is intimately tied to perceived government solutions to contemporary economic problems, as discussed below.

WHY HAS THE CURRENT PERIOD OF ECONOMIC PROBLEMS NOT CAUSED WORKER PARTICIPATION TO BE ECLIPSED BY TRADITIONAL BREAD-AND-BUTTER UNION ISSUES?

Economic recessions are associated with adverse wage trends that force unions on the economic defensive. Wage increases may have to be foregone, employment security becomes an overriding issue, and the prestige of union leadership hinges on the ability to uphold past gains.[27] Such conditions seem to mean less attention and lower priority for union demands, like worker participation, which are not centered on the bread-and-butter basics. Moreover, recessions diminish or eliminate the shortage of workers, which, as mentioned in relation to Sweden, was a major force motivating employers toward acceptance of worker participation in management. As security consciousness on the job increases, absenteeism, quality sabotage, and turnover become less of a problem from a managerial point of view. There is less need to motivate workers through participative and democratic reforms. And this is just what Maslow's need theory, mentioned earlier, suggests. Demands for participation and self-actualization are viable only when basic economic needs are met.

Or is this really the case? There are several reasons to resist going along with the common opinion outlined above. First, there is the manifest fact that worker participation has continued to be an expanding issue in a number of European countries in spite of the onset of worldwide economic problems in the early 1970s. This alone suggests other factors are at work.

Perhaps the most important other factor is the common perception of workers' participation as a possible solution to economic problems. In the British case just cited, for example, *The Economist* has echoed government opinion in saying, "Industrial stagnation is the British disease. Participation could be one step towards its cure. Shared decisions could at last bring the radical industrial change the country needs."[28] Earlier, Fiat's Agnelli was cited to the effect that worker participation might constitute the basis for a return to "more productive management" in Italy. Such opinions have now become rather common.

Governments, in particular, have been drawn toward the industrial democracy movement as a significant form of response to economic problems. In the present volume, for example, Martin has described how the Swedish Social Democrats, hurt by the failure of their economic policies in the 1960s, and unable to cope with economic problems, needed an alternative basis for attracting voter support. The issue of industrial democracy, Martin noted, seemed to offer the most promising possibility. In Germany the Social Democrats saw in the extension of codetermination both a method of improving productivity and competitive position in world markets and a major reform that did not involve major new expenditures. Through expansion of participation, Schmidt believed, the government could satisfy demands for social reform in a way that would improve the national economy and not constitute a welfare drag upon it. Without such newfound government support, economic adversity would indeed have been the basis for the decline of worker participation as a political issue in the 1970s.

WHY HAS WORKER PARTICIPATION NOT CAUGHT ON IN THE UNITED STATES?

Of course this lack of government support could be cited to explain why American labor has not picked up the lead of their European counterparts in moving toward greater workers' participation. Certainly this is a factor. Given the high unemployment levels in the United States in the 1970s, there has not been the labor shortage that has underlain the participative trend in Sweden and elsewhere. And given the manner in which the oil crises of the 1970s work to the competitive disadvantage of European manufacturers compared to American, it is not surprising that the productivity issue—to which worker participation in large measure is addressed—has become more important in Europe. Finally, to state the obvious, the very lack of a successful socialist tradition in government or labor deprives the rhetoric of industrial democracy of much of its legitimacy and ideological force in the United States. For reasons such as these it might seem surprising if workers' participation did become a major reform in this country.

Yet this is not the whole story. Many have predicted that the United States will inevitably be drawn to follow the European model in some form. Macbeath, writing for the British North American Committee (a predominantly business group), for example, noted, "North America will not be able to avoid some invasion by the slogans of participation and industrial democracy . . . [as] these various devices and slogans express the same common aspiration in all developed countries."[29] Maslow's theory about needs for self-actualization (participation) following fulfillment of economic needs suggests conditions should be at least as favorable in the United States as in Europe for development of interest in workers' participation. Many of the same motive concerns are present in the United States: "blue-collar blues," overeducation of the work force, rise in participatory political values and slogans, an increasing productivity problem, alienation from traditional union forms. A good argument can be made that workers' participation ought to catch on in this country, and it may seem paradoxical that this seems not to be the case.

Much of the seeming paradox can be removed by noting that American labor has moved toward wider powers, and that European accomplishments in the realm of participatory control of work are themselves not so radical or extensive as yet. American management has led in the introduction of participatory management techniques outside Scandinavia, for example. And the Scanlon Plan companies and numerous other experiments at companies like General Foods, Kaiser Steel, and International Group Plans have gained wide attention. In some cases, as at the Harman International plant, the unions (the UAW in this case) have begun a collaborative relationship. More important, union collective bargaining has expanded in scope to include many matters of work organization, productivity matters, health and safety matters, and other subjects that constitute the routine fare of European works councils. American unionists are in fact prone to deny that any substantial difference exists between the United States and Europe in the degree of actual workers' control over management.

American labor's antipathy toward the symbols of codetermination (works councils, board representation) derives from its peculiar history. Without detailing how the American idea of industrial democracy came to be equated with collective bargaining apart from direct worker participation in management,[30] two major points may be mentioned briefly. First, the AFL itself arose in opposition to the producer cooperativist principles of the Knights of Labor. The Knights' commitments to worker cooperatives were perceived as being opposed to a strategy based ons strikes and bargaining and were thought to be the cause of defeat. Second, during the 1920s a major union-busting drive was undertaken by businessmen using in large part the cover of employee representation councils. These the labor movement rightly branded as "company unions," but in the process worker representation came to be closely identified with managerial manipulation. Finally, some importance must be attached to the personal influence of George Meany, the longtime strong man of the AFL-CIO. Unlike Leonard Woodcock, mentioned frequently as a prime candidate to replace him, Meany has been entirely unsympathetic to the notion of direct labor participation in management. This in turn reflects his conservative-Catholic background as business agent for the plumbers' union, whose constituency is strongly infected with a small entrepreneurial ideology sharply at variance with notions of workers' control.[31]

The factors cited in favor of a movement for economic democracy in the United States focus on the individual worker (for example, his or her over-education, alienation from work, absenteeism, and so on), not on governments or unions. At this individual level, there is a strong potential for a workers' control movement. A study by the author on American autoworkers, for example, showed majority support for works councils and other mechanisms of workers' control.[32] More significant, a national opinion survey by the Hart Poll in 1975 found that a majority of Americans favor employee ownership and control of corporations and would support a presidential candidate who advocated employee control of U.S. corporations.[33]

In spite of individual-level support for workers' control concepts, further movement in this direction in the United States is frustrated by lack of government and union support. Unions tend to see workers' councils as organizational rivals, and government, for reasons noted earlier, finds little motive to push participatory reforms in the absence of union support. The result has been an absence of actual working models of the workers' control concept in the United States, apart from limited management-identified experiments. Jaroslav Vanek has attributed the relative lack of movement toward workers' direct participation in the United States to this failure. "A pragmatic civilization such as the United States," he wrote, "will not be convinced by theoretical argumentation; . . . if anything can generate a movement . . . it must be a strong demonstration effect—and that for the moment is missing and will be for some time."[34]

It is for this reason that supporters of the workers' control concept in various forms have focused their efforts toward providing demonstrations. In terms of limited forms of participation, this has been the thrust of the various quality-of-working-life centers, or of HR 14269, a proposed 1976 bill to fund demonstration projects on productivity issues, including employee participation. Supporters of more extensive forms of workers' participation have organized the Federation of Economic Democracy to fund worker-controlled enterprises. For the moment these remain isolated and small, however. American workers may yet become involved with the politics of industrial democracy, but that development will await changes at the level of government and union officialdom.

CONCLUSION

Workers' control is neither utopia nor simply a management trick. If it has the potential to grow into decentralized socialism, so too it has the potential to revert back to human relations management. But in the main it has been neither, certainly not in Western Europe. The West European versions of workers' participation have not undermined capitalism, or, as yet, even proved to be the sort of "nonreformist reform" of which André Gorz has written. Instead European capitalism has been increasingly drawn toward the codetermination model and other forms of worker participation. This tendency has appeared as a hopeful partial solution to economic problems and has been imposed, in the main, from above. It has not appeared from below as an uncontrolled consequence of dire contradictions of the economic order. On the other hand, workers' control remains predominantly a part of the ideology of the left. Its prime proponents, the German unions, see it as a useful vehicle for the extension of their powers and programs. And even in countries with a tradition of voluntarism in labor relations, unions are increasingly favorable to legislated rights of direct labor participation in management.

There is every reason for expecting a continued increase in worker participation. At the individual level, as a study by the European Association of National Productivity Centers (EANPC) has noted, the factors currently creating pressure for industrial democracy will increase. Notably this includes increased workers' abilities and training, overeducation in relation to work responsibilities, and consequent worker dissatisfaction.[35] At the level of shop-floor work democratization, the prospect is the same: the same study concludes that structural democratization as typified by the works council and autonomous work team tends to develop further even where it has not been fully effective in the past. Such shop-floor democratization seems to create motivation for greater direct participation in more remote representative mechanisms.[36] And at the union level, not only in Germany, but also in countries as diverse as Sweden, England, and Italy, both the mechanisms and scope of issues associated with workers' control are being increasingly accepted. With old ideological obstacles being eroded in practice if not always in rhetorical label, the prospect is for further development of collective bargaining in the direction of increased workers' control. Finally, governments too are showing an increased receptivity toward (and greatly reduced fear of) industrial democracy for reasons rooted in economic productivity needs in the context of adverse competitive situations. As this too will increase in the future, as the oil shortage disproportionately hurts European manufacturers, one may expect many administrations to find irresistible the tempting optimism with which Chancellor Schmidt, for example, appraises the economic effects of his nation's system of worker participation in management.

The obstacles to change in the direction of greater workers' participation are also great. Some of these have been indicated by Max Elden in a study for the European Conference on Personnel Management.[37] In this document Elden warned European businessmen that participative reforms could necessitate costly changes in machinery, physical work surroundings, layout, and could even affect the nature of the enterprise's product. Not only this, but managers cannot count on an enthusiastic response from either workers or middle-level supervisors. The former are frequently distrustful of the management motives behind proposed changes, while the latter feel their roles will be reduced in status or even abolished. Unions still, not uncommonly, perceive direct workers' participation as an end run around collective bargaining, and governments, placing a premium on industrial stability, may prefer inaction to displeasing one sector or another. It is hardly surprising that the end result, as described in the studies in this volume, has been a quite limited version of workers' control. But within this context of limited reform, the movement for industrial democracy in West

Europe has—in very diverse ways—significantly extended labor's powers vis-a-vis management and has revitalized the European left by rendering the demand for workers' control a contemporary and viable one.

NOTES

1. See Jaroslav Vanek, *The General Theory of Labor-Managed Economies* (Ithaca, N.Y.: Cornell University Press, 1970).

2. David Jenkins, "European Report," *World of Work Report* 1, no. 1 (March 1976): 3.

3. Victor Turovtsev, *People's Control in Socialist Society* (Moscow: Progress Publishers, 1973), p. 35.

4. Alexander Matejko, "Some Sociological Problems of Socialist Factories," *Social Research* 36, no. 3 (Autumn, 1969).

5. Jim Kaplan, "Introduction to the Revolutionary Left in Italy," *Radical America* 7, no. 2 (March-April, 1973): 1.

6. Ernest Dowson, "The Italian Background," *Radical America* 7, no. 2 (March-April, 1973): 12.

7. Roberto Massari, "La gestion ouvriere des luttes: des comites unitaire de base aux Conseils d'usine," *Autogestion et socialisme*, no. 26–27 (March–June, 1974): 138.

8. G. Frederico Micheletti, "Technology is not enough," *La Stampa* (Turin), April 21, 1976; translated in *European Press Roundup*, National Quality of Work Center, Washington, D.C., n.d.

9. "Problems Faced by the Manager: An Interview with Agnelli," *La Stampa* (Turin), June 16, 1976; translated in *European Press Roundup*, National Quality of Work Center, Washington, D.C., n.d., p. 5.

10. David Jenkins, "Italy: Metal Workers Ask Broader Consultation," *World of Work Report* 1, no. 1 (March 1976): 8.

11. Commission of the European Communities, "Employee Participation and Company Structure in the European Community," Document COM(75)570, Luxembourg, November 12, 1975, p. 114.

12. Jenkins, "European Report," op. cit., pp. 3–4.

13. Quoted in A.H. Raskin, "The Workers' Voice in German Companies," *World of Work Report* 1, no. 5 (July 1976): 6.

14. "The Germans Know How," *The Economist* (London), September 4, 1976, p. 80.

15. Abraham Maslow, "A Theory of Human Motivation," *Psychological Review* 50 (July 1943): 370–96.

16. See, for example, Ronald Inglehart, "The Silent Revolution in Europe: Intergenerational Change in Post-Industrial Societies," *American Political Science Review* 65, no. 4 (December 1971): 991–1017.

17. Gerald I. Susman, *Autonomy at Work: A Sociotechnical Analysis of Participative Management* (New York: Praeger Publishers, 1976), p. 20.

18. George Berkley, *The Administrative Revolution* (Englewood Cliffs, N.J.: Prentice-Hall, 1971).

19. For example, see Special Task Force to the Secretary of Health, Education, and Welfare, *Work in America* (Cambridge: MIT Press, 1973), p. 115.

20. International Labor Organization, "Symposium on Workers' Participation in Decisions within Undertakings," Document D.1 of a conference at Oslo, August 20–30,

1974 (Geneva: ILO, 1974), pp. 24–25. Later reprinted as *Labour-Management Relations Series*, no. 48 (Geneva: ILO, 1976).

21. Lars Ødegaard, "Direct Forms of Participation," in Oganization for Economic Cooperation and Development, *Workers' Participation: Documents Prepared for an International Management Seminar Convened by the OECD* (Versailles, March 5–8, 1975) (Paris: OECD, 1975), p. 13.

22. Innis Macbeath, *The European Approach to Worker-Management Relationships* (London: British-North American Committee, 1973), p. 13.

23. Bjørn Gustavsen, "A Proposal for Legal Regulation of Jobs and Work Organization," mimeographed (Oslo: Work Research Institute, n.d.), p. 10.

24. "Plan on Worker Participation," *Common Market Reports: Euromarket News*, no. 389 (July 1, 1976): 5–6.

25. "Labour-TUC report calls for more state intervention," *The Times* (London), May 24, 1976, p. 1.

26. Nancy Foy and Herman Gadon, "Worker Participation: Contrasts in Three Countries," *Harvard Business Review*, May-June 1976, pp. 71–83.

27. Albert Rees, *The Economics of Trade Unions* (Chicago: University of Chicago Press, 1962), p. 58.

28. "Workers at the Boardroom Door," *The Economist* (London), September 4, 1976, p. 91.

29. Macbeath, op. cit., p. 69.

30. See Milton Derber, *The American Idea of Industrial Democracy* (Chicago: University of Chicago Press, 1970).

31. Joseph C. Goulden, *Meany: The Unchallenged Strong Man of American Labor* (New York: Atheneum, 1972). For example, of his plumbers' union background, Meany said, "I think I had been re-elected three times before I realized that we had any problems in the world other than how to lick the steamfitters." Goulden comments on Meany's parochialism: "As a Catholic and building tradesman, he could be trusted to keep his progressivism on the safe side of radicalism."

32. G. David Garson, "Automobile Workers and the Radical Dream," *Politics and Society* 3, no. 2 (Winter 1973): 176–77.

33. "Americans Favor Sweeping Economic Change," *Common Sense* 3, no. 3, insert, p. 1. *Common Sense* is the organ of the People's Bicentennial Commission, which sponsored the survey. The survey was based on 1,209 randomly sampled individuals and was taken on July 25, 1975. The Hart Poll is an established polling organization used, for example, by major television networks and national newspapers.

34. Jaroslav Vanek, *The Participatory Economy* (Ithaca, N.Y.: Cornell University Press, 1971), p. 165.

35. European Association of National Productivity Centers, *Industrial Democracy in Europe: The Current Situation* (Brussels: EANPC, March 1976), p. 25.

36. Ibid., pp. 25–26.

37. Max Elden, *Participation* (Endhoven, Netherlands: N. V. Philips, for the Committee on Participation, European Conference on Personnel Management, n.d.), pp. 54–56.

ABOUT THE EDITOR AND CONTRIBUTORS

G. DAVID GARSON is Chairman of the department of political science at North Carolina State University, Raleigh, and is an editor of *Workers' Control: A Reader on Labor and Social Change* (1973) and of *Organizational Democracy* (1976). He is also the author of *Political Science Methods* (1976) and of *Power and Politics in the United States: A Political Economy Approach* (1977).

STEPHEN BORNSTEIN is a Fellow of the Center for European Studies of Harvard University and is completing a doctoral dissertation on the *Confédération Française Démocratique du Travail.*

ALFRED DIAMANT is Chairman of the West European Studies Program of Indiana University and is the author of *Austrian Catholics and the First Republic* (1960). He has also contributed to scholarly books, journals, and conferences on West European politics.

KEITHA S. FINE is on the faculty of political science at the University of Massachusetts–Boston and is a Faculty Research Associate of the Center for European Studies of Harvard University, doing research on the French and Italian left.

DEREK C. JONES is an Assistant Professor of economics at Hamilton College in Canada and is currently a Visiting Fellow at the Industrial Relations Research Unit of the University of Warwick in the United Kingdom. He is presently writing a book on British producer cooperatives.

ANDREW MARTIN is a Faculty Research Associate of the Center for European Studies of Harvard University and has taught at Columbia University, the University of Massachusetts–Amherst, and Boston University.

MARTIN SLATER is a postdoctoral Fellow at the Center for International Studies of the Massachusetts Institute of Technology, conducting research on migrant workers' conflicts in Italy and France.

INTERNATIONAL LABOR AND THE MULTINATIONAL ENTERPRISE
edited by Duane Kujawa

*A FULL EMPLOYMENT PROGRAM FOR THE 1970s
edited by Alan Gartner,
William Lynch, Jr., and
Frank Riessman

*IMPROVING PRODUCTIVITY AND THE QUALITY OF WORK LIFE
Thomas G. Cummings and
Edmond S. Molloy

AUTONOMY AT WORK: A Sociotechnical Analysis of
Participative Management
Gerald I. Susman

*WORKER MILITANCY AND ITS CONSEQUENCES, 1965-75:
New Directions in Western Industrial Relations
edited by Solomon Barkin

THE SCOPE OF BARGAINING IN PUBLIC EMPLOYMENT
Joan Weitzman

*Also available in paperback as a PSS Student Edition